The River Runs Uphill

The River Runs Uphill

A Story of Success and Failure

Robert Aickman

J. M. PEARSON
Burton on Trent

First impression 1986
by J. M Pearson & Son (Publishers) Ltd.,
The Midland Railway Grain Warehouse,
Burton-on-Trent, Staffordshire.

Typeset by Characters of Taunton and
Dorchester Typesetting, Bristol.
Printed and bound in Great Britain by
A. Wheaton & Co. Ltd., Exeter

British Library Cataloguing in Publication Data
Aickman, Robert
The river runs uphill
1. Inland Waterways Association – History
I. Title
386'.06'041   HE663

ISBN 0-907864-38-4

Contents

List of Illustrations

Acknowledgements

The drawing of Robert Aickman by Peter Scott was photographed by Hugh McKnight and is in the possession of the Upper Avon Navigation Trust. Special thanks are due R. J. M. Sutherland for his kindness and efficiency in disinterring thirty year old photographs from his filing system and David Cooper who skilfully catalogued Robert Aickman's photographic collection.

The publishers extend grateful thanks to Felix Pearson, the author's literary executor, for her enthusiasm and her unstinting help in the preparation of this book. Thanks also go to Harry Arnold, Hugh Potter, Niall Allsop, Joy Hales, Janet Hoult, Mark Curnock, Chris Brown, Roslyn Discombe-Down and all concerned with the production of this volume.

I dedicate this book
To those who did it
Including those who should be named
But are not
And those who should have received mention
But have not

Great souls are not those which have less passion and more virtue than common souls, but those only which have greater designs.

LA ROCHEFOUCAULD

Englishmen habitually distrust the most obvious truths, if the person who advances them is suspected of having any general views. To produce any effect on their minds, you must carefully conceal the fact of your having any system or body of opinions, and must instruct them on insulated points, and endeavour to form their habits of thought by your mode of treating single and practical questions. When you have gained a high reputation with them for knowledge of facts, and skill and judgement in the appreciation of details, you may then venture on an enlarged view; but even then, very cautiously and guardedly. A journal which should start by a systematic exposition of far-sighted views would not have twenty subscribers.

JOHN STUART MILL

Publisher's Note

I met Robert Aickman only once, some months before his death. He had consented to a rare interview, duly published in "Waterways World" (September, 1980). All that hot afternoon in his South Kensington flat I was acutely conscious of being in the presence of A Great Man, and it was there for the first time that I learnt of the existence, in manuscript, of "The River Runs Uphill". His publishers hadn't been able to come to terms with it and so it had been consigned to gather dust for over a decade. That callow interviewer could scarcely have credited that it would be he who, six years later, would cause that lost classic of waterway literature to see light of day. And even then, it was not of my own prompting, but rather through a friend of a friend, that the approach was made for my company to publish this book.

Nearing the 40th Anniversary of the Inland Waterways Association, it seemed appropriate to move quickly, not for a moment thinking that publication would be met with anything other than joy and celebration; particularly from within the ranks of the Association which Aickman had founded those long years before. Thus we could scarcely credit an ensuing refusal by the present Council of the IWA to carry paid-for, pre-publication advance publicity for "The River ..." in their Association's controlled circulation magazine, without prior sight of the manuscript. Their request smacked of censorship and appeared unprecedented – they had never asked to see any of our other titles regularly advertised in their magazine before. What do the present incumbents of Aickman's legacy have to fear? Are they trying to re-write history or, more pertinently, trying to suppress its recording at all.

But, controversy apart, I would not be honest, were I not to express an element of frustration which grew within me as we went through the process of putting "The River Runs Uphill" into print. Minor masterpiece of its genre that it is, there are serious flaws. I longed fervently for him to be still alive so that we could thrash it into some sort of mutually acceptable shape. The faults lie – not so much in what is written, but what has not been written, or, more tellingly, what had been edited in the violent re-draught which took place. Aickman, it transpired, had erased virtually everything of personal import. All reference to his wife for instance, heavily involved in the early years of the Association, was obliterated in the re-write. So that we are left with, at best, a one-dimensional narrative, barely autobiographical in approach at all.

Nevertheless, this book had to be published, and I feel nothing but pride in our involvement. It is important to point out however, that we have left it in the tense in which it was written and made no attempt to update its mid-sixties viewpoint. The reader must take the book as he or she finds it. At its worst it frustrates attempts to even read between the lines. At its best "The River Runs Uphill" is an inspirational chronicle of a post-war battle against the indifference of Authority which, forty years on, still remains to be lost or won.

MICHAEL PEARSON

Proem

The Inland Waterways Association succeeded more than almost any other voluntary organisation in modern Britain, in the sense that in 1967 the Government promulgated a reversal of the closure policy for rivers and canals that had predominated for over a century and been prosecuted overtly and with rigour since "nationalisation" in 1948. The Government now said that most (though by no means all) of the nationalised waterways that were in controversy, were to be retained as "cruiseways". This almost unparalleled recantation of what successive Governments had been asserting for a generation was attended by all manner of booby-traps and bunkers: the ancient right of the public to navigate, the ancient obligation upon the navigation authorities to maintain "the Track", were alike swept away; instant closure, whether the waterway was nationalised or not, was made easy; all that is left of the "publicly owned" system (the greater part of the whole) is a People's Park of Rest and Culture, with the people admitted only by favour, and the entire administration in the hands of Government nominees. This state of affairs constitutes a total reversal of the deeper purposes which the Association long aimed to promote.

This book tells something of the techniques and sacrifices by which an outstanding victory was won; and something of the reasons why a defeat was sustained also. I have taken the story up to the Market Harborough Festival of 1950, after which the first fine rapture ended.

The most difficult problem has been that of organising and selecting from the truly vast quantity of material that survives. I have sometimes compared the direction of the Association with the direction of the Holy Roman Empire: multiform, fissiparous and grinding. Even so, I had not realised quite how much we did. In the interests of compression and better organisation, I have been compelled half to rewrite the book after completion of the first draft.

My original purpose, stated in the Proem to an earlier autobiographical volume, "The Attempted Rescue", of endeavouring primarily to illustrate "the interaction of public life and private character, to me one of the most fascinating themes, the theme of 'Coriolanus'", has, I fear, suffered somewhat from the care I have had to exercise for reasons of discretion and delicacy. But the campaign for the waterways, even at its most rigorous and conflictual, was by no means my whole life; and it is a main implication of this book that the campaign would have lost greatly in effectiveness if it had been. I hope to show that the specialist and the expert are almost always among the poorest of guides. If I have anything to teach, it is that. "Fortunately", as David Hutchings puts it in his lecture on the rebuilding of the canal to Stratford, "we were none of us experts, or we should all have known it was impossible".

ROBERT AICKMAN

I

How?

The idea of foundation as one of the basic categories for the understanding of history has rarely been discussed. In America, the term "Founding Fathers", and occasionally Goethe and Stefan George refer to the concept of "Grundung", the laying of foundations: and I myself am of the mind that this is one of the most crucial principles of historical understanding.

Historical founders and historical foundations imply a special quality. It is not identical with genius, though most founding fathers have shown that elusive trait we call genius. But it is not genius alone that I speak of; it is rather the plenitude of possibilities, the planting of seeds that will nourish future generations, which makes for founders. We find examples of this potential in all fields of history, and it would be a fascinating undertaking to scrutinise world history from this point of view.

GERHARD MASUR

Towards the end of the Second World War, I noticed in "The Observer" a review by Sir Compton Mackenzie of a book about the canals of England called "Narrow Boat". The review was highly favourable. Having always had a mild interest in the subject, and being born in Cancer, with its strong watery affinities, I bought a copy and read it. The author was named L.T.C. Rolt.

Mr. Rolt had converted a working narrow boat, romantically, and a little mysteriously named *Cressy*, into a mobile residence. His book describes a slow voyage aboard her with his wife during the last months of peace and the first months of war; a voyage that was virtually the couple's honeymoon. Mr. Rolt used this voyage as the foundation for sundry observations not only on the problem of the waterways but also on the plight of modern England, indeed of modern man; which the problem of the waterways appeared somewhat to symbolise. The problem of the waterways seemed in Mr. Rolt's view to be that they were beautiful, and could be useful, but that Authority would have none of them; refused to help or promote them; sought only to close them.

The first canal I could myself remember to have identified as such was the Grand Junction (after 1929, Grand Union) where it traverses Cassiobury Park, near Watford. On many of those long walks with my parents of which I wrote in "The Attempted Rescue", we crossed this canal by a certain white bridge to which we descended through what was then the Earl of Essex's park. The River Gade, swift and silky, runs close by the canal, with Ophelia-like greenery streaming in the crystal water. Nearby stood a wooden watermill, then disused, now demolished; which later I learned had connections with Frederick Delius, whose music has long meant much to me. There were enormous, ancient beeches, and, on the other side of the canal, a grass bank which I then thought steep and high. It was, in fact, a charming spot: beautiful, characterful and a trifle exotic.

Traffic was still heavy on the Grand Junction, so that, more often than not, we heard from afar, while still on the slope of the hill, the inimitable tutter-tutter (Sir Alan Herbert's term) of the boat engines, and the long rattle as the crews allowed the sluices ("paddles" in the south to professionals) to drop unhindered through the racks – an improper procedure, because bad for the gear, but less wicked in those days, when the gear received more attention. For immediately above the white bridge was a lock, and, seldom did one have to wait more than a few minutes to see a pair of narrow boats (which normally trade in pairs – 'boat' and 'butty') work through it. My father would hoist me above the bridge parapet in order to get a good view; I did not really like being held out over the water, nor did the grimy scurrying, uncommunicative apparitions of the boat families below, at all reassure me. There are some whom they disconcert to this day.

When I first knew the lock, a single-storeyed white lock-cottage, like an illustration to a German fairy story, stood at the foot of the bank on the far side of it. I can even remember when the cottage housed a lock-keeper. But soon I was told that the tenant was now an ordinary person, because a lock-keeper could no longer be afforded. I can still recall my father sounding sad and angry as he said it, but hopeless. In the end, the lock-cottage was pulled down. I scrambled, incredulous and aghast, among its foundations until my father called me away because of the filth and litter that had already accumulated from passers-by.

Among the vilest of all the vile things that Authority has inflicted upon the beautiful waterways of England, has been the steady process of demolishing the waterside structures; the policy of Making a Desert. But behind the demolition of that particular lock-cottage is said to have been a particular explanation.

It is related that when, at the very end of the eighteenth century, the canal was being built, a local landowner objected strongly to the entire operation; to the rowdyism of the construction gangs, to the threat which the completed waterway offered to the tranquillity of the area. When this man failed in his opposition, he was instrumental in the appointment of an enormous negro ("a real giant," people said, "as well as coal-black") to keep the lock I later knew so well. The appointment was unusual but the lock-keeper's secret instructions were more so; they were that he was to do all in his power to harass and impede every boat that might appear, and to discourage all who sailed with her.

The lock-keeper did what he had been appointed to do, and did it for a surprisingly long time, mainly because his strength was as the strength of ten, and his very aspect appalling. But, in the end, a group of boatmen banded together to teach the lock-keeper a lesson. It was agreed, for obvious reasons, that some hour of darkness would best suit. This was not difficult, as the season was late. So much is known (it is said), but little more; because when the chosen December night came, the simple fellows, stumbling about in the cold blackness, overreached themselves so that what had begun as a lesson ended as a homicide, and all concerned had to lose existence in the murk and be never seen again.

Thus that particular lock-cottage came to be 'disturbed' (not, of course, that it is the only one); and the boat families grew into the habit of hiding away the children if ever the boats crossed Cassiobury Park at or near the time of dusk. They will tell you, if they can be made to speak about the matter at all, that sometimes just as twilight is finally becoming night, the figure of the huge negro can suddenly be seen, bounding in great leaps along the canal towpath.

It is, no doubt, a narrative of the kind that one takes or leaves; but there is on record at least one piece of what may stand as supporting evidence. Cassiobury Park passed long since to the Watford Corporation, so that by now Delius' corner has inevitably picked up a tinge of the Mayor's Parlour, and the few working boats that remain, seem almost hectically vivid and vital, more so than ever before, however diminished in their actual decorations. During the 1930s, it was deemed necessary to cut down one of the big trees that I have mentioned, as being hollow and a danger to the public. Inside the hollow trunk was found an accumulation of windlasses. The windlass or key is an instrument without which the locks on that waterway, or on many others, cannot be operated; and one of the charges made against the negro was that he had made a practice of stealing and hiding boatmen's windlasses.

The next place where I became conscious of canals as canals was Brentford. Then a country town, with many good specimens of that Middlesex brickwork which John Betjeman has so penetratingly particularised as one of the especial regional beauties and ornaments of all England. When visiting my alarming relatives at Worton Court, I used to be whisked by Paine, the chauffeur, or to glitter in a London United tramcar with my parents, across the wide bridge that in Brentford spans the same

Grand Junction Canal, and in a sense marks the point at which the atmosphere of the river, the Thames, changes into the very different atmosphere
of the canal. The difference is so great that Brentford Bridge almost brings
to mind the transformation scene in a pantomime.

I remember that at each end of the bridge the tram tracks left the centre of
the road, swinging out to cross the cobbled bridge closely alongside the two
pavements. It was a thing that would have pleased me (as it would now), but
it never prevented me from noticing the truly vast aggregation of painted
boats always to be seen moored, tight as floating logs, in the pool above the
bridge, with washing aflap from every cratch to every cabin, and the
dark-skinned crews either behaving with incredible domesticity or else
engaged upon ploys even more unknowable than their exercises on the
move. No-one told me that it was the same canal as in Cassiobury Park. This
was because no-one knew. People have the oddest ideas about what canals
are and where they go.

I can remember no more, as one remarks after rescue from drowning,
until I came upon the canal at Stratford upon Avon. It was during the 1930s.
I was visiting the town and the Shakespeare Memorial Theatre with my
parents. One day, I took myself off on a solitary walk. My intention was to
walk up the towpath to Wilmcote, there to visit the house of Shakespeare's
mother, Mary Arden; and that I accomplished. The map showed many
locks on this stretch of the waterway, but, in reality, there were many more.
Only upon later representations from my Association did the Ordnance
Survey inaugurate a policy of, when practicable, showing every canal lock
separately. Occasionally, there are so many in a short distance that the scale
of the map makes it impracticable.

These unrecorded locks, when Ordnance Survey maps were (and are) in
all other respects so dependable, were the first element of fantasy; but far
more fantastic was the state of the waterway. Wild vegetation abounded; the
water was shallow; the locks were leaking and crumbling, many with gates
either flapping or jammed. It struck me as being not so much a region of the
dead, but a region of a life that I knew nothing of. There was not a boat in
sight, but I did not at that time realise that no boat could pass. On the
contrary, I simply wondered how boats *did* pass, and reflected that there
was much I had to learn if I wished to know about canals.

But as I went on, a third element of fantasy was inescapable. Everywhere
there were threatening notices, all stamped out on iron plates, and all in the
name of the Great Western Railway Company. Many were stuck about at
odd angles on heavy supports. I was at a loss to understand how the Great
Western Railway Company could come into the scene at all. In its proper
place, I loved and revered the Great Western almost as much as anyone,
which is saying much, because few other railway companies attracted such
deep and sustained respect (perhaps only the Midland), but all these black,

iron notices, almost military in their array, entirely military in the rigour of their language, were depressing and frightening. I could not then know that most were required by Act of Parliament. As many of them were directed against trespassers, it was remarkable that I found the audacity to continue on my way. I remember quite well how I did manage it. I recall feeling that everything around me was, as I have said, fantasy: unreal and unlike the rest of the world, though I had no idea how or why: and not least of all those black notices. It was an initiation. No-one who lacks that feeling about the rivers and canals of England has come anywhere near the heart of the matter.

When I had returned home, I consulted books and soon lighted upon what is the basic fact about the entire waterways situation in Britain: that during the nineteenth century, about one-third of the river and canal system was bought up by railway companies; a bit here and a bit there, so that, in the end, the railway interest acquired a grip on virtually the entire network. The books seemed to imply that this had not necessarily been in all respects advantageous; but I did not pursue the matter. Seething with indignation about ills that are entirely unnecessary but entirely beyond one's power to remedy, is a major cause of unhappiness.

After reading "Narrow Boat", some years later, I wrote to Mr. Rolt, entrusting my letter to the care of his publishers. I said how much I admired his book and how much I agreed with the view of life it reflected. I wondered whether even now the waterways prospect had inevitably to be as bad as the book seemed to imply. I suggested the formation of a society to campaign for a new waterways world.

Mr. Rolt replied at length; kindly and with enthusiasm. He invited me to visit him aboard *Cressy*; which, he wrote, was then moored at a place in the Midlands named Tardebigge. The name was so improbable that I checked it on the map before replying. It lay a mile or two from Bromsgrove in Worcestershire.

I walked with my map from Bromsgrove station, and my host began well by saying that I was the first visitor who had had the initiative to do so. It was a clear, sunny afternoon, not too hot: *Cressy*, beautifully painted and lovingly converted, was enchanting; Tom Rolt, as I soon found myself calling him, was welcoming and well-informed; his wife, Angela Rolt, was hospitable and personally fascinating. She was a direct descendant of King William IV through one of his many children by the lovely Mrs. Jordan; and the odd thing was that she looked exactly like that monarch, whose features were distinctive. One could have identified her anywhere. As hostess she achieved a degree of elegance that I have seldom known equalled on any of the numberless boats I have since visited, and that then took me utterly by surprise. The entire afternoon and evening were excellently calculated to enhance the fantasy of the waterways. Even the weather was *exactly* right;

which does not happen more than once or twice a year, and almost never when is it really important.

The visit was followed by an invitation to a voyage a few weeks later. *Cressy* had lain at Tardebigge for a long time, while her owner worked for the Ministry of Supply at Birmingham. Now, the war over, he wished to take her for the next winter to Tooley's boatyard at Banbury.

Almost immediately after casting off, I went through my first canal tunnel; and then through two more, one of them (West Hill Tunnel) more than a mile and a half long; and canal tunnels seldom fail to enchant (unless one is a claustrophobic), however many times one traverses them.

This was the summit level of the Worcester & Birmingham Canal. Canals, being man-made, have normally to be supplied with water from man-made reservoirs, sited as near as may be to the canal's summit level. The reservoirs which feed the Worcester & Birmingham Canal, adjoin the waterway and resemble lakes. They are beautiful, and much of the summit level itself is beautiful, unbelievably so when one sees from the road how greatly the surrounding terrain has been built up. But that is still the usual state of affairs: almost all canals remain beautiful – provided that you don't depart from them; and a problem in writing about them is how best to avoid a monotony of superlatives.

I was astonished by how beautiful and dreamlike the Worcester & Birmingham Canal proved to be. I remember that my first meal on a canal voyage was a picnic luncheon at a mooring by the inlet to Bittall Reservoir. Angela Rolt's regime combined elegance with a variety of hand-picked, home-baked ingredients, in accordance with her husband's philosophy. She even made the bread eaten on *Cressy*, and very special it was. We moored the first night in an eldritch, wooded cutting not far from the heart of Selly Oak; and not the least queer thing about the generally queer atmosphere of the place was that we were left almost unnaturally undisturbed. "Canals", as I have remarked on many different occasions, "stretch green fingers into towns".

The next day, we descended Farmer's Bridge and Aston Locks; at the heart of the city, and one of the most heavily, densely industrialised "flights" anywhere in Britain. I encountered the other side of the canal fantasy at its most intense: the mysterious alloy of involvement with detachment. To those attuned it means even more than the faery domain of the remoter rural waterways; so that a good test of devotion and understanding among professed canal-lovers is a preference for the Birmingham Canal Navigations or the tough passage through the Potteries. At the second or third of the Farmer's Bridge locks, I encountered on new terms my first working boat. At that time, the B.C.N. was still busy, and I should say we met ten or twelve working narrow boats before we had completed the descent and reached Salford Junction. For me, the spell was complete:

"wound up", as the Weird Sisters put it in "Macbeth".

I recall, too, the long, brightly painted line of *Cressy* when she lay at the top of an embankment in Fazeley while we went ashore to shop. Seen from a distance, she looked as long as a liner; and there was a special delight in the adaptation of so capacious, even luxurious, a vessel to the windings, bridge clearances, and other working intricacies of the often seemingly tiny canal. I found the successful relativity of it all remarkably fortifying in a world where proportion has virtually ceased to exist: proportion not only as understood by an expert such as Vitruvius or Prince Matila Ghyka, but as once apprehended by everyone, and manifested unconsciously in every aspect of living, as all can see in any collection of bygones.

On this first canal journey of mine, *Cressy* stopped at Braunston, once the great working boat centre of the Midlands, and an excellent example of the many villages that are household (or boathold) words to the canal community but of no particular note to any landsman. In Samuel Barlow's boatyard at Braunston, I met Frank Nurser, one of the most noted of all boat painters, who, alas, died not long afterwards; and he undertook to paint me a can, a stool and a dipper of my own. This he punctually did; and, in later years, the three resplendent objects came to be exhibited, first, in the Lion and Unicorn Pavilion at the Festival of Britain, and, second, at the Brussels World Fair. They are with me in this room as I write. They have become slightly dingy, but one can hardly paint over the work of Frank Nurser.

It is a most remarkable thing that boat-painting cannot be satisfactorily imitated from outside the working boat community. One might expect that to be a pleasant figment, but, in my experience, and somewhat to my surprise, it is not. On a number of occasions, I have known artists (or art students) either knock off a roses and castles job in no time, or according to temperament, work carefully and slowly and lengthily upon it. Sometimes they have set about it after assimilating one of the fairly detailed published descriptions of how the true boat painters do it. On occasion these artists succeed in selling the products to London shops, even in establishing a mildly lucrative connection with the trade buyers; but never, in my observation, have they produced artefacts that could for a moment be mistaken by the informed for the real thing. At the best, they produce accomplished but lifeless imitations of the real thing: what Olde Tyme Music Hall is to what the Bedford or Canterbury theatres were. Needless to say, this state of affairs throws much light on the character not only of popular art but of all art. I shall return to the roses and castles in due course.

In time we reached Banbury. George Tooley, associated with the actual conversion of *Cressy*, had once, like his father before him, been a boatman ("bargees" are seldom found on canals); and the short street which led to his yard was a favoured spot for boatmen to live after their retirement. It was called Factory Street, much as the street that leads to the canal in central Birmingham is called Gas Street. Through the windows or open front doors of the little houses, one could see the traditional boat decorations, now come ashore: tiers of brightly polished brass knobs, and the highly distinctive paintwork, the "roses and castles". On a corner was a small public house, where the boatmen of all generations congregated with their wives for sing-songs and clog-dancing. Known to all as "The Strug", its full name was "The Strugglers", and its sign depicted a man struggling through an egg-like world, his feet projecting at one side of the egg, his head at the other. An inscription beneath the world-egg indicated that the man was glad he only had to do it once.

George Tooley was by now dead, but his son, Herbert Tooley, sustained all the traditions, the craftsmanship and the ancient pace of things; as, most happily, he still does. Mr. Tooley knows all there is to know about every aspect of building a boat, and he is also the finest painter of roses and castles on the cut (as the canal – or, for that matter, the entire canal system – is called by the working boat families); his father having been a noted master of the craft before him.

The voyage over, and *Cressy* stoutly secured at Tooley's yard for the winter (Tom Rolt's progress was sedate, his precautions comprehensive), I returned from Merton Street station, travelling via Bletchley. It was not the quickest route to London, but I thought that its rural wanderings through Buckinghamshire would not be available much longer, and they were not.

I cannot claim that I leapt into public action: despite all the joys and enchantments I had met with; despite the obviously urgent need for extremities of knight errancy. On the contrary, I spent a period of time that approached the traditional nine months, thinking about things. Some of my thoughts are summed up in the next chapter. Nor have I any doubt that over my head tocsins were tolling, ravens predicting, and vampires flitting.

But I assessed the accomplishments that seemed relevant: past experience had suggested that I could write, orate, organise, lead; nor was I one to worry very much about being popular with all men. A probable handicap for any kind of public life was that about the things I cared for at all (which were many and various), I tended to care too much; so that caring tended more to hurt than to rejoice me. As I cared nothing about machinery or any kind of engine, and as I disliked both beer and pubs (I am one for cafes on the continental model), I could have no prospect at all of keeping up with the boys. I knew almost no-one in the waterways or aquatic world – though I surmised at once that they might not be the people best able to help. I was aware that I had potentialities in other directions, which I should have to neglect and frustrate, and which, for such ill usage, might revenge themselves on me unpredictably. Nor could an all-consuming campaign to breathe life into a corpse be regarded as a promising source of income. At that time I benefitted under my Great-Aunt's trust to the extent of about £400 per annum, but was otherwise dependent financially upon writing and general opportunism. A corpse-reviving campaign was unlikely to enter financially into the latter category. It duly never did: indeed, by the end it had gone far to ruin me.

When one thinks and thinks about a thing, bystanders become impatient and assert that the more people think, the less they are able to decide. In my experience, this is seldom true. On the contrary, I have noticed how much gain there can be in really protracted and sustained thought, even sometimes about quite small matters. The world must be made to wait at such times. Still, there is a limit, and for each person the limit is reached at a particular point. When that point is arrived at, decisions seem often to be taken almost on whim, or on the strength of a small, chance happening; but the truth is that, as George Groddeck always insisted, we do not live, but *are lived*, so that decisions (other than between Daz and Omo) are reached outside our conscious minds. This does not mean that the time we give to conscious thought is wasted. On the contrary, it is a necessary preliminary to the unconscious, the totality, doing its best for us. In Japan, men struggle to discharge the arrow from the bow, in order that, ultimately, at very long last, something else, something that is not the will, may discharge it.

The inaugural meeting of what I suggested should be called the Inland Waterways Association, took place in this room in May 1946.

At that time I knew only one watery person (other than Tom Rolt) who seemed to me suitable to be invited; but he was a most remarkable man, Commander Luard, who long before had founded the extremely successful Little Ship Club. Astonishingly good-looking and amazingly charming, he had invented a variety of navigational aids and secret naval devices. He was among the most prominent people in ocean racing. He was much involved with ensuring the survival of the Cornish fishing industry. He had strong views, that closely coincided with my own, about the way the world is run. And he wrote novels and short stories; by no means all about the sea, but about other human passions and extravagances as well. I am glad that he accepted my invitation and was present at the start of the Association. Unfortunately, he was able later to contribute little; not from lack of interest, but from lack of time. It is, of course, always the problem with the talented; they have been over-committed from birth.

Also present at my invitation was R.K. Kirkland, who is an authority on all that moves. I felt from the start that if there was to be any hope for the waterways, it was essential to emancipate them from the sole concern of the small and ever more inturned group that was specialising in them. Tom Rolt invited Charles Hadfield and Frank Eyre, who had collaborated in a book on waterways that had been published by Collins.

Just as we were sitting down, the front door bell rang once more. A stranger stood outside. His opening words were: "Is this the meeting of the Inland Waterways Association?" He said his name was Captain Smith, and he was welcomed in. The name for the organisation had not by then been formally agreed upon. No-one ever admitted to having invited Captain Smith, and I do not think anyone had. I never learned where he heard about us. I admit that I never actually asked. From the very first, he made extremely valuable contributions to our deliberations. His advent among us was part of the waterways fantasy; the first occurrence in what came to be known as "the best traditions of the I.W.A." Both impressive and strange many of the traditions were, while they lasted.

II

Why?

Belief in absolute values, illusory as it always is, seems to me a condition of life.

THOMAS MANN

I believe that the key to the modern world lies in Samuel Butler's suggestion that the machine is an evolutionary development, and that it is in the process of reducing man from homo sapiens to homo mechanicus; virtually to greenfly status. That machines have their own purposes and intelligences, though entirely different from the purposes and intelligences of men, and that they are rapidly taking over from men, seems to me plain, when once the concept is grasped and the totally different constitutions of machines from that of man is even fractionally allowed for.

The preoccupations of men are changing.

The religious view of life as being primarily a preparation for another life or, alternatively, one life among many lives in a series or rotation, is vanishing. It remains to be seen whether man can remain man without it.

Art, which concerns me much, for primarily I am an artist, is becoming like archery: something that was once a necessity (even a legal obligation), and is now a pastime that a surprising number of people are interested in at weekends and on odd evenings. Here the impact of the machine has been direct. The art of painting had been destroyed by the camera, and what is now called painting is bubble-blowing: neither practically useful nor spiritually questing; too vacuous, for the most part, even for use as wallpaper. Jazz music, and its not very differentiated popular descendants, may aetiologically derive from the primitives of Africa, but it draws its extraordinary power from the power of the machines which beat through every bar of it (so that when one becomes aware of this, one cannot bear to listen). The music with higher claims, has gone the same way: it is so tangled with the machine, that it is no longer human. Painting and music in their human connotations are dead; and literature is palpably dying. Man, even the intellectual, is more and more ready to do without the written word at all, and is evolving philosophies to correspond. Literary style is anti-democratic.

Even love, as hitherto understood, romantic and faithful in varying proportions, is being superseded by veterinary approaches. And veterinary approaches mean mechanical approaches, as any farm animal will confirm.

We live more and more by the mechanised torture of farm animals; the progressive eradication of wild animals.

It is agreed that if we do not blow ourselves off the world, we shall crowd ourselves off the world. Conceivably, life can still be made comfortable; but nothing in sight can make it human – make it worth living. And if this life is felt to be not worth living, there is now no other life permitted us. It seems that we have to become homo mechanicus, a new species; or vanish altogether, like the dinosaur, through incapacity to adapt to changed conditions. Homo sapiens has no future.

The above observations will still be regarded by many as too exaggerated for serious consideration; though the number who will agree with them is growing, and to some they will be too obvious to need recapitulation. I am not seeking to convert: conversion is seldom a product of reasoned argument, and I have condensed and pared down these beliefs to the stark skeleton, omitting all examples, the cumulative and interlocking force of which is great.

I need, however, in this matter of why I started the Inland Waterways Association, to lay special stress upon the poor quality of daily living in the later twentieth century.

Quality of living is, in the first place, very much a matter of outlet for aggression.

In all of us there is enough aggression to equip us for living in a cave and strangling intruders upon our territory. In terms of evolution, that was only yesterday; perhaps only ten minutes ago. We are still that man.

Down the ages there have been three main outlets for this aggression.

The first has been war; which has been not merely socially approved but socially applauded; mayhem, adventure, applause, and even the hope of loot, all amalgamated.

The second has been a stable social order; with each man in his "place", receiving society's support in dealing with his frustrations.

Most important of all, however, has been the steady, unceasing, inescapable, day-by-day struggle with the environment: with the weather, with disease, with the landlord, with life itself, with God.

War has now been made, not perhaps impossible, but certainly impracticable. It can no longer serve its former cathartic and emancipatory function. Hence the angst behind what has been well called the Violence for Peace movement: the true, though largely unconscious, anxiety is not that there will be a war, but that there will not; that so ancient an outlet for aggression has now been sealed off.

The state social order is everywhere in dissolution. No one knows where he stands. Pre-supposed new horizons for all are rapidly narrowing to a universal, collectivist, egalitarian tyranny: to which our ministers offer no alternative.

In the culture of the West, by means of which the evolutionary process has destroyed or is destroying all other cultures, the struggle with the environment has also been decisively modified, through the welfare state, the enforcement of equality, and kindred devices.

Homo sapiens is likely to die of frustration and boredom; perhaps attempt racial suicide to escape his torment, his emptiness and uselessness.

The great difficulty with all schemes of economic enfranchisement is the quite remarkable lack of evidence that most men and women are equipped for any such destiny. The almost total failure of compulsory education to educate; the fact that all the diverse schemes for economic betterment at such very different stages the world over, really offer in the end no more than higher heaps of mass-produced mechanical junk for all: these things predicate world-death from ennui, probably from self-destruction.

One reason (though only one) why education has achieved so little is that teaching is a vocation; and that very few teachers have it.

Every activity that matters is a vocation; and in no field are there remotely enough people who have it. Currently, the gaps are filled by well organised humbug: managerial techniques, public relations, and egalitarian lies.

Rule is a vocation; so that, at the very best, democracy is a negative technique (though negation has an important part in the field of government), and of value only if votes are in some way weighted in favour of the discriminating, as Winston Churchill at one time advocated. The problem of government is, and always has been, the problem of how best to find and to promote the few people who have a real gift for it. Hereditament, now so absurdly despised, will do something; but the problem is complicated by Plato's observation that only those are fit to govern who do not want to. One thing is certain. As Yeats put it: "A great country is a country which promotes its great men".

I thought that in the waterways system, vast in relation to the size of the country, beautiful, potentially useful, neglected and forgotten but still legally and technically alive, I might have found a field for a modest social initiative and adventure: something that might touch the fringe of the cosmic dilemma. A social *adventure*, I emphasise; not a social experiment. A social experiment is something inflicted (or bestowed) upon people; a matter of duty and conscience. A social adventure, as I saw it, is something in which free individuals participate jointly, and perhaps joyfully.

Today, a higher proportion of our population is committed to work that offers no direct satisfaction of any kind in the doing. The only comment upon this that strikes me as hopeful is that put forward by the ingenious Professor Parkinson, who says that the boundless proliferation of pseudo-work is an inevitable and therapeutic phase in the transition from real-work to no-work. It remains to be seen whether man in the mass can face no-work. On the other hand, recreation is not merely becoming more passive (watching the television or sitting in the car, instead of visiting the theatre or going for a ten-mile walk) and more congested (so that escape from official amenity has become very difficult), but is losing its inner justification as it is more and more pursued merely for its own sake, and alongside everyone else.

On the waterways, it seemed to me that there should be less than the usual gap between work and pleasure: steering even a blackened coal boat is a vocation; and, on the other hand, every pleasure boat that passes, helps the campaign to keep the waterway in being at all. On the waterways, unusually little seemed to be either compulsory or handed out; those being the apparently opposed, but, in fact, almost identical concepts that at once restrict and mask the richer world around us.

There was, and is, a widening gulf between utility and beauty. For all the talk of 'industrial design', and all the town and country planning, things that are regarded as useful, grow even uglier; and the fact that the new ugliness is not of grime and squalor but of uniformity and lifelessness, is by no means necessarily a change for the better. Dirt can be washed off. A New Town is difficult to remedy by any means. What outsiders call squalor, may be true, real, and personally authentic living to the participants, Jane Jacobs, the American prophetess, points out; and can therefore in the end enhance the living of outsiders also. It is hard to imagine anyone but experts visiting the new town centres of the world, unless compelled. On the other hand, that which is officially regarded as beautiful, tends to have a neat railing round it, a list of bye-laws, and a corona of souvenir kiosks encircling the coach park. On the waterways, beauty and utility mingle: souvenir kiosks are few, even today; and from very earliest record down to John Masefield's dirty British coaster with its salt-caked smokestack, it has been agreed by all that even the grimiest, most work-worn boat manages somehow to be a thing of beauty.

It further seemed to me that even by 1946 there must be enough people who shared these views, to make possible a campaign to take possession of the waterways system (which Authority implied that it wished only to be rid of), and develop it as an enclave where our philosophy could be put into practice, and might have room modestly to flourish, and us with it. I thought that then the message might spread to other fields of endeavour: a prescription for making-your-own-life. I was not so hopeful as to think we could modify society in general. I did think it possible that a fortress could be built, which could not easily be either stormed or assimilated, and which would, therefore, continue to influence. These were the convictions and hopes that for eighteen years of misunderstanding and abuse, together with some startling and quite unexpected personal sacrifices, made it seem still worthwhile to continue the struggle. The campaign appeared to be the maximum contribution I could sensibly make towards the resolution of the world dilemma.

The campaign achieved astonishing victories (though the intensity and bitterness of the resistance was the most astonishing thing of all); but it failed, almost totally, to accomplish its main purpose. For this, obviously there are reasons appertaining to the deeper reality of man; but there was one almost technical miscalculation that I (and no one else) made from the outset. I believe it to be so precise and so important that I do best to dispose of it at once.

As one reads one's morning paper, one observes that seldom does a week seem to pass without it being stated that some enterprise or activity is about to close down or cease because "it can no longer be made to pay"; and commonly an enterprise or activity to which one was particularly, though sometimes vaguely, attached. If trouble is taken to follow up such cases, or if the case somehow enters one's own life, it is frequently (not, of course, always) found not that the enterprise in question cannot be made "to pay" at all, but rather that it cannot be made to pay well enough to attract or to hold capital (and sometimes labour) which can obtain a better return elsewhere. It is by this process that everywhere smaller enterprises are losing their identity in larger; and larger enterprises in still larger. The almost inevitable end is a single enterprise in each field; followed by state ownership of one kind or another. Believers in nationalisation are, indeed, frequently heard to welcome in private the development of the 'monopolies' they inveigh against in public. The entire course of events is the grand high road to the junk state, universal impersonality, and ubiquitous boredom.

In 1946, the narrow boat carrying industry was in the condition I describe. It was not, as the official interests concerned with closing the waterways claimed, that it could not be made to pay at all. It was that an investor from the outside world could get a better return from something else or a worker, better wages. I suppose that the vocational appeal of the narrow boat life, which by a large number (much more than enough for the purpose) was eagerly, even fanatically, proclaimed would suffice to produce the quite small amount of support the industry needed, even though a higher income could probably be got elsewhere.

I was wrong. It seemed that almost no one is prepared to sacrifice income in exchange for what he himself proclaims to be the good life; the life he wants. Though some time had to pass before it could become clear, I should perhaps have seen sooner that it was a crucial discovery. The point touched other important aspects of the waterways situation than narrow boat carrying (such as the retention and proper development of the beautiful waterside structures); and, in any case, it suggested that what I was taking in the spirit of reality, too many others were taking in the spirit of pastime.

III

Ideals and Shadows

Charles Joseph Bonaparte's little speech upon taking over his office as Secretary of the Navy was not reassuring. "I hope we will all get along well together," he said, "but if we don't, since you can't discharge me, I suppose I will have to discharge you."

DAVID STACTON

At that first meeting, I was elected Chairman; Hadfield, Vice-Chairman; Rolt, Honorary Secretary; and Eyre, Honorary Treasurer. I agreed to make available a room in my house for use by the Association rent-free; an arrangement which lasted for more than four years. The room is known to a few of my older friends as the Waterways Room still. I offered to direct the organisation, on what is known as an honorary basis, for two years; after which we should be successful enough to pay a full-time professional organiser. This proposal was accepted, mainly, I think, because no one could think of anything better – or, indeed, of anything else that was possible at all.

With the oracular power that comes upon one at such times, I observed that the secret of success for any campaigning organisation was the engagement from the outset of a paid employee. We had settled the annual subscription at one guinea, so that even after enrolling several known well-wishers, we had less than twenty pounds in prospect, but I lent the Association another thirty, and we engaged a young woman suggested by Charles Hadfield, to dwell in the Waterways Room on two mornings a week, despatching literature and writing out receipts.

It was hardly a dynamic or progressive employment in those first weeks, and the young woman soon bettered herself. She was replaced by Elizabeth Jane Howard, most beautiful of women, and also one of the most brilliant. She was at that time working on her first novel (and, in my view, still her best), "The Beautiful Visit"; which, when published, was immediately so successful that she soon outsoared the shadow of our night and has dwelt in the empyrean ever since. Jane Howard was so beautiful that continuous problems arose, especially when, at a later date, she joined the Association's Council. Little in the way of completely normal business was possible or sensible, when she was in the room. I had previously thought that the power of Zuleika Dobson was exaggerated. I now learnt that it was not. Jane's presence had the effect of making everything else in life seem worthless and absurd beside her radiant identity. By merely existing, she promoted loves and hates which, through no fault of hers, left some who felt them, fevered and wasted. She was like a creature from the Arabian Nights. She was also an inspired and devoted worker (soon for much more than two mornings a week) at often very dull jobs. The Association was fantastically fortunate to have such a person in its employ for such a critical period of years.

Jane Howard wrote a short story named "Three Miles Up". It is not merely one of the best pieces of canal fiction, (which is to say little, as there is almost no canal fiction of repute) but also one of the best of all ghost stories; which is to say much more, as there are perhaps only twenty-five or thirty good ghost stories in European fiction. Moreover, I know of no story that better captures the atmosphere of canal cruising. Like most good ghost stories (fiction), it derives from first-hand experience: the waterway described is the canal between Fazeley and Fradley in the Midlands, where the navigator will be able to detect many of the geographical and social features described by the author, though not the terrain of the terrifying dénouement (which, however, can at times be lighted upon elsewhere).

The Association began by sending to the press letters signed by the Chairman and Honorary Secretary and appealing for support. They were very innocuous letters; saying no more than that those with any kind of interest in an obviously neglected field, should join us. Many editors found space. Members began to come in at once. In September, the late Sir William Beach Thomas, most poetical and persuasive of writers on the countryside, commended us in "The Spectator"; our first round of applause from an independent critic of note. At no time, did we lack funds to pay the paid secretary's wages, and soon my small loan could be refunded.

There are some simple basic rules for a 'voluntary organisation'. I do not say they are rules for success, but I do say that success is unlikely to attend those who disregard them.

A fundamental policy booklet should be available to all enquirers; describing the character of the problem, and the solution which the organisation exists to advocate. Organisations which offer no solution, or a too imprecise solution, or alternative solutions, seldom achieve any end beyond the recreation of the membership (which, however, more commonly than not is the true end, even though perhaps unconsciously). Our policy booklet, named "The Future of the Waterways", was originally written mainly by Rolt, but was later progressively rewritten by me, as experience was ingathered.

The booklet should be supplied free to all members upon joining, so that they can properly inform themselves upon the movement's character and objects; and should be on sale to all others. It can be supplemented by a briefer summary, available free to all as a leaflet, or in the apt term, throw-away. Many voluntary organisations never even start to advance in the world of external action, because they have never sufficiently defined where they aim to go, let alone done all possible to make sure their members comprehend.

New members should be asked to complete a printed membership form, which should then be filed and brought out twelve months later when the subscription is due to be renewed. It is much better for subscriptions to run for twelve months from the date of joining than to be all renewable at the same date: the slow and difficult work of collection can then be spread throughout the year; all subscriptions become of equal value; and potential members can be assured that they will receive their full money's-worth from the outset.

The method by which the renewal of subscriptions can best be applied for, is very important. Every member has a right to an advance reminder indicating the amount of the subscription, and the date when it falls due in his or her particular case. I am amazed by the number of organisations which either expect members to renew their own subscriptions without reminder of any kind (and send a pained note when the member fails to do so – the first the member hears of the subject); or send reminders which do not indicate the amount due, so that the member, if enthusiastic enough, has to look it up in last year's cheque book. The organisation should be provided with at least two subsequent forms, to be sent, normally after standard intervals, to defaulters. The second reminder should be only slightly pained. The third (or perhaps fourth) should indicate with precision that if the subscription is not received by a stated date, then the membership will lapse. These final intimations tend to be criticised, but not by those who will be of real value to the organisation's campaign. Compliance with the above rules will help to keep the renewal rate as high as it was in our own early days.

Efficiency in office work is of the first importance to a voluntary organisation, though seldom productive of gratitude, and not always rated highly by the inner group of enthusiasts for the cause. The formal words of thanks at the annual general meeting can sometimes seem to those concerned so bitterly inadequate as to be better omitted altogether; but a keen and well-run 'General Office' is as important to the director of a public campaign as a keen and disciplined staff to a general waging a war. To a campaigning voluntary organisation there are two things that really matter: an inspiring, imaginative and energetic leader (whatever may be his or her exact title in the organisation), and an efficient office. Committees are of less importance altogether, though it is essential to be able to handle them so that they offer of their best; so that, to put it plainly, they advance the cause, and not only themselves. The shortcomings of committees are groaned over by all who have to deal with them, but are not always accurately diagnosed or most effectively palliated.

Committee rule is initially subject to the two-headed drawback that there are far too many candidates for whom membership of the committee is their only claim to importance, while those persons who might be of real value to the cause, are usually too busy elsewhere to join the committee at all, and certainly too busy to give to its work the time and attention that the members of the first group are eager to give. The members of the first group struggle with passion to join the committee and to remain on it, governing their actions, like Members of Parliament, primarily (often exclusively) by the need to retain their places; which means, in the main, the need to avoid unpopularity. The members of the second group have to be wooed to remain at all, and tend to clutch, consciously or unconsciously, at every chance of departing, and thus lightening their load. For of those few who have a real vocation for governing or administration, most live in a state of ambivalence; divided between drive to rule and nausea at what ruling is, its unreality in the outer world (at least in modern times), its waste of spirit in the inner.

Men are not organised to agree among themselves for long. Committee rule involves the continual frustration of personal self-expression; and hence, notoriously, tends to produce a colourless, compromise product which is not really wanted by anyone, but, like the majority of the committee members themselves, is moulded as far as possible mainly with the aim of avoiding positive unpopularity. The well-known boredom of committee meetings originates in this all-round-the-table frustration of personal creativity: boredom is a positive, not a negative, condition; a by-product of repressed aggression. Many with experience of committees will agree that they work well only when dominated by an effective chairman. The proper function of a committee, in short, is advisory; and perhaps (like the proper function of democracy itself) restrictive.

In a voluntary organisation, the upshot of committee government, un-avoidable though committee government may be at this moment in history, tends to be that the supposed cause receives less and less attention, as the committee concentrates more and more on social and other accessories. Under committee rule, I can see no way of preventing this. How best to advance the cause must be controversial; so that, as people say, "all the time is spent in talk". Equally important is the fact that the advancement of the cause involves those concerned in hard, real, and difficult work; in meeting the resistance of the environment. That may be a proper activity for most men, lacking which, as I believe, homo sapiens becomes homo mechanicus; but it is an activity which a committee inevitably finds vastly harder than an individual, and it is also an activity which people expect, unconsciously if not consciously, to be paid for undertaking – and not without some reason. Such concern with the cause as may remain, tends, therefore, to be mostly preaching to the converted; but by far the easiest and most popular (though unacknowledged) line in a voluntary organisation is to concentrate upon social events, which though not free from controversy (far from it), yet evade engagement with a hostile or indifferent outside community and world.

Nor, of course, is this line of least resistance confined to members of the committee. In most voluntary organisation memberships, there is a small proportion that is more pugnacious in the cause than the committee, but a large majority that cares for the cause much less than the committee does. In my experience of very diverse voluntary organisations, the greater number of them really exist primarily in order that people who have a particular interest of some kind, may meet other people believed to have the same interest. I was told by a man extremely important in the organisation of the Labour Party, that in his view (I think, in the view that was generally accepted), more than seventy per cent of those who went to the trouble of actually becoming a party member, joined "solely for social reasons"; to meet others with similar views and interests, hardly at all to advance the crusade for nationalisation and social justice. In the waterways cause, where, on the one hand, a tremendous and sustained battle was required to overturn an entrenched and established negation of considerably more than a century's standing, while, on the other, much of the advocacy had, in the nature of the case, to be concerned with advocating pleasure of one kind and another (boating and the look of things), life was, from the outset, obviously going to be difficult. From the beginning, I wondered whether the job could not best be done by a small, dedicated group. At the start, it was not a practicable possibility: I had no such group, and no idea where recruits for it could be found. So from the outset the Association was at the mercy of the people who paid their guinea and employed the superstructure others had built up, to advocate random ideas of their own, often directly opposed to those which the Association has been formed to promote.

If one really means business with one's cause, one must decide upon a precise aim or set of aims; preferably after giving much thought to the matter – if only because subsequent going-back or wavering is, on balance, deeply disadvantageous, both to the cause and to oneself. The inconsistency and mutability which are essential to the proper conduct of life as a whole, indeed to remaining fully alive at all ("consistency is the hobgoblin of little minds"), should have no place in one's work for the cause. This is partly a technical matter – or technical limitation: politicians are less respected if they proclaim reversed objectives too frequently; and a medieval crusade-leader would have been very nearly lost if he had decided, after further thought and additional experience, that it did not really matter if Jerusalem was recovered from the Infidel or not. Public life, like the art of the popular theatre, is rough stuff of its nature. Too much subtlety is simply out of place; though integrity, contrary to some appearances, is in the long run very important. The promoter of such a cause as is now in mind, should, in fact, be more a prophet than a politician. And thus adherence to the objectives is important inwardly also: a prophet cannot sufficiently believe in himself if he becomes aware that much he has proclaimed, was wrong. This is true, however sincere he was at the time he proclaimed it. The integrity that it required is precisely the integrity of inner conviction. Given that, and all is dust without it (dust and tea-parties), then the prophet should realise that, in the context of his work, he is promoting a cause, not living a life; and that the two have very different, often opposed, rules.

Having settled his aims, after all the time and thought necessary, the promoter, and all who are with him, must uphold them and press them upon the world at all appropriate seasons and on all appropriate occasions; and must do all possible to keep them in the forefront of every single activity the organisation embarks upon. This sounds like a programme for surfeit. It is not. The promoter will find that after shouting, whispering, writing, and insinuating the same, simple thing (including, often, to the same people – though this should be avoided) for years on end, most of his hearers and readers will still have it badly wrong; if, indeed, they have not reversed it, at least when it comes to putting it into any kind of practice. This is because man is made to project: for the most part, what he loves in another is the image of himself that he ingrafts there; what he hears, is what he has heard already, and long, long ago. This outcome saves the promoter and his group from succumbing to the weariness of incessant repetition. The response is always so unpredictable.

Equal in importance with constancy of aim and ubiquity of attack is disregard for unpopularity (the double negative being carefully chosen). If one's ideas are of any value at all, they are bound to upset many people, merely as ideas; certain to make entirely justified enemies (because not everybody's interests can be identical with one's own – and it would be dreadful if they were, as under ideal Marxism). But it is the promoter himself who arouses far more antagonism than his ideas: modern man, more than any man before him, struts through the meadow, like Tarquin, cutting off the heads of all the tallest flowers. He does it almost without thought.

Similarly, the promoter is wise to proclaim no other interests than the cause; to admit to little life of any kind outside it. He may have a spouse but certainly not a love life.

All the same, if he is to hope for success, he should *be* outside, while not proclaiming the fact. When it comes to advancing a cause, the expert and the specialist are self-defeating almost by definition. The need is for one who cares more for the wood than for the trees, and more still for the landscape as a whole; also for one who has, or can make, connections with individuals and groups who know little about the cause but are in a position to advance it.

In such company, he must not obtrude the cause, but be able subtly to link and mingle it with the diverse interests and advantages of his auditors. Actual talents not directly connected with the cause, can be very important; as talents for oratory, literature, flirtation, and travel. These, it will be observed, are none of them so much skills as arts. It would seem that the successful promoter must himself or herself have an artistic variation in his or her character. Few generalisations are truer than Shelley's proclamation that poets are the unacknowledged legislators of mankind. The promoter finds himself, then, in a new ambiguity: the face he shows to his general membership may have to be very different from the face he shows to the wider world.

As the waterways cause advanced, I often reflected that the world was will and idea; though not in the least as Schopenhauer applied those terms. Facts do not exist: most supposed facts are a matter of actual controversy, and all facts change into quite different facts as history proceeds. The world is first flat and then spheroid (with some still saying it is flat). There are ideas only; and most of the ideas are chosen (and upheld as facts) according to the interests, the pleasure, and, in fact, the will of those who assert them. On the other hand, when will is being consciously exerted, it has to encounter ideas only, not facts.

This formulation does not lighten the campaigner's task as much as might be expected, but it does identify it. From the first, the dug-in opponents of the waterways movement asserted and continually sought to prove that the facts of the situation were against it. After twenty years, the facts suddenly dissolved and almost completely reversed themselves; entirely because the official will had been so worked on that it changed its direction. If my thorny tale offers any message of hope, it lies there. A prophet can greatly prevail if he identifies his task correctly, and steadily asserts his ideas against the official ideas. The distinctively contemporary element in the martyrdom of man is closely connected with his belief that his task in life is the accumulation of more and more facts. Facts, terrifying in their number, mutability, irrelevance, and threat to individual happiness, weigh man down until he loses all direction of his destiny, and staggers like a crippled mule.

Life is not fact but poetry. It was by steady adherence to that truth that the waterways battle was so considerably won. To be able to say this, is for me the most important prize from all the victories gained. I now do not merely believe but know that a quality of the imagination is all that matters in life. I can proclaim it from the heart.

The struggle, and the waterways field itself, may seem so miniscule as to make such utterances ridiculous. I do not think this is true. I think the field was well chosen. I do not think any other could be found that was at once so big (about three thousand miles of waterway system, reaching into most parts of England) and, for historical reasons, so available; nor many where the opposing force of fact and accepted opinion, official and unofficial, was so strong. When the campaign began, most of the waterway "enthusiasts", few in number at the best, were as gloomy about the prospect as any official. Many of the experts are exactly the same today. Indeed, I believe the waterways to have been so specially appropriate to such a campaign for man that I doubt, with much sadness, whether what we did can ever be repeated.

IV

The Problem and the Programme

*Those who are in opposition must not expect to be attacked for what they really are or really
want, but for what the party in power is pleased to think they are and want.*

JENS PETER JACOBSEN

For a century and more at the time we began, the British system of
inland waterways had lain in a coma: it had become the national
Sleeping Princess.

The two basic events in the modern history of the waterways were the
taking-over of about one-third of the system by railway companies; and the
foundation of the Inland Waterways Association.

Whereas in other lands, action of some kind was usually taken, after the
development of railways, to prevent the railway interests merely buying up
the waterways and killing them, we in Britain proceeded, I shall not say on
the opposite principle, but on no principle at all.

We are pragmatists not theorists. What happened here was that railway
companies, attempting to manoeuvre through Parliament Private Bills for
the construction of their lines, and meeting, inevitably, the warm
opposition of river and canal companies already serving the districts in
question, were compelled (pragmatically) to buy out the canal companies,
often at a very high price, as the only means of building their lines at all: and
that, in this way, the aforementioned one-third of the waterways system
passed into railway ownership before most of those not immediately concerned had realised what was happening. The one-third, moreover, being
made up of a bit here and a bit there, bestowed upon its new possessors a
virtual grip upon almost the entire network; a development of which the
railway interest (no doubt in its deep unconscious) was certainly well aware
from the beginning.

As one writes about waterways, one hears always the phantom voices of
the advocati diaboli: Mephistopheles being, as Goethe pointed out, strictly,
and merely, the spirit of negation. Already they speak: claiming at this point

that the waterways of Britain are not, and never were, a system or network at all. The support put forward for this contention is that most of the waterways were constructed (canals dug out, and rivers made navigable) by local interests acting largely on their own, and sometimes going in for peculiarities of 'gauge' (size of locks and of navigable channel). Though this is true, the upshot has had little bearing on the national situation: while the differences in gauge are certainly irritating and obstructive to development (a boat to go everywhere must not exceed 46 feet in length or 7 feet in width), they are really much fewer than might have been expected; and the product of all the local efforts has long been a single mesh of navigation serving a surprisingly wide total area of country. This last will be apparent to all who glance at a comprehensive waterways map. But it is evidence of the conditions prevailing, before the Association was founded, that, to the best of my belief, the description of the waterways as 'a system' was first employed by me! The wood and the trees. From first to last, parochialism and extreme narrowness of interest were major problems; but that, of course, is only to say that the Association belonged to this world. Nor by any means is parochialism wholly an evil. Very far from it. It was merely a difficulty in the waging of a campaign which had to be national or fail.

The railway companies gave considerable attention to diverting all possible traffic. Frequently the procedure was to raise the tolls for carrying by water while offering specially reduced rates for carrying by rail. Then, when the traffic had been secured, to raise the rail rates to more than they had been in the first place, while failing to maintain the increasingly deserted canal, thus making a return of traffic to it unattractive and hardly practicable.

The railway companies raised the tolls for using the canal, cut down on the maintenance (and, of course, on any kind of publicity), and instituted a variety of inconveniences, crude or subtle. On the notorious Kennet & Avon Navigation, across the waist of England, from the Thames to the Severn, the Great Western Railway forbade fires in moored boats; concern for public safety was cited, but the ingenious regulation froze out the boatmen literally as well as figuratively. The remarkable thing was that any traffic survived under such conditions: that much did, until quite recently on most of the waterways, provides striking proof of an intrinsic strength in water transport.

The *advocati negantes* naturally claim that the railway intervention was a quite minor event in waterways history; a negligible contribution to the decline. One reason, at least in the Association's first years, for the warmth behind this counterclaim, was that many of the individuals who had been closely linked with railway policy, were still fixed in employment on the waterside. But it would be a mistake to make too much of that: many waterway workers at levels below the top, were cordially on the

Association's side from the start, and people's opinions are far more a product of their temperaments than of their circumstances or true financial interests. Those who wish to assess for themselves the impact of the railway intervention upon the waterways of Britain (the waterways of Scotland and Wales, suffered, proportionately, even worse than those of England) are referred to the multi-volume Report of the 1906–1912 Royal Commission on the subject. It contains an astonishing aggregation of sworn evidence which will leave very little doubt on the subject.

The railway companies did not find it as easy as they would have liked actually to close waterways; even the waterways they owned. Traditionally, most navigable waterways are 'statutory navigations' (a status considerably whittled down by recent legislation aimed at reducing maintenance obligations and facilitating closure): governed by a specific Act of Parliament, negotiated by the persons who constructed the navigation in the first place, and normally laying upon them and all their successors fairly standard obligations of upkeep and access to all traffic that offers. A statutory navigation can usually be closed only by another Act of Parliament, known as an Abandonment Act though, in recent years, certain other procedures have sometimes proved efficacious, such as Abandonment by Warrant of the Minister of Transport, available when opposition to the abandonment lacks strength, and even abandonment by the Minister of Agriculture, in cases where land drainage interests are very powerful. (Land drainage authorities want to keep water levels as low as possible, and unimpeded by locks and weirs, so that the normally unused depth of the watercourse will be available to run off sudden flood waters.)

The national character enters here, as at so many points in our chequered tale. As a nation we commonly allow an obvious evil to run on until the last extremity, and then (sometimes) conjure up a desperately overdue national clamour. As with the belated reaction to the Nazis, left until things were almost hopeless. What tends to happen is that a waterway is allowed to fall to pieces, even for generations (waterways being startlingly tough and durable), without anyone doing anything much beyond grumbling about the smell, the leaks, the unsightliness, the anachronism, and (in latter years) the danger to the kiddies; but that when They, the ubiquitous, anonymous, possibly non-existent, but omnipotent They, propose to take the last step of all, and actually to set about closure, then there is a national protest: letters to the press, to officials, to Members of Parliament, and to Ministers; a local preservation committee, even a national utilisation committee; patrons, honorary secretaries, delegations by special coach, resolutions, volunteers of all ages with mattocks and secateurs, persons brewing successive waves of ever stronger tea . . .

Railway companies and others (but mainly railway companies) succeeded, none the less, in closing about a thousand miles of navigation before the Association was founded; but the main policy became merely one of neglect and oblivion. Infrequently, the working boat still crawled about a considerable mileage of the system; dragging along the bottom, pushing through weed, stemming leaky locks. As, owing to these handicaps, they could often be loaded only to half capacity, they were very much less efficient than when the canals they traded on had first been opened, in the eighteenth century. It was a miracle that they survived at all; and soon few of them did. More and more, the younger members of the 'boating families', a group almost as tough, self-sufficient, and distinctive as gypsies, were leaving 'the cut' to seek work on 'the land'. Carrying by inland waterway was hampered by a system of charging by toll on every ton carried; the rates varying not only according to the commodity, but also according to the geography of the proposed journey, and being seldom even posted or otherwise disclosed in advance. It was a replica of the turnpike road system, abolished on the highways a hundred and fifty years before, as a menace to the national economy. There was almost no attempt to develop supplementary revenues: pleasure boating was discouraged, sometimes forbidden; and little attempt made to sell water to industry. It was hard to find a hopeful word anywhere; including, as I have remarked before, among the self-proclaimed amateur enthusiasts. The Association was founded far too late, but if it had not appeared when it did, and if it had not fought with insight, ferocity, endless persistence and refusal to compromise, then there was nothing that could have prevented most of the rivers and canals being closed to navigation. However bad the reasons for their plight, the nation as a whole lacked the moral energy to save them. The official argument was always that because this or that waterway was in especially bad shape, therefore it should be among the first to be closed, without regard for how its bad shape came about ("raking up the past") or for its relative importance in the national scene. And, naturally, some of the most potentially valuable waterways were, for that very reason, among those that had been most savaged.

It was necessary to propound a revolution.

The Inland Waterways Association proposed the following programme, and thereafter prospered in the degree to which it adhered to it:-

All the navigable rivers and canals (whether – after 1948 – 'nationalised' or not) should be transferred to a new National Waterways Conservancy; administered by representatives of the interests concerned, from carrying companies and local authorities to boat clubs and angling societies; and required to pursue a policy of multiple use, exploiting every navigation in all its functions and potentialities, including commercial carrying, pleasure boating, water supply, land drainage, and angling (the proportionate potentiality of each, naturally varying from waterway to waterway). There should be no more abandonments or closures under any circumstances, but, instead, at a later date, a drive for re-opening certain rivers and canals that had been already lost.

In due course, the Association proposed a two-stage approach.

The first stage in a national waterways policy should be making the existing system viable under a conservancy and a policy of multiple use.

The second stage should be a programme of enlargement and modernisation, as in France, Germany, Holland, Belgium, the United States, the Soviet Union, and many other lands; "bringing British waterways into the modern world", as it is sometimes called. In the countries mentioned, more and more goods travel by water each year, and more and more money is spent on modernising the waterways. It is extremely unlikely that all these countries, with their differing political systems, are wrong, and we, who neglect our waterways, right; though advocati negantes have regularly claimed that British geography presents peculiarities which unsuit the United Kingdom to inland waterway transport.

The two questions about waterways and the Association that I have been most frequently asked down the years, are "How did you come to start it?" and "Is the Association concerned with trade or with pleasure?" When to the second question I replied that the Association was concerned with both, and with much more besides, the enquirers would commonly depart visibly baffled and visibly sceptical. Nothing has proved more difficult than persuading people to open their eyes and minds widely enough. I have found this disappointing, because all possibility of success for the waterways cause is a matter of the wider vision. And nothing has more convinced me than this difficulty of finding a vision wide enough, that the Association truly has stood for a new view of more than inland waterways.

V

Early Amenities

That fact-finding is a substitute for decisions is very generally known. What we fail to recognize is that fact-finding is also a substitute for thought.

PROFESSOR NORTHCOTE PARKINSON

When the Association's first letters appeared in the press, rejoinders followed from representatives of the two trade associations that then existed; one representing waterway carriers, the other representing navigation owners. These rejoinders took the line that there was no need for a new organisation, because those that existed – indeed, had long existed – could look after the situation perfectly well. The implication was that nothing was materially wrong with the waterways. The response to this was not difficult. Readers in doubt were invited to visit a canal and insert a walking stick to see how soon it reached the mud. The number applying to join us steadily increased.

The two trade associations then combined in inviting Rolt and me to dinner. The feast took place in an hotel near Victoria Station. A feast it was: much trouble must have been taken in that period of patchy, post-war supply. It was also a curious occasion: the first of a longish series in my life, as the waterways movement advanced. The curiosity lay in the character of the dialogue. Our four generous hosts, stated, much more than once, that their lifetimes had been spent in the canal industry, and, sometimes, that their finances were deeply involved with it, yet expressed little but pessimism about its future; while Rolt and I, involved only by idealism, seemed full of hope and even confidence. The point upon which we concentrated, not only on this occasion, was that if things were as bad as was claimed (which, as far as it went, we did not doubt), then the industry should be exceedingly grateful for the appearance of a group concerned disinterestedly with fighting its battles in the public arena and with arguments in support of it, based upon the public good. We made little impression. A critical difficulty had made its appearance.

Our hosts and their associates feared our already public proposal that the waterways system should be regarded and retained as a single, comparatively uniform, entity. The view of the two organisations was that such public money as was likely to be available for the regeneration of the waterways (very little, they supposed, and with good reason), should be directed entirely to the shrinking mileage on which their members traded. Plainly, they thought that our policy of regarding the system as a whole, was more disadvantageous to their position than our general advocacy could be helpful. That distinctly short-term assessment had to be added to the scepticism with which the businessman regards the philosopher. (Often the businessman has all my sympathy). The discussion did not begin until most of the splendid food was eaten, but, when it did begin, it lasted for hours, so that Rolt and I departed slightly exhausted, though unconceding. The two sides of the table (as the saying goes) had found almost no common ground at all. I had even then seen enough of the canals not to be greatly surprised, but it was plain that the Association was going to be even more on its own than some had hoped. Already, it seemed possible that a new generation of carriers was going to be required, as well as a new type of waterway administrator. As for our hosts, we suspected that they decided upon a policy of waiting for our Association to die. By accepted standards, it seemed very likely to happen.

When, after two years, the Association was not only alive but becoming strident, I (alone, this time) was invited by one of our former hosts, to another feast, a gorgeous luncheon. The conversation followed exactly the same course. The spokesman for the carriers, prominently connected with a well known and long established firm, made a great impression upon me by saying of the industry, with obvious sincerity and feeling, "I only hope it lasts out my time", and implying that it would be childish to hope for more. Nationalisation had come about by then, and plainly the Association's advocacy of equal treatment for the whole system was regarded with more alarm than ever. There was no sign at all that the new authority for the nationalised waterways agreed with our aim (very much the reverse), but presumably there was a danger of bureaucratic crackpots coming together with philosophical crackpots. It was my last encounter of that kind with the carrying trade, but the dialogue passed on to the nationalised authority and was continued almost intact as the years went by.

One reason why dialogue with the trade flagged, was that carriage by water had dwindled and dwindled, until the Association had become far more powerful than the trade, as I write with regret as well as pride. The policy of steady contraction, whether advocated by the trade or by the bureaucracy (who proved to be even more wedded to it), was fundamentally a hopeless one for all concerned: as, of course, my friend at the magnificent luncheon had in his own way recognised. Every closure of a waterway weakened all the other waterways, instead of strengthening them, as was always alleged; and led but to further closures. The neglect of one length of waterway, regularly spread to the next length and the next. As the branches were cut off, the tree was killed. The railway system has since been killed in the same way and with the same arguments, though not against the do-or-die opposition that we put up.

Even in that first phase of the Association, it was true that narrow boat carrying, and some other forms of waterway carrying also, were already in the predicament I have referred to at the end of Chapter II: they were by no means hopelessly impracticable and uneconomic, but they were far from a good investment on the open market. The shortcoming of the trade lay in the failure to propose (or, at least, to press for) any effective programme of modernisation and enlargement. From long before I and my friends had come on the scene, the trade had passed a point of no return. Frequently devitalised by railway infiltration, made intensely conservative by its eighteenth century origins and perhaps by its very way of life, it had been finally rotted (or, alternatively, fossilised) by traffic-sharing, traffic-guaranteeing agreements introduced during the Second World War, and still much in the background during my early days. The industry was eminently the product of the odd Sleeping Beauty regime that had prevailed for more than a century. Its almost total failure to emulate the example of waterway developments in other countries, possibly foreshadowed also some major element in Britain's total decline.

At the Association's first Council Meeting, I was put in charge of the Kennet & Avon campaign, which proved to be the most maddening and frustrating of all; and Captain Smith agreed to investigate the case of the Essex and Suffolk River Stour. Once navigable from the sea to the pleasant country town of Sudbury, the Stour is among the best known of English rivers, owing to its associations with both Gainsborough and Constable. Now most of the locks were in a state of wild dereliction; while the four at the bottom, though in much better order, seemed to be padlocked and unavailable. Captain Smith tracked down a navigation authority, the River Stour Commission; about which organisation its Clerk imparted two facts. The first was that the actual Commissioners had all died out or retired. The second was that, in any case, the Commission had "powers but no duties". Historically, this revelation constituted the Association's first achievement for the waterways. It was a significant one.

It is worth pursuing the tale of the Stour to its present end. As in the cases of many derelict or neglected navigations, the only effective authority proved to be the local River Board. River Boards (formerly Catchment Boards, and now River Authorities) are constituted to deal primarily with the drainage of the area. In the case of the Stour, it transpired that the four bottom locks (theoretically advancing the navigator as far as the village of

Stratford St. Mary) had just before the Second World War been rebuilt by a water company as part of an unusual bargain with the River Stour Commission under which the water company became entitled to extract more water from the river. There seems to be no record of the new locks ever being used by the public (their availability having not exactly been advertised), and when the Commission virtually ceased to function, the River Authority chained them up and closed them.

At a much later stage in the Association's history, an enquiry was instituted into the ownership of the River Stour lock sites and adjoining land. We were advised by Counsel that, the Commission being by now, as it seemed, finally defunct, ownership was probably vested in the Crown. We evolved a scheme ("we" being, as usual, mainly a single enthusiastic Member, in this case, Mr. John Marriage) for the establishment of a local trust, which would negotiate the transfer of the locks from the Crown, raise funds for their repair (still not a big undertaking), and thereafter administer them on a charitable basis for the benefit of the public; with, of course, the hope that in the end the remaining, much more run-down locks would be restored also, and the river returned to the state that had been taken for granted in Constable's time. In order that the new trust should appear solid and respectable enough to take over land from the Crown, it was regarded as essential that it should be linked with the National Trust. As at this time, the National Trust was just completing the restoration of the Stratford Canal, largely with resources, of both money and labour, derived from waterway enthusiasts, and as also it owned several properties on and near the section of the Stour in question, including the famous Willy Lott's Cottage and Flatford Mill, there seemed every reason to count upon its support. But the hope was disappointed: the Trust's local organisation and supporters took the view that they preferred their river without nasty boats and nasty trippers; in fact, they preferred it dead. So opposition was implied rather than help offered, and the Stour continues to fade.

It was especially sad in that the Association had previously played a prominent part, financially and legally, in frustrating at least two separate schemes for the extraction of still further water from the already shrunken Stour. There are many rivers and canals from which much more than the present income from water supply could reasonably be derived, especially when, as often, the water is 'returnable' to the waterway after industrial application, usually for cooling electrical plant. But, even before our time, the Stour had been pumped out for direct consumption by south-east Essex, and salt water was advancing far inland, rendering brackish the land, and injuring the trees. If more fresh water had been taken out the hypersensitive residents would indeed have had something to complain about. The whole sad story of the Stour might have been designed to illustrate the need for the National Waterways Conservancy and the wider as opposed to local view.

In November 1946, appeared the Association's first Bulletin; distributed free to Members, offered for sale to others. The title was significant: the publication was not intended to be a general waterways magazine, but a periodical statement of progress or regress in each campaign; and that it remained while I remained. In all, I edited 71 issues of the Bulletin, the later issues running to 20,000 or 25,000 words each; and of the total content, I wrote perhaps ninety per cent; though other contributions, frequently brilliant, regularly appeared also. As far as number of words go, I could instead have written four or five average-length novels. Every quarter (but production was not always as regular as it might have been, partly because big waterway events would happen at editorially inconvenient moments), I used to set aside three or four eight or ten-hour days; enlist a really tough and enduring typist with a sympathetic personality who could also spell; and dictate the Bulletin from matter I had accumulated during the quarter in a log basket, and had laid out in heaps all over the floor during the night before the work started. At the end of each three or four-day period, I spent one further day working over the typescript. The Bulletin soon acquired a certain reputation for elan. But when devoting to it so much literary and dialectical care, I knew well that very few of the Association's Members read the Bulletin at all. Not that this prevented them complaining when it was late. Or that it mattered much to the campaign: the Bulletin *was* read by the real campaigners. the few, the tiny minority upon whom, everywhere and in everything, all that is good depends.

The first Bulletin already announced the death of a member. Mr. Montagu Aubrey Lloyd had died after his cruiser had sunk on the Gloucester & Berkeley Canal. His daughter-in-law completed the book he was writing on the voyage, and, published by Imray, Laurie, Norie, and Wilson, a very ancient firm that specialises in aquatic works, it made a modest success as the first inland cruising book to appear after the Association's establishment. There had been a few precursors, mostly ancient and odd: Dashwood's "From the Thames to the Solent" (through the long defunct Wey & Arun Canal); the novelist Temple Thurston's "Flower of Gloster" (through the Thames & Severn Canal, also defunct); and Bonthron's remarkable "My Holidays on Inland Waterways". Bonthron travelled in state: when he and his party neared a forbidding flight of locks, they were apt to "hail a stout fellow on the bank", and themselves "repair to a nearby hostelry". But he covered almost every single navigable mile in England, including a passage through the Surrey Commercial Canal in a racing eight with all the men in whites. Recounting wondrous feats, his narrative is four-square, his epithets almost Homeric in their conventionality.

Bulletin 1 also referred to Mr. J. F. Pownall and his Grand Contour

Canal.

This remarkable man was already a Member, and I had already met him. Mr. Pownall had discovered long before the Association's time that a canal built along the 310 feet contour could reach to the most astonishing number of important places, with locks required only for descent to estuaries at the terminals. He was also a pioneer of multiple use: the Grand Contour Canal could virtually solve the water supply problem of England, while taking much of the slow-moving industrial traffic off the roads, and making possible through shipping from such places as Birmingham to such places as Basel. The cost of the Grand Contour Canal would be high (though much reduced by consequent savings in the construction of new roads), but I know of no project before the public in any field which would bring three such vast, separate advantages from a single outlay. Naturally, therefore, Mr. Pownall, though (as I must emphasise) highly esteemed in his own profession of civil engineer, has spent much spirit, and much substance, in storming the citadel of authority without exactly capturing it. One might go so far as to say that he belongs to the very type of which authority (inevitably committed to norms and averages) most disapproves: original, profound, and right. As can be told by looking at him, Mr. Pownall is properly an eighteenth century man; comparable with James Brindley and Thomas Telford. Then he could have peregrinated from Earl to Duke, and on to the Elector Palatine, or a Prince Bishop, until he had found a patron, and a patron rich enough and powerful enough to act. Now there is only one patron and it has no head to reflect with, to lose, or to be parted from. Mr. Pownall is a man, who, presented with a problem that has baffled one for months or years, instantly and ingeniously solves it with a pencil diagram on the back of a matchbox. Only those who think big can do that. I have often noticed it.

Psychoanalysts say that "it is all there at the very first interview" with the patient – if only it can be grasped. Bulletin 1 informed the Members that "We propose to get out extensive statistics, for use by trading enterprises, of the real costs of canal trade." This was a first push at a vast golden door into the void. It proved to be a perfect case of the world being will and idea, rather than fact. Soon it became "an enquiry into the real costs of transport"; stimulated, at the outset, by increasing experience of how very unreal most actual transport costs, not least canal costs, seemed to be.

Again and again, I received cautious enquiries from large, and often famous, corporations. They were not completely satisfied with their present transport arrangements. They wondered, just wondered, whether the canals could help them. Commonly, a representative was sent to stand me a lovely luncheon. (Au Jardin des Gourmets in Greek Street was a favourite establishment for the purpose.) "We are both moved and delighted," I would say at last, over the bombe surprise, "that your group thinks of returning to canal transport; but it is only fair that I should mention some of the difficulties. Not only has the British waterways system hardly been updated since the eighteenth century, but it is today little more than half as efficient as it was then, owing to neglect (and other things too). The authorities administering it will be found at the best to be indifferent to new traffics; and often actually hostile. One has to cite the letter of the law against them continuously. What is more, the surviving carriers are so under-equipped and so dispirited that they also have little interest in new business. Any enterprise contemplating large-scale waterway transport, has virtually to begin by building its own fleet. This might have advantages as well as disadvantages, were it not that there are very few canal boatbuilders left, and those few utterly unequipped, either materially or mentally, for big orders. And there is one other thing the newcomer has to do, and the most important of all: he has to prepare for combat, for a struggle, likely to last for years, with almost every authority concerned, starting with the Government." White and bewildered, the representative would invariably exclaim (and how justly!): "But everyone knows that water transport is the cheapest in terms of real cost!" To which I had to reply, as he summoned the bill: "Everyone knows it, and we, in particular, undoubtedly believe it; but it cannot be proved. No proof exists, because no one knows the real costs of any kind of transport." This made the representative feel that entertainment had been extracted from his employers almost on false pretences (with the possibility that some of the blame might be fixed on him); and also that the entire discussion had been of an abstract, highbrow order not to be taken seriously by a practical business man. Sometimes, however, the representative rallied to say that he had been very glad to meet me personally.

I tried to send him away with some of our literature, and, often too, his employing organisation would, a week or two later, return us a thoughtful contribution (ten guineas, maybe); sometimes even join us, so running the risk of being cited by us publicly as a supporter. Hovis (concerned, Heaven help them, with the possibility of carrying on the Kennet & Avon) joined us in our first months. Shell-Mex did much for us at various times; assisting in kind and with services, notably at the Market Harborough Festival, as well as sending an annual subscription. The Distillers Company, whose luncheon I recall to this day, my mouth slightly watering, subscribed for years; having sent a letter with the first subscription to the effect that our chance of success was regarded as remote in the extreme, but that our spirit was impressive, and our cause potentially of importance to all with goods to shift. I have received so many letters like that in my time, often on the most beautiful paper, that I have sometimes thought of asking a friend to bind them into a pale keepsake for sentimental recourse in my imminent old age or hopeless mental incapacity.

Few find it easy to believe that no one knows the real cost of transport. There was one of our Members, an extremely important person in an extremely important company – a man of high military rank also, attained in actual combat – who would have none of it, and became quite aggressive. It was after a very pleasant dinner in (this time) his club – an extremely important club, in or near Pall Mall (I must not be too exact). "I just don't believe it," he summed up, glaring at me. "But I know one thing; our research department will find out if you are right; and if you *are* right, then they'll find out the answer to the question." I expressed unreserved delight. "It's what they're for," said my host. "How long do you think they'll take?" I asked, adding that I had no wish to rush things. He thought for a moment: "Not more than ten days." Some time later, we were both guests of a common friend. The man of war spoke first: "Our research people have been on this thing of yours for more than a fortnight now. The whole lot of them. I don't know how much longer we can give to it." He spoke as if the enquiry had been embarked on as a favour to me and as if it had proved far more difficult than I had led him to believe . . . And, in fact, I heard no more of the matter at all. I didn't like to ask, because asking would be too much like crowing; crowing in a case where I had no wish to crow. The real cost of transport continued unknown.

The government department concerned do not, of course, admit that the real cost of transport is unknown; nor ever have admitted it. But here a point arises as simple as it is crucial: the answer to be obtained from a government department (with much difficulty, and after much passing from hand to hand, shifting from foot to foot) is no more than the answer upon which government policy is based at that time. It is no more than an idea given substance by will. In the first place, it changes detectably from government to government (though it is true that the Ministry of Transport, in particular, takes and sticks to a very solid line, against which individual Ministers break their careers comparatively in vain). Much more important is the fact that completely different answers, all equally well argued and supported, can be obtained at all times from such bodies as the road haulage associations and the National Council on Inland Transport (concerned with making transport in its totality as civilised as Society will bear): answers as different from one another as all are different from the official answer.

And here, of course, one finds oneself driven into the metaphysics of definition and relativity: what are 'real costs'? Do costs agreed to be real, cease to be so when the costs in neighbouring countries are added into the analysing process? . . . If the matter is gone into deeply enough, I think it will be found that there is no bottom to it short of individual or social will. Within a very wide range of possibilities, we can have the transport we want to have. Economics are 'rationalisation' only. Not only that: we *do* have the transport we want to have. Transport is not the only field in which a few, not necessarily very civilised, but still very determined people do all the effective wants; with the rest of the community geared, beneath the clouds of paper and of jargon and of jobs, to do their will.

My Association's task, therefore, was not to argue economics (except by way of persiflage – very important at many junctures so that one had to be able to do it convincingly), but to alter the public will, the accepted way of seeing things. It was more difficult than making economic smoke, but, at least, more real.

In particular, we had to contend with the extremely fashionable idea (in every field) that if only enough facts could be accumulated on a subject, then in the end a decision would 'emerge' almost on its own. Much labour is often bestowed on this fact-gathering, but most of it is really laziness, and an escape from the labour that is really necessary. It is an escape from the rigours of decision; from the controversy and personal unpopularity that inevitably follow decision; from the sorting into grades that life insists upon. By pretending that 'objective facts' will decide on their own (if only there are enough of them), the egalitarian illusion is sustained that no man has had to give others an order . . . In the real world, facts can decide nothing; partly because facts are what their finders make them. If individual men will not decide, then we shall enter a world of the mechanised collective in which decisions no longer exist at all, or are even possible . . . Those who have had to enquire, as I have, into where the power of decision lies now, will agree that we are near to a world of no-decisions already.

A popular misconception concerning the Association has always been that it is an organisation of boatowners – of pleasure-boat owners. In recent years, the error has been compounded by Authority, because it is only as an organisation of pleasure-boat owners that Authority is willing to recognise the Association's existence. Before long, it may well become such an organisation. But at no time hitherto have boat-owners of any kind been more than a minority of the Membership; and originally it was a tiny minority. In the early days, boatowners were few in number anywhere; and, though the number of boatowning Association Members has enormously increased, so has the total Membership. In its first years (though not nowadays), the Association was sometimes in other quarters believed to be a trade organisation; a commercially activated pressure group for the carrying interests. People found it difficult to understand or believe in a campaign for a comparatively impersonal ideal, especially when the campaign was fought in the open, at public meetings, through business luncheons and dinners, and in sessions with changing Ministers and Parliamentary Secretaries; though it was precisely this heart of philosophical idealism that made our campaign real, and raised it above the usual voluntary organisation level of aspiration and introversion. The aims of many voluntary

organisations are too narrow and too specialised. They ask for too little to
have any hope of getting the much less they really want. That is the way to
official acceptance and to official disregard. Official tolerance might be the
locution that best covers both things. An important rule runs: that which
officialdom acts upon, it cannot acknowledge. So it is as well to demand the
moon. You will then be at least in the running for a little cheese.

Most of the Association's early Members were either friends of mine who
had been unaware of much previous interest in waterways, or (the majority
– Rolt's friends prominent among them) enthusiasts for narrowboat
carrying and its attendant culture, symbolised by the roses and castles. I was
far from popular when I insisted that there was no possibility whatever of
the narrowboats surviving on their own merits for longer than another year
or two, grievous in every way though this prospect was; and still less
popular, hard though it is to believe now, when I said that an important
aspect in the multiple use concept which I prescribed as the only practicable
treatment, should be advocacy of canal pleasure-boating. At the very best, it
would be impossible sufficiently to revive narrowboat carrying in time to
prevent most of the canals being closed.

The majority reaction, corduroyed and shaggy-locked, was that drifting
along the working canals in a little cruiser was soft. It was dodging the real
issue (I remember that phrase well); and would interfere badly with both
the efficiency and the morale of the working boat families. One had to be
hardy even to claim that an increase in pleasure-boating would at least fill
the gap until carrying could be really resuscitated. To claim more, would
have been to be thrown out. At that time, and away from the Thames and
the Broads, there were only two or three hire-craft firms on the entire three
thousand miles of the surviving waterways system; none of them large. On
most of the system, privately owned pleasure boats hardly existed, as I have
said; and I remember counting one at a time over the years, the accessions to
the number of 'converted narrow boats' such as *Cressy*.

At the very start, there was just one other known to us (though there were
probably a few more, occupied by the canal recluses who were then one of the
basic forms of life in our community). The one we knew was named *Imogen*.
She had been converted by a baronet, Sir John Jardine, who soon joined us,
and who claimed that his conversion was the very first of all. I have heard
him claim it (on the telephone, as a matter of fact), but I am not going to
adjudicate upon the claim. Sir John was a man from a different world: he
sat, in yachting array, at the prow of *Imogen* while a professional crew
navigated her, and a butler in tails served drinks on trays to him and his
guests. One problem with a narrow boat conversion is internal headroom.
Sir John Jardine had met this problem (I cannot say solved it) by providing
down the length of the vessel what railway-coach designers used to call a
"clerestory roof". It looked attractive, but as one could walk completely

upright only along the very centre of the craft, I am happy to be able to say that there are better ways of dealing with the practicalities of the matter. After Sir John's death, *Imogen* was acquired by our Member, Mr. Filmer, who operated a box factory by the City Road Basin off the Regent's Canal in the heart of London. Most generously, he used to allow participants in our Saturday afternoon canal outings, a whole clambering multitude of them, to take their teas in his factory canteen. His voyages in *Imogen* included a transit of Telford's Pontcysyllte Aqueduct in North Wales, the first and most famous of the Seven Wonders of the Waterways; in those days a very rare feat for a boat based on London, and a narrow boat conversion at that. (Oddly enough, there really and truly *are* Seven Wonders of the Waterways: seven constructions decisively more notable than others on the waterways system.) When last I heard of *Imogen*, she was moored on the Thames at Staines, where she belonged to another Member, an attendant in a cinema car park, a genuine original among men. Possibly she has since changed hands again; possibly more than once. Converted narrow boats seldom die, nor even fade away.

The third vessel of the kind that I can remember visiting, lay at Kingston, on the less titivated Middlesex shore of the stream. The owner had not merely "put a top" on her but had also bolted railway lines longitudinally down the hull bottom. The object, he explained, was to strengthen the vessel against the Channel crossing which he was proposing to undertake in the near future. We neither of us knew any record of a Channel crossing by narrow boat, but our member had decided to be a pioneer. I was very interested to hear it, because there was no doubt that the accepted range of narrow boating had, like so many things, lately contracted: formerly they had traded regularly on the Thames tideway from the Regent's Canal Dock at Limehouse as far downstream as Woolwich, and occasionally as far as Sheerness. I wished our Member the best of luck, and cordially shook his hand; but soon afterwards he abandoned the project, owing, he said, to attacks of rheumatism, and later, I believe, sold the boat altogether.

Since then narrow boats have crossed The Wash on several occasions (the long crossing too, from the Witham to the Great Ouse), and, though I have yet to hear of the first across the Channel, the common view seems to be that it could be done if enough time were available: time to wait for completely ideal weather in which to make each single stage of journey, the stage round the North Foreland being probably the trickiest. In many whole summers there might not be enough suitable days for the total trip from Limehouse to Calais, but it is an exploit of the kind that is always accomplished in the end. I contributed personally to an adventure in salt-water narrow boating, as I shall relate in due course.

In the early days, I myself set about converting a narrow boat, influenced by the beauty and fascination of *Cressy*, and as a contribution to the development of pleasure-boating; at a time when the idea of pleasure-boating as a possibly significant element in the canal scene (and revenues) had hardly dawned and was regarded with distaste by the few who had even thought about it. I bought a narrow boat, a 'hull' (as people put it in these cases), from Walkers of Rickmansworth, now no longer on the waterside but then the nearest yard to London with boats to sell. My boat was named *Phosphorus*, and Walkers gave me an estimate for converting her to a plan of my own. Tom Rolt advised me in the selection of the hull, and, though I had received some architectural training of my own, I was much indebted for help in planning the conversion to my friend, Victor Mayo, who was an engineer, and also one of those who had come upon the waterways movement through me, and were among the Association's first Members.

I still have a blueprint of this conversion plan, and I still think it useful and reasonably ingenious. What caused us most difficulty was the dining table in the saloon. A narrow boat is only seven feet across (outside measurements), and conversion does not (or should not) widen it. If two rows of people sit longitudinally down each side of the table, not only are those in the centre of each row hopelessly penned in, but the table cannot be wide enough properly to bear the dishes, and the participants in the feast have to eat right into the faces of the people eating opposite. If the eaters sit along one side of a longitudinal table, all of them are confronted merely by the impersonal side of the boat; which lowers the level of sociality quite disproportionately. If the table is set across the width of the boat, it is apt to be difficult to stow when out of use, and must also, when set up, be a barrier between the end of the vessel where the galley lies and the other end: it might not seem that this would matter much, but experience soon proves that it does, either domestically, or navigationally, or both. Victor Mayo and I met the problem by setting the table across the boat, but cutting it in half and fixing each half to a hinge against the boat's side. When there were no more than three or four people at a meal, only one of these hinged flaps would have had to be used. Even when both flaps were in use (when six people could eat concurrently), there were no table legs to tangle with human ones. When not in use at all, the table would be entirely out of the way; its two sections flat against the upper parts of the boat's super-structure, each secured at the top by a bolt. It would have been better still if the two undersides, visible all the time the table was out of action, could have been suitably decorated . . . Victor and I also designed six square seats, providing maximum room for the six eaters. Domestic chairs can be spiky, space-wasting nuisances, when the area available is so small. They also look out of place.

With Rolt and others, I paid many visits to the slowly evolving *Phosphorus* at Rickmansworth, but within months it became clear to me that while I was directing the Association, I should never have time to make much use of her, and also that it was astonishing how much time and labour boat-ownership involved throughout the year, apart altogether (often far apart) from time devoted to the joys of cruising. There are a thousand different jobs to be done, and, notoriously, no boatyard will care for a boat unless the boatowner is accepted as caring himself, which means caring visibly and appearing in person at all times. It is precisely this maintenance aspect of boat-ownership that, as I later realised, appeals to so many: all that is epitomised in Kenneth Grahame's famous commendation of "messing about in boats". This was a form of words that, through absolutely no fault of its own, came to fill with nausea the tougher of our campaigners when encountered, as it regularly was, in the press or at a public meeting, during some wild struggle to keep a particular waterway in being at all, and commonly after a campaign had continued for months or years without apparent advance. Few were the occasions when some well-wishing stranger failed to sum us all up in Grahame's words; and with the air of one who had happily lighted upon the profoundest, most conclusive of bon mots. There was nothing, absolutely nothing, we must all agree, like just messing about in boats: nor, it was implied, much more to be said about the problem in hand . . . This formula, now that it had been lighted upon, would save the waterways magically.

I am not a messer about in boats. I enjoy once-and-for-all jobs like planning the layout of *Phosphorus* and designing the table. I could tolerate the full stretch of running the waterways campaign, though I have never decided whether or not I positively like it (Plato would have pointed out that if I did, I should have been the wrong man for the job). But, between these two levels of labour, I have much sympathy with the Frenchman of the ancien régime who exclaimed "Living! We leave that to our servants". Like my Father, I am most easily brought to a standstill by the detailed repetitive necessities of daily, individual existence. Still, I was enchanted by the prospect of my lovely ship; and what really led me so soon to sacrifice her was the increasing realisation that I should have little time for dallying if there were to remain many (or any) waterways to dally on. But it was not only that I gave up boating to make boating possible for others. That would be touching (preferably if said by someone else); but not quite true. Whenever I see others lovingly fiddling with a boat-engine (by law of nature, or will of man, so enormously more recalcitrant than any normal car engine), or patiently exploring the damage inflicted by a cold winter upon the woodwork of a hull, I rejoice that I withdrew for a noble motive before being driven by a less worthy one. On the other hand, I know of a number who gave up the campaign for the waterways in order to go boating. The two are always hard to combine.

With the conversion hardly started (workers in canal boatyards seldom move at the double), I sold *Phosphorus* to our Member, Mrs. Dorward, who made of her something quite different. Thereafter, Mrs. Dorward, the wife of a classics professor at Liverpool University, was often to be seen at the helm; a statuesque figure, like Isolde, with abundant hair streaming in the wind. Later, *Phosphorus* was one of the narrow boats that crossed the Wash, and the last time I saw her was at Cambridge.

Another aspect of the mild *Phosphorus* incident strikes me as I write: I wonder how I ever afforded the escapade. It was not until years later that I first received an "honorarium" for my waterways campaigning (£200 per annum at the start; rising to a triumphant £600 at the conclusion), and before that time I was, in effect, paying the Association's office rent also (which I continued doing until 1951). And yet we all know the answer: it lies solely and entirely in the different value of money. It is a strange thing, and crippling to the best in us, that we have for all our lives to budget for an accelerating erosion in the value not only of all we have (the rust and the moth), but also of the medium which is supposed to symbolise the value of all we have. It is as if continually a yard shrank from its original thirty-six inches. A pound weight is no less an abstract symbol than a pound sterling, but it does not inflate (though there are many whose purposes would be served, if it did). The reason why the idea of the pound sterling is not defined by tablet in Trafalgar Square as is the idea of the yard length, lies not in some stronger element of reality in money but entirely in the common attitude. Money is laden with guilt. In consequence, it is as if one could not get a firm price for building a house, because no one could tell what the inch would be worth by the time the job was completed. All through my childhood I used to hear that inflation of the currency was prominent among the proofs of the Roman decadence. Our own society has evolved in such a way that its economy cannot function unless the value of money continually diminishes (Keynes's most eagerly adopted contribution to practical economics). It would not be much mistaken to say that the most important Member the Association ever attracted is Mr. Eric de Mare, who knows what is wrong with the economy and the currency and how to remedy it, where the experts do not (and often, like the gifted Keynes, thrive on the wrongs); whose many, patient writings on the subject will be familiar to some of my readers; and who, of all men and women that I have known, is the most truly a prophet . . . In the meantime, I shall merely add that I could not think of buying, converting, and maintaining *Phosphorus* now, in the way that caused me no anxiety (no financial anxiety) in the later 1940s, when, in number of pounds, my income was considerably less.

It was in Victor Mayo's abode that I first met Eric de Mare, and later his remarkable wife, Vanessa, original thinker on every subject, storm centre of recondite powers, and erstwhile toast of the Fitzroy; and I first met Victor Mayo in my lonely days of early youth. I met him in a theatre queue. It was a queue to see Mona Inglesby's International Ballet: an enterprise which for a number of years maintained a quite unexpectedly high standard on a private enterprise, publicly unsubsidised basis that would now be as impracticable as for me to purchase *Phosphorus*. He was then Hans Victor Mayer, and, as a refugee from the Nazis, was limited by the British Government to a minor and ill-paid job, far below his capacities. He introduced me to large circles of fascinating people, whom otherwise I should never have met: German, Dutch, Czech, and other refugees; fantastically buoyant and cheerful, considering the terrible things that lay behind in almost all their lives, considering even their basic plight of being stranded, penniless and suspect, in a foreign, in most cases an enemy, land. Meeting these people was among the most important events of my life up to that time. It was my first experience in any depth of continental civilisation and culture; and it was an unforgettable demonstration of how quickly and effectively men and women could rise above the extremest adversity, not only in heroic ultimates, but (which seems to me to matter at least equally) in quality of daily living. It is hard to judge what Britain did for them. I myself incline to the view that the much-abused National Conservative Governments did the very maximum that public opinion would permit. One of the most striking things of all was that, for years and years, there was almost no social contact between by friends and the English population around them. In many cases, I doubt whether there is much now. I find little appreciation, little knowledge, among my neighbours of the advantages to Britain brought by these resilient exiles.

I fell in love with one of them (who would have none of me) and another accompanied me on one of my visits to Borely Rectory, "the most haunted house in England". I travelled considerable distances with Hans Mayer himself, all by public transport and on foot. I remember a party of us hiring a punt on the Thames at Staines, and navigating it up the tributary Colnbrook to the point where passage is obstructed by a mill: Hans (as we then called him) displayed great finesse in paddling the punt back down the quite swift current. This kind of skill was then new to me. For some time, Hans maintained a boat of his own at Olney on the Great Ouse, but gave it up because he said that the air of the region never changed from year to year. He moved his boat to Borth-y-Gest, where he said it did. In the end, he succeeded in achieving British citizenship and, wishing to alter his name, but to something not ostentatiously John Bullish, adopted Mayo at my suggestion. Later, he became an American citizen instead, and soared to enormous heights of administrative tycoonery with an engineering company that had big interests in Europe. He married, multiplied and magnified.

VI

Ten Aspirations

Favouritism is the secret of efficiency.

ADMIRAL OF THE FLEET LORD FISHER OF KILVERSTONE

At the end of its first year, Sir Alan Herbert agreed to be the Association's President. As Bulletin 2 put it: "No single name is more closely associated anywhere with the subject of British inland waterways, and no alternative possibility arose as to who we should approach."

A.P. Herbert's fame in the canals context was mainly a matter of his book, "The Water Gypsies", which was then the best known work of fiction with a canal setting, even though the canal geography in its pages becomes a little nebulous beyond the village of Northchurch, north of Berkhamsted, and though the author's confident description of the boat families as "gypsies" was far from popular in the circles concerned (though very possibly more accurate aetiologically than the boat families assert).

I was disappointed when one dark evening in his Thames-side garden, Sir Alan repudiated another of his books with an aquatic title, "The House by the River"; in my opinion, an incomparably better one. He spoke of it as "early stuff, best forgotten", or in words to that effect. It would seem that at a certain stage in his career, Sir Alan decided, consciously or otherwise, to concentrate almost entirely upon the recipe of entertainment, sentiment, and propaganda for mixed causes (often splendid causes) which he has made distinctive. He has had great successes thereby: the reform of the divorce law, the brilliant "Misleading Cases" (unquestionably among the classics of British humour), the beautiful house by the river itself, the entry into British folk-lore of its owner; but one is aware of a very different and far greater artist who has been suppressed. A.P. Herbert's most important book is likely to remain the tragic "Secret Battle" ("the story of a valiant heart tested to destruction", as Winston Churchill said of it) though neither it nor "The House by the River" would make the author a British folk-hero.

An inner conflict inevitably remained. Certainly, our President, though at one historical moment of battle, was a brilliant deus ex machina, adroit and sure, the man who more than any other saved the day, yet he at no time displayed much interest in either the details of the waterways situation, personal or impersonal, or in the philosophy which underlay the campaign. One could never be in doubt that he had a score of other irons in the fires of advocacy: from a campaign for a "public lending right" for authors (a matter of life or death to the profession of letters, goodness knows), through a campaign for renaming the stars (which seems mistaken), to a campaign for ending 'Summer Time' (strongly supportable in theory, but un-sympathetic – to me, repugnant – in application). Our "dear old battle", as he sometimes termed it, was possibly something he thought he had out-grown. Every year he used to say to me that he would really have to resign. I never found him an easy man to talk to, and at our last encounter of all, when the mass suffrages had ceased to be with me, I consider that he treated me very badly indeed. None the less, there is no doubt that his mere name at the top of our lists counted for a substantial and potent legion. He linked us with known values.

Bulletin 2 announced also the appointment of our first Vice-President: Peter Scott. I had known him for some time, and have had a considerable amount to do with him since, at one point and another.

Among a variety of other things, I assisted with the organisation of a number of lectures he gave during the 1950s at the Royal Festival Hall; the first events of the kind to take place in that large arena. At the first lecture of all, the size of the attendance for this occasion without precedent was naturally a preoccupation, but there was no need to worry: the Hall was packed out. Suggesting a programme of ornithological music for Mr. Felton Rapley to play on the organ while the audience assembled, was one of my more light-hearted tasks. For the printed programme, I wrote a short note on the lecturer. I wrote it under the pseudonym of Aquarius, but I am sure that by now I may admit to the authorship, and reprint from it.

"Many of our age relate to the fact that more and more people, instead of broadening with the years, diminish and narrow under the pressures of specialisation and social restriction. To those who still succeed in remaining what the sage called totus atque teres, whole men and round, we owe a particular debt: they uphold and assert the true dignity of our species through this uncomfortable bridge passage of history.

"To introduce Peter Scott to a new field of activity is to know that sooner rather than later he will be a master of it, and will be out-distancing nine out of ten of the established and specialised practitioners. He has a special confidence and concentration that carry him swiftly to the heart of the mystery, towards which the progress of others is that of toiling journeymen. He was born not so much with a silver spoon in his mouth as with a silver key.

"But of course, he too has his specialities: the difference is that there are so many of them. The author of books as various (and successful) as WILD CHORUS and THE BATTLE OF THE NARROW SEAS, is also the painter whose works, original or in reproduction, almost beyond doubt hang in more British homes than the works of any other contemporary. And the number of his bird pictures should not overshadow the distinction of his portrait drawings. He has sailed single-handed for Great Britain in the Olympic Games, and won the Prince of Wales Cup on three occasions.

"Lately, in his glider, he has conquered less a new world than a new heaven. He served in the Battle of the Atlantic and in the Light Coastal Forces. He has explored unmapped territories in the Canadian Arctic; and has privateered in the struggle to preserve our own beautiful inland waterways. He has stood for Parliament, and would certainly have prevailed in the same constituency had he stood again. A remarkable example of his capacity for almost effortlessly compassing new skills was his single venture as an actor: none in the distinguished professional cast but acknowledged that the triumph of the production was his. Long a notable voice on the air, he has lately achieved new prominence on television. Currently, he is writing his autobiography.

"There remains to mention his most special creation of all: The Wildfowl Trust at Slimbridge; the largest collection of waterfowl in the world; which is also every winter our island's concours d'elegance for wild geese. About this, and about the New Waterfowl Gardens at Peakirk, there are other words herein."

Since that time, Peter Scott has progressed to the foundation of the World Wildlife Fund; concerned with preserving the natural heritage all over the world, and by far his most important work, because among the most important works that can be imagined. Primarily, it is not so much the wild creatures that are at risk, but man, homo sapiens. As man destroys the wilderness, he destroys himself too. I am very honoured to be a member of the Fund's Advisory Panel; and was honoured too to be put on the map when a Canadian archipelago was named the Aickman Islands.

Peter Scott, providing another instance of the dreary rule that those with talent are seldom left with time, was able to do only a limited amount publicly for the Association, but he travelled long distances by waterway, entered very fully into the intricacies and difficulties of the administration, and on several occasions played a crucial, though unobtrusive, part in seeing that events went the right way. He was a Vice-President to be relied upon, for the excellent reason that he understood and cared for what the campaign sought to achieve.

Bulletin 2 records the first public shot in the Association's first successful battle. Our Member, Lord Methuen, had put down a Question in the House of Lords concerning the fixed bridge that obstructed the Stratford

Canal. He was to continue putting down Questions on this subject for some time.

The Stratford Canal is in two parts: an upper section from a junction with the Worcester & Birmingham Canal (that on which I had first cruised in *Cressy*) at Kings Norton, to a junction with the Grand Union Canal (the main waterway from London to Birmingham) at Kingswood; and a lower section from Kingswood to Stratford itself. Since the acquisition of the whole canal by the Great Western Railway Company, the lower section had fallen into dereliction, and was the navigation I had encountered, as already related, in my childhood. The upper section continued in intermittent use, until an incident with a drawbridge at Lifford Lane near Kings Norton. The bridge carried a road across the waterway, and was designed to be lifted for the passage of boats. One night, it was claimed, the bridge had been damaged by a lorry. Instead of being repaired, it was merely clamped down so that no boat larger than a canoe could pass beneath it.

We regarded this obstruction of a statutory navigation as illegal; and Lord Methuen, then our only Member in either place of legislature, kindly asked Question after Question. At the end of many months, an answer was given to the effect that the bridge would be lifted upon twenty-four hours notice being given, and that posters indicating the fact would be affixed in the area. We immediately gave the notice (which had probably not been expected of anyone), and Tom Rolt prepared *Cressy* for the voyage. On the morning of 9 May 1947, we cast off from the beautiful lagoon at Kingswood.

It was a revealing occasion.

In the first place, we could find none of the promised posters, until I lighted upon one on the *back* of a lengthman's small hut at the top of a steep and nettled bank. In the second place, the railway company had thoughtfully provided a maintenance boat to go first and see us through; a full-sized narrow boat, named *Bilster*.

Bilster was not a success. She drew more than *Cressy* and, instead of helping us, had continually to be helped by us. When she stuck beneath a bridge ("in a bridgehole", as the idiom of 'the cut' puts it), it was we who found an agricultural tractor that was willing to descend to the towpath and drag her on. Later, it seemed best for us to cease following behind her, and instead to go first and take her in tow. Even that had to be given up, to the sincere embarrassment of her crew. In the end, *Bilster* was just left in a random spot at the bottom of a cutting and, as afternoon was drawing on, the crew disappeared to report. Later we heard that *Bilster* had been torn to pieces by local hooligans that same night.

We were now drawing near to the fatal bridge, and somewhat apprehensive lest the lifting gang might have gone home too.

Before the bridge is a short tunnel. When we emerged at the far end, we began to hear a sound that seemed familiar, but which we could not at first quite identify. Then we did identify it: it was the sound one hears when fairly close to Wembley Stadium before the match begins on Cup Final day; the strangely impersonal, almost non-human murmur of a large crowd.

We rounded a few more corners, and there the crowd was: lining both banks, several deep; on roof-tops, up trees. A mild, sarcastic cheer met our belated advent. The obstruction had been raised by a large gang. *Cressy* passed beneath it, though with a clearance of only an inch or two. The applause became a little warmer. We made statements. We posed for photographs. We signed autographs. We accepted cups of tea. We proclaimed a great new future for the canals of Britain.

The Association was only twelve months old but our cause had arrived.

In the meantime, the gang was swiftly at work (it was now evening) refixing the obstruction. Further voyages would be necessary.

One of them was undertaken by Peter Scott. His Severn Wildfowl Trust (now simply the Wildfowl Trust) had ordered a narrow boat conversion for use as a hostel by visitors to their collection at Slimbridge, which stands beside the Gloucester & Berkeley Ship Canal. She was named *Beatrice*; had been converted by Spencer, Abbott's yard (now vanished) at Salford, in the northern part of the Birmingham conurbation; and was now on her maiden voyage in her new incarnation. There is a difficult turn on to the Stratford Canal from the Grand Union at Kingswood. I had been accustomed to narrow boats landing members of their crews to pull the vessel round on lines from the towpath. Peter Scott at the helm took *Beatrice* round, in fading light, on a single steady course: possibly the first time it had ever been done, though more is expected now than then of narrow boat virtuosi. The next day, the Lifford Lane obstruction was passed as before, but with even more press publicity. Some of the publicity was sceptical: the "Daily Mirror" asked what this prominent personality thought he was doing in adding to the charges on the taxpayer? But this time the trick was done. An announcement was made that the opening bridge would be reinstated. It was a triumph not only for our cause, but for our method.

Perhaps the crowd for the first assault had been the most important revelation. Here was evidence that people cared. A public campaign, however right, good, and necessary, will not succeed unless it speaks to some need in the mass unconscious. William Willett laboured for years in the cause of daylight saving, and spent much money; but at the time of his death, his advocacy of BST was still regarded as an aberration in an otherwise commendable career. A few years later, daylight saving was adopted for less idealistic reasons than Willett's. It was immediately accepted, almost as part of the natural order; and has continued to be accepted (and extended) ever since, with few beside our President to dissent.

The audience at Lifford Lane started me thinking upon the need to widen our net as variously as possible. Some people would care for diversification of transport; some for pleasure-cruising; some for efficient water supply; some for history, or town and country planning; many for the lush waterway's sentiment. At the core of my purpose was the unification of these diverse things, but, to succeed, it would be necessary to reach out also to those interested only in any one of them, and often without having previously thought much about it. Happily, there could be few among those who thought at all, to whom no single aspect of the waterways would appeal. Moreover, there should be some to whom the vigour of our attack upon a whole small world of century-old abuses would appeal in itself. A successful cause must not only reflect the deep unconscious but mould it too.

It was clear also that the Association would have to be 'strictly non-political' in the party sense. During the years that followed, I went to much care in this matter; so that my pleasure was great when I learned that at least one of my many internal critics had been in the habit of confiding in hushed voice "And another thing. Did you know the man's a Communist?".

In 1947 this non-party claim was important, because 'nationalisation of transport' was imminent; most of the railways, many of the lorries, only a proportion of the river and canal system.

When the Transport Bill first appeared, we were surprised, as far as its waterway content went, mainly by the omissions from the "Schedule of Undertakings to be Acquired". It was not that collectively we were in favour of nationalisation; or collectively opposed it. Either attitude, albeit natural, even inevitable, would have been unthinkable: or, at least, strategically and tactically unwise. If an organisation such as ours decides, however seemingly objective (even expert) its reasons, to follow a line that coincides with the line taken by a political party, then the organisation forfeits every kind of public influence, and not least with the political party in question, which now loses all reason for wooing and ingratiating the organisation. A loud and frequent bawl of total independence is essential from first to last. The patchiness of the Transport Bill, therefore neither gratified nor antagonised us. It merely puzzled us.

No provision seemed to be made for the acquisition of the Manchester Ship Canal, the largest and best known in the country. Nor was reference made in the list to a large group of waterways among which the common factor seemed to be that all were situated in the eastern half of England. Finally, there appeared to be no direct reference to the proposed acquisition of the railway owned waterways, which at that time amounted to about one-third of the system, as already stated.

L.T.C. Rolt and I formed ourselves into a deputation and secured a meeting with an official at the Ministry of Transport. He had a room to himself, three drawers to his desk, and a carpet on the floor. These were his answers.

The Manchester Ship Canal was to be "the subject of a separate bargain". Possibly the Government thought it too big to swallow whole. Moreover, it was, and is, controlled by the Manchester Corporation, which acquired a steadily increasing financial stake in the venture as private finance became discouraged by difficulties in the process of construction. There has never been a "separate bargain". The waterway continues to be directed by the Manchester Ship Canal Company, with the Corporation as majority shareholder.

As for our second question, it was true, we were told, that the common factor among these waterways was their location in the eastern part of the country. The Government's strategic advisers had reported that they were unsuited to nationalisation. Further details of this plate-armour judgement were neither vouchsafed nor to be expected.

When we came to the railway owned waterways, our informant looked up and enquired: "Oh! Do we get them too?". I think he was a little hazy about the impact of the past century of waterway history. . .

But my readers must not lie awake wondering if they own the once railway owned waterways. In the end, these waterways did pass into "national ownership". They passed under provisions in the Bill for the transfer of the railway companies' "ancillary assets": initially, no doubt, such items as railway hotels and refreshment rooms. In the same way, although the Bill did not attempt directly to nationalise the canal carriers, certain carrying enterprises passed to the Government because they were subsidiaries of navigation authorities in the schedule. Possibly their arrival caused surprise too.

Thus (in part) was transport – for better or for worse – nationalised and bestowed upon the electorate. A comment may be made not upon the principle of nationalisation but upon the form: the form took little account of transport's needs, and still less of the ever intensifying impact of transport upon society at large, but concentrated almost entirely upon the political question of ownership. Most will now agree that thereby a chance was lost – probably for ever.

Before the Bill became an Act, the Association prepared a memorandum upon it, of which copies were sent to the Minister, the members of the Standing Committee considering the Bill, various other Members of Parliament who had shown an interest in waterways, and the press. This resulted in a larger deputation meeting the Minister, Mr. Alfred Barnes.

It was an interesting experience, and a notable success for an organisation still less than a year old: but it made no more impression on events than our written memorandum. The Ministry of Transport was then in Berkeley Square House, one of the most hideous buildings in London (even to this day when there is so much more competition). The Minister was encircled by a court of helpful civil servants, rather like a boy emperor. Mr. Barnes was not, of course, alone in this. Most Ministers, when one meets them officially, seem to be boy emperors, or Gullivers under the net, or (in the end) merely sad buffoons. Very broadly, the three conditions correspond to the particular Minister's degree of Ministerial experience. These official meetings with delegations are seldom more than ritual: they give pleasure to the delegations (especially when seemingly social cups of tea or coffee are included), and are not intended to affect events. Compliance with the ritual can advance the delegates, but seldom their cause. If events can be affected at all when they have attained the Parliamentary level, one must attempt to reach the Minister privately, and without public mention; that is, in the absence of his civil service staff, who, in the nature of things, act mainly as spies upon him. They are permanent as the hills, where he is ephemeral as the cloud that crowns the hilltop. It is commonly said that private approaches are unavailing also. Often they are, again in the nature of things; but occasionally something useful can be achieved. At the back of all this is the overwhelming difficulty of determining where, if anywhere, power really lies.

Bulletin 3 informed our Membership that our memorandum had "beyond doubt already achieved the position of the most important modern document on our subject". I do not think this was an exaggeration, especially when competition from other documents was so limited. I truly believe that the memorandum contributed significantly to the process of change which in the end became a volte-face, public and official. Such change processes have nothing at all to do with official utterances or public occurrences. They are always undetectable, both because they are glacier-slow and because their working is deliberately concealed by those worked upon; and they are never acknowledged – even less when the walls have fallen than when the first faint tappings are heard. At the most, cautious tribute is paid to some puppet created for the purpose of receiving it.

Our deputation to Mr. Barnes included our President and me, Tom Rolt, Captain Smith, and a Mrs. George Smith (unrelated to the Captain), who was an unusual woman. Sonia Smith had been an actress; pupil, I believe of Michel Saint-Denis' London Theatre School. During the war, an appeal had been made for women volunteers to work the narrow boats. Most who responded were women of character, as would be expected: many remained inebriated for long after with the dense canal brew. One became a Duchess; several wrote books about their experiences – and even went on to write other books. They were known as the Idle Women (I.W. for Inland Waterways), which is the title of Susan Woolfitt's book about them. (Emma Smith's "Maiden's Trip", however ambiguously entitled, is another authority to be consulted – for literature, as well as for lore). Sonia Smith had been one of the number, but she had gone further than most by marrying a working boatman. George Smith, who belonged to one of the best known families on 'the cut' (but where are the Smiths not among the best known families?), was a blond, curly-haired Adonis; and I am sure he could have strangled the wildest of boars with the barest of hands, had occasion arisen. For years, Mr. and Mrs. George Smith operated, all by themselves, a pair of working boats, named *Cairo* and *Warwick*. In the cabin of the butty (the boat which comes second, being towed by the boat known as the motor), one would come upon the collected works of Dostoievski, not at that time common reading on the waterway, but apt to the fiery character of Sonia Smith. Later, she, for a spell, joined the Association's Council, being plainly well qualified to speak for the working boat community, sometimes too inturned (and too busy) to be articulate in a hostile world.

Mr. Barnes indicated that a representative of the Association might be invited to join a Users' Consultative Committee he was proposing to attach to the body he had in mind for the administration of the nationalised waterways. He went to considerable pains to emphasise that this Committee would not be a mere facade to cover decisions arrived at elsewhere, but would, he hoped, play a real part in the resuscitation and management of the industry. Alas, the real sources of power were too strong for Mr. Barnes' hopes and our hopes. We were not asked to be represented on the Committee, partly because there never was a Committee.

That was just as well for the waterways; as such committees divide movements such as ours into those to whom an easy "honour" (a seat on a public body) and an easier life prove irresistible, and those who care more impersonally for the cause.

We issued a broadsheet listing our ten aspirations for the immediate future. They were impeccable, unanswerable.

1. The navigations in use, should be better kept up.

2. The navigations not in use (but not actually abandoned) should be recovered.

3. Abandonment proposals should be subject to specific consultations, which we listed.

4. The system of charges should be modernised.

5. A minimum water depth of five feet should be enforced.

6. There should be a survey of enlargement possibilities.

7. There should be an enquiry into the real costs of water transport (not yet of all transport).

8. Very much more should be done to stimulate pleasure-boating, including that by foreign visitors.

9. The working conditions of working boatmen should be improved: sympathetically not schematically.

10. New and better equipped repair and construction yards should be fostered.

It is remarkable how little has been done to this day about any of these things. It is a corrective to over-exuberant claims on any of our parts. And yet who would claim that any one of our ten points was other than an obvious necessity?

At the end of the day, as a later Prime Minister was wont to put it (sometimes at the end of each day), it transpired that about two-thirds of the surviving navigation system had been taken over by the Government (officially described as "the public"): about 2000 miles, out of about 3000 miles. One immediate development, which continues to this hour, was that official spokesmen began to speak always of "2000 miles of waterway", so that most people believe that is all there are. It is a consequence of there being no National Waterways Conservancy. When the system was at its peak, the mileage amounted to 4000, but 1000 miles had been permitted to drop off, in one way or another, before the Association was founded. Official maps are invariably very misleading as to the extent and character of the national waterways system as a whole. All the official publicity speaks only of 2000 miles.

The nationalised waterways were placed by Mr. Barnes under the direction of a Docks and Inland Waterways Executive, responsible to his over-riding British Transport Commission. The Docks in question were those that had been owned by former railway or canal companies.

Peter Scott invited Lord Hurcomb, the first Chairman of the Commission, to dinner at the Carlton in order to meet me. Lord Hurcomb had already spent a lifetime in the Civil Service. He was as old as the rocks on which he sat. I asked him, merely for interest, why the Derby Canal had not been nationalised. After all, it linked the nationalised Trent & Mersey Canal with the nationalised Erewash Canal, passing through the gay city of Derby en route. "Ah," said Lord Hurcomb, "that was one I managed to miss." The Derby Canal was in poor shape and had behind it a confused history even by British waterway standards. Lord Hurcomb's response was all too prophetic: from first to last, the nationalised authority acted on the lazy principle that when a waterway was exceptionally run down, however bad the reasons, then it was not worth bothering about, however great the potential. During the rest of the discussion at the Carlton, Lord Hurcomb was not as forthcoming as he had been about the Derby Canal. After all, he had been suddenly required to know all about the railway system (almost the entire railway system) as well. The conversation soon passed to bird-watching; an activity which Lord Hurcomb pursued round the edges of the Grand Union Canal's Wilstone Reservoirs, near Tring.

Another elderly career civil servant was appointed to the Chairmanship of the Docks and Inland Waterways Executive. Sir Reginald Hill was a less craggy figure than Lord Hurcomb. Indeed, he even wrote poetry; some of which was printed in the Executive's official organ, "Lock and Quay". I do not mean this sarcastically; Sir Reginald's verses were far more charming than anything else in the paper. He was a gentle, rather melancholy man, who had obviously formed a realistic view of the world. He could make a cultivated speech, and it was impossible not to like him. He was perhaps unfortunate in being set at the head of an enterprise which the gods scarcely intended to prosper. I call it an enterprise because we were repeatedly assured that it was not a government department. It was a very-end-product of the decision, associated originally, I believe, with Herbert Morrison, that business activities taken over by the government should, as far as possible, seem not to be run by the government, even though the government appointed everyone who did run them. In retrospect, it seems impossible that *any* of these transport "Executives", frail and intricate as ivory pagodas, can have been even meant to succeed. But the answer to that is short: public transport has been infinitely worse, and infinitely worse managed, since they were superseded.

In the Association's first twelve months, we invited Mr. George Cadbury to be a Vice-President. Bournville made considerable use of the canals (the slightly mysterious 'chocolate crumb' traffic was famous), and Mr. Cadbury, a much respected figure in the canal world, was President of the National Association of Inland Waterway Carriers, and part-author of a stubborn canal classic, usually referred to as "Cadbury and Dobb". Mr. Cadbury replied that advancing years and declining health made him feel unable to accept any further such distinctions. Shortly after this reply his appointment to the Docks and Inland Waterways Executive was announced.

A seemingly more robust old gentleman added to the Executive's number was Mr. Robert Davidson from the Leeds & Liverpool Canal, the finest in England. Conscious of his Yorkshire background, he was a man who stood no nonsense. It was impossible not to be awed by him, and the Executive never seemed the same after he unexpectedly died. He was a man of action, and we all missed him very much.

There is a maxim that public committees should include (at the tail end of the appointments, of course) a trade unionist and a woman. The Executive included a trade unionist from the first, but had to pass through several transformations (plus ca change . . .) before it came to include a woman, though this was achieved in the end for one brief period. The original trade unionist, I recall, seemed to expect the waterways world to be like the general world of industry; indeed, to be determined to make it like that if he killed it in the attempt.

By now, Frank Eyre had retired from the Association's Honorary Treasurership. He was replaced by Ninian Hislop. I first met Hislop when he wrote generously offering to help the cause by voluntary work. I asked him to come and see me. When he arrived, I enquired what he did. He said he had a part time job with a specialised motor club that I knew about. This sounded promising: the Association had work and to spare for people with part time jobs. What were his hours? Well, he began at 9.30 and usually managed to get away by 5.30, though on most evenings he had to take work home. I reflected. What about Saturdays? He had been told by the Club that his Saturdays would be completely free, but it hadn't worked out like that at all: far from it. Sundays? On Sunday, he usually went for the "Evening News" walk with his mother or a girlfriend. After a heavy week in the office, he needed the exercise. I observed that it hardly seemed to be a part time job at all. He replied that he was beginning to think that, but that the pay was certainly on a part time basis. I believe that it was through connections within the Association that Hislop extricated and bettered himself. If so, he made handsome acknowledgement when he undertook the exacting task of watching over our accounts.

VII

First Dissensions

Whoever makes good progress in the beginning has all the more difficulty later on.

LAO-TZU

It was not until 8 March 1947 that I made my first speech on behalf of the cause. The occasion was not a minor one. There was to be a debate in Newbury Town Hall on the nationalisation of transport. Mr. F.J. Erroll M.P. and Mr. Anthony Hurd M.P. (later Lord Erroll and Lord Hurd) were to set about an attack, Mr. Hurd then being the local Conservative Member; Mr. Ian Mikardo M.P. and Mr. Ernest Popplewell M.P. to undertake a defence. All four of these were already more prominent Parliamentary personalities than the average. The Mayor of Newbury was to be in the Chair. Local Members of the Association had contrived that invitations should be sent to Rolt and me to address the meeting on the subject of the Kennet & Avon Navigation, the local waterway.

We had a great success. Our strictly non-party case was greeted with considerable relief and, in the end, great enthusiasm by almost the entire audience, which was a very large one. Mr. Hurd and Mr. Mikardo, who summed up for their respective sides in the debate, both expressed strong approval of the Association's arguments; and the Mayor, by definition a non-party man himself (while in office), referred to us with even warmer benevolence.

The Kennet & Avon, acquired long before by the Great Western Railway Company, had been in all kinds of trouble for many years. But what seemed in 1947 to be the most pressing inconvenience was 'reinforcement' of steel girders inserted during the war under a road bridge in Reading, to strengthen (it was alleged) the bridge for the possible transit of tanks: it undoubtedly restricted very seriously the size of craft that could use this otherwise 'wide' waterway. (Technically, every waterway is 'wide' which can pass boats of more than seven feet in beam.) Our first reference to the "Bridge Street Bridge obstruction" appeared in Bulletin 2. In one way or another, the pressure for its removal never ceased; but twenty years passed, and numerous vicissitudes and upsets within the Kennet & Avon campaign (let alone the outer world), before the pressure was successful. During the first years, the bare legality of the obstruction was doubtful; but here the position was later to be complicated by new legislation suspending all statutory obligations to maintain the Kennet & Avon any better than it was being maintained at the time of the Act – which, from the navigator's point of view, was hardly at all, most of the waterway being impassable.

The new legislation was an oblique tribute to the vigour and persistence of the Kennet & Avon campaign in its early days, but we had learned long before that laws designed to protect waterways are, in any case, remarkably difficult to enforce. Often enforcement is possible virtually only at the behest of a party with a business interest in the waterway; and our experience was that even when all business had not already been driven off, too many plaintiffs showed a human and commercial willingness to desist from the pursuit of an injunction requiring the navigation authority to maintain 'the track', in exchange for a settlement in cash, with which road lorries could be bought to replace the stranded boats. The prospect grew worse after a judicial decision in our time on the Kennet & Avon itself: certain owners of trading craft, assisted by advice and evidence from us, persisted in seeking an injunction but were defeated by a judgement in which the Court took the initiative in saying that a payment of damages would suffice. After that, I took to pointing out, in moments of cynicism, that a speculator had merely to buy a few boats, arrange a few orders, and seek to trade on a neglected navigation: if he handled things properly, it should be a comparatively easy way to a substantial sum of money. I think it was true, but it was hardly a state of affairs that helped the waterways of England. Since those days, the ancient safeguards, which were of great service, and often of decisive importance, to our campaign, despite their working imperfections, have been skilfully whittled down, almost year by year, so that the Government has by now acquired a completely free hand in disposing of what is supposed to be (two-thirds) public property, and are under no surviving obligation to heed the public's interest or wishes.

The real need is for the more positive legislation which the Association always used to advocate. Every member of the public should have the right of recourse to the Courts when default in maintenance or in service is alleged. Frivolous complaints would be restricted by the likelihood of costs being awarded against those losing their actions: though in an ideal society there would be a very high court indeed for the hearing at public cost of reasonably authenticated complaints against all organs of government. There is an ancient court of this type in France. There should be a modern one in England.

Within our first twelve months, Charles Hadfield resigned his Vice-

Chairmanship; and soon he was writing letters to the press in opposition to mine, especially on the subject of narrow boat carrying. He has since written a number of exceedingly lengthy and detailed books on the canal history of various regions of England and Wales. These works are often treated with great respect, and no doubt rightly; but to me Hadfield seems a man more interested in canal beds than in canals. In his books, he not infrequently suggests that this or that canal should never have been built at all. It was not an attitude that was likely to appeal to me, or that seemed to me conducive to the advancement of the Association's extremely difficult struggle.

I was convinced that the Association should demand, on the contrary, the retention, and, where necessary, revitalisation of the entire surviving system. I had several strong reasons for this.

The first and strongest was (and is) that this over-populated country cannot afford to lose a single navigable mile, even though some of those miles may have been, at the time they were built, more difficult to justify, in profit-and-loss or balance-sheet terms, than certain other miles. (How could it have been otherwise?)

A second reason was (and is) that it would be difficult to run a national campaign while admitting to many enquirers that it was not proposed to do as much for their local waterway as for various others. Most enquirers are naturally interested in their local waterways first. Any attempt at discrimination would have resulted in the weakening of the national campaign (anyway at that early stage) by the atomisation of the single body into numerous merely local societies, all more or less powerless; much to the gratification of opposing authority. Certain small waterway societies of this type did appear in later years, so strong is local feeling – and the urge to hold paper office; and authority has duly done what it can to foster this development. By that time, however, it mattered much less to the campaign. If I, and those who agreed with me, had not prevented it happening in the early years, there would have been no effective campaign at all, and many hundreds of navigable miles would have been lost.

A third reason, almost as strong as the first, was the utter impossibility of obtaining agreement upon which waterways mattered more in the modern world, and which less. All the effort would have gone in trying to agree upon what we were prepared to fight for.

Similarly with Hadfield's economic arguments against narrow boat carrying. It was a time when every single boat, every kontiki raft, every boy in a canoe, counted for the survival of the waterway it moved on; and working narrow boats counted not merely as by far the most important, vessel by vessel, but as part of an industrial argument that existed independently of the number of craft, and as part of a strong world of popular sentiment also. The survival of each single narrow boat was as a nugget of gold on our side of the controversial scale. Hadfield's letters to the press in antagonism to mine, even if justified within their economic frame of reference (which I do not accept – and at the time of writing I have been for some years on the board of a narrow boat carrying company), seemed to me, on balance, a remarkably ill service to the cause. But it was clear enough even within the first months of the Association, that Hadfield by no means agreed with me as to what that cause should be; and also that a certain number of our Members agreed with Hadfield.

In like manner, I doubt whether Hadfield much participated in the popular sentiment about the roses and castles. The critical necessity seemed to me to be to attract the greatest possible volume of support, and the utmost diversification, without actual inconsistency. Thus, while I myself wholly share the popular sentiment about the roses and castles, and about the entire working-boat way of life also, and believe it to be a rare insight into the true quality of things and into what matters, and although I have no such personally warm feelings about angling and all that goes with it, I tried, year in and year out to attract the anglers and add their support to that of the other interests, practical and emotional, behind the campaign.

I have referred to a certain number of the Association's Members who were more in agreement with Hadfield than with me. In accordance with my general view of things, I believe this to have been more a consequence of personal temperament than of waterway discussion; and thus outside the scope of argument, probably outside the possibility of change. I think most disagreements are no more and no less than conflicts between differing temperaments, and that temperaments are unalterable (including by psychiatry), and are the only true raw material of society. I have always believed strongly that a small group of people whose temperaments and (therefore) aims are closely akin, can virtually conquer the world, if that is what they wish to do; whereas a much bigger group will usually be found on close examination either to be limited to sociabilities, or to be far more concerned with internal debate than with any kind of external action. Of the big voluntary organisation this becomes all the more true as its size leads to its steady and stealthy incorporation into the authority it was originally constituted to oppose. There is a point in the history of every successful voluntary organisation when any real power it may have had, becomes symbolic power only. Nothing fails like success, as Dean Inge so well observed (of the British Empire in particular). At that point, the organisation should wind itself up; but it is always the point when the membership, having, as it thinks, something at last to show for all the work, is more than before eager to continue.

As party canvassers have long been instructed, one cannot hope to convert by argument. The intellect itself is a very superficial, and strictly luxurious, acquisition of man. Men are governed either by tradition or by force: it was Disraeli's deepest utterance. All that the canvasser can do, for the waterways cause as for any other, is to reach and awake those already in potential sympathy. The wide problem of governing the state cannot be left at that, and the case for democracy lies in its negative and restrictive aspects; a strong case, as government is an evil in itself. When it comes to a voluntary campaigning group, the situation is different. The aim is (presumably) positive. No one is compelled to belong, as all are compelled to belong to the state. Accordingly, there is no honest justification for those who disagree, continuing to belong. They can always depart and form a new organisation. It will then emerge which of the lines of thought offered more truly represents the public will (or the public unconscious – they are much the same). Several splinter groups did much later break away from the Association; and the test proved conclusive, because all remained tiny.

The playboys of the waterways world remained, in their own being, a serious problem. From the start, it was often taken for granted that our view was akin to that of the groups who try to acquire and operate disused railway lines, primarily so that they themselves can at weekends drive the engines. As a Committee Member of the National Council on Inland Transport, I am very far from suggesting that all the groups that have tried to save this line or that from the official holocaust, are made up of playboys. Some of the groups operate a serious transport service, and make an extremely important contribution in a field that has become (has been made) as difficult as the waterways field at its worst. It is urgent that legislation be introduced to require the transfer of officially discarded railway routes at a reasonable price to suitable private takers. At present, the official railway interests act like the official waterway interests: they either refuse to hand the line over at all, and indeed direct more energy to ripping it up than they have for a long time applied to making it efficient; or they attach financial and other conditions to the transfer that are quite unjustified commercially, and palpably intended to dampen and discourage. One might have thought it better for a service to be maintained under almost any auspices, provided that reasonable requirements for safety were complied with, than for the route to go drearily to ruin; but that is very much not the attitude of either the railway bureaucracy or the waterways bureaucracy, as all who have tried to take over a disused railway or a disused waterway are bitterly aware. None the less, it remains true that the playboys are a strong element among the railway enthusiasts, and that their attitude had contributed significantly to the scepticism with which authority has been able to meet the whole movement.

The critical point about the playboy, in our context, and perhaps in others too, seems to me to be that he is one who is prepared to accept the existing order of things and aims merely at extracting from it as much personal entertainment as he can. It is a not unreasonable attitude to life and society as a whole; at all times incomprehensibly complex, latterly a Kafka nightmare. But there is a difference between responding in this way to the state, from which none can escape, and to a voluntary and private campaigning organisation, joined at individual will. An organisation that means business is bound to be greatly hampered by the playboy member's attitude. While he seems to give support, often more vocal and enthusiastic support than most, his purpose is, in fact, almost the reverse of the one that brings results. There is always far too much work for the volunteers to do, and the playboy greatly adds to it instead of helping to reduce it. He has joined the organisation "for what he can get out of it", as he not infrequently admits, even proclaims. He is not a man to agree that one gets far more from an organisation in pursuit of an impersonal ideal than from one which explicitly aims at the pleasure of the Members.

In the early years, I conversed several times each day on the telephone with strangers enquiring for particulars. About one in three asked what they would "get out of joining". I would reply with all possible firmness "Nothing. Members receive a Bulletin which has been well spoken of. There are fairly frequent meetings, and dinners, and trips on the waterway. Many seem to think they are well run and enjoyable. But none of these things are reasons for joining. They are all adjuncts to a campaign. The only reason for joining is belief in the campaign". Of nothing am I more sure than that ten who fully understand and fully agree are stronger than a thousand who are but generally interested. It is for the generally interested that time and money have to be spent in internal administration instead of in campaigning. Nor is this the only reason why on balance they weaken rather than strengthen the organisation. Authority has good reason for professing not to take an organisation seriously until it has become safely unwieldy.

Of the link between use and beauty, the poet is John Betjeman. I mention this because John Betjeman's position is so widely misunderstood. So far from being the sentimentalist of the branch line for its own sake, and of the past for its own sake, he has a rigorous understanding of the truth that use and beauty benefit man only when in equilibrium: that, in a sense, neither even exists without the other. The mass alienation of man, about which so much is said, results from their forcible disengagement.

In 1947 appeared Tom Rolt's "High Horse Riderless", which I regard as his best book. It offers a detailed account of this same alienation (before the term had spread far beyond a purely clinical use); based upon the author's direct observations of English mores. It makes fascinating reading. It does not offer much in the way of solution, but that may be set to the account of integrity, as most solutions so far offered are no more than symptoms of the disease. What is especially notable about "High Horse Riderless" is its precise formulation of the dilemma: the need is not for the rejection of all machines, after the manner of the Erewhonians, or for the acceptance of all machines, after the manner of the twentieth century, but for selection between machine and machine, accepting the life-enhancing and repudiating the death-advancing (spiritual as well as material). Our guide should be that Son of Heaven who, when gunpowder was invented, ruled that its use should be confined to fireworks, and when the power of steam was demonstrated, ruled that it should be applied only to toys. Tom Rolt does not show how the human race as a whole can rise to such wisdom, but nothing less than that will do if the human race is to survive.

VIII

The Blue Windmill

Everything in the world must surpass itself in order to be itself. There must be something
limitless in a human being and in his activity for either to have definition and character.

BORIS PASTERNAK

The Association's first Annual General Meeting took place on 31 May
1947. It began in my house, with sandwiches and sociabilities, and
passed on to the premises of the Association for Planning and Regional
Reconstruction in Gordon Square, one of the several bodies that were
already regarding our work and beliefs with sympathy. About sixty people
appeared. Peter Scott was in the chair, and later presided over a large,
informal dinner at a Greek restaurant named the Blue Windmill, which the
movement often patronised at that period, and until the plump and genial
proprietor, known to all as Chris, bettered himself and moved to higher
things. After dinner, about twenty people came back to my house and sat on
rugs upon the roof until a late or early hour. As Bulletin 6 expressed it: "The
weather on this occasion was of record-breaking heat and humidity; so that
the attendance and enthusiasm were especially commendable."

Donations were announced from Peter Scott; Michael Bratby of
Scrimgeours, the gallant and entertaining first Honorary Secretary of the
Wildfowl Trust; and Lord Egerton of Tatton. The last-named, who was
also the last of his line, was the bachelor descendant of a pioneer in the
building of the Manchester Ship Canal. One of the Association's first
Members, he asked Rolt to pay him a visit. Having crossed the vast expanse
of Tatton Park, Rolf found Lord Egerton in a proportionately vast mansion.
Having taken Rolt on a tour of many wonders, including huge sporting
trophies and very early motor cars, he summed up gloomily: "Of course, I
am a hawk among sparrows." His contribution to our cause was a very
handsome one, critically timed. The enormous Tatton Park estate has now
passed out of the family. The sparrows have mastered the hawk.

We used to adjourn for dinner in what amounted to a private room on the first floor of the Blue Windmill after every Council Meeting. It was in Windmill Street, between Tottenham Court Road and Charlotte Street. The decor, though simple, consisting largely of pale blue paint and very thick flowered carpets, was strikingly spick and span, and no one had to think of paying much more than five shillings for a large and excellent meal. When we started a Midlands Branch, and from it came Cyril Taplin as a Council Member, I used on the occasion of each monthly session to walk with him from the Blue Windmill to Euston Station for the midnight train to Birmingham; through the dark streets, with (in those days) little traffic at that hour, and through Euston Square gardens. I attached great importance to this regular social sequel to the business meetings, and it was noticeable how the Council lost colour and cohesiveness when, as it increased in number, individual Members began to say that they thought they had better get home to their families without waiting for dinner.

The Association's first waterborne outing for its Members occurred on 26 July in the same year. We felt that the event should take place on a canal rather than on a river (with the usual object of widening the scope and acceptance of things), and we selected the Lancaster Canal because it seemed to be the only one on which suitable boats were available, there being a company, already established, and at that time unique in the land, which offered regular or private canal trips from a place named Hest Bank, north of Lancaster, set between the navigation and Morecambe Bay. The great expanse of the Bay is to be seen at close quarters from an appreciable stretch of the canal. We were extremely uncertain what the response would be from our Membership: I (then but a child) thought it might, including Members' friends, be 150; Rolt thought it might be zero. Rolt was nearer the mark. The exact figure was judiciously muffled in the report which appeared in Bulletin 7, but I recall it (I am unlikely ever to forget it) as being about half a dozen, apart from Rolt and me and our party. Accustomed as I had been to much matter-of-fact journeying about since early childhood, I had failed to appreciate the effect of the distance between the Lancaster Canal and the areas in the Midlands and South where most of our Membership then resided. In the event, only one single Member came from the Home Counties, outside our own party. In the course of the trip, however, I met for the first time Mr. Douglas Pole Welman, a prominent and exceedingly shrewd businessman, then and now; one of the many such whom the waterways have slightly fascinated but slightly baffled. ("I am interested in nothing but the trading possibilities," Mr. Welman would say.) He then lived in what he claimed to be the most rained-upon house in England, high up in the Pennines, and had a repertory of truly extraordinary tales concerning the romance of commerce from his own first-hand experience. On the day of the outing, the rain fell by no means only upon Mr. Welman's upland seat, but it takes more than rainfall to prevent a right-minded man or woman enjoying the Lancaster Canal. Indeed, many think that it looks at its best in winter twilight when snow is descending.

It once ran from Preston to Kendal. There was also a southern section from a junction with the Leeds and Liverpool Canal to a remote spot named Walton Summit, standing high above Preston on the south bank of the Ribble. It had been intended to link the section of the Lancaster Canal north of Preston with the shorter section to the south, but impetus had flagged after the invention of the railway (as on the waterways happened so often and so disastrously), and the link was made only by "tramway", with a special bridge, of charming design, across the Ribble. When, during the nineteenth century, the tramway fizzled out, the bridge was converted for use by pedestrians. From it, at the time of the Lancaster Canal outing, I saw the biggest swarm of gnats that has ever come my way. A compact but agitated column of them towered upwards in the evening light until it seemed to reach the grey clouds. In my time, Walton Summit had come to resemble a lost city of the Incas. Low stone warehouses adjoined big stone-edged basins, all long unused; with no life but cows, sheep and no doubt, llamas.

The northern section fared better, even after the all too customary acquisition by a railway company, the London and North Western; afterwards part of the L.M.S. Despite its isolation from the rest of the waterways system (apart from a link to the agreeable little port of Glasson on the River Lune estuary), it carried a modest traffic until the L.M.S. promoted a mass-closures Bill during the early 1940's, when the nation was preoccupied. The L.M.S. achieved almost everything it wanted, closing the beautiful Welsh Section of the Shropshire Union in its entirety, the almost equally beautiful Cromford Canal, the Huddersfield Narrow Canal across the Pennines, and much else; but the Lancaster Canal it failed to close, largely owing to opposition from the local authority at Kendal. The upper, and more beautiful, portion of the waterway, above Tewitfield Locks, then fell into progressive disrepair; was abandoned, section after section, by the British Transport Commission; and finally destroyed, beyond reasonable possibility of reopening, by driving across it in several places the M6 motorway at towpath level instead of by bridging. The attempt to resist this final piece of national folly was one of my last campaigns for the waterways. The low level motorway has cut off one of the loveliest sections of navigation imaginable, and killed a recreational alternative at the entrance to the increasingly congested Lake District. The Minister responsible was Mrs. Castle.

What, I used to be asked, can be the *real* explanation for such decisions? Why should the Association's campaign meet with such determined, persistent, self-renewing, and often unscrupulous resistance?

At the bottom of the resistance lay, beyond all doubt, the disastrous intervention of the railway companies during the nineteenth century. This afflicted the entire system with advancing administrative arthritis; fostered defeatism at every level of the staff; prevented almost all modernisation (so that even by the end of the nineteenth century, the remarkable thing was that any traffic survived at all); and kept up a steady and pervasive pressure for abandonment. Then came the "hard-headed business" attitude, of which we used to hear so much: because the waterways had fallen so sick, they were not worth reviving; because they were less profitable than the manufacture of breakfast foods, they were not worth retaining at all. Hard heads do not always imply long sight. Over all lay more than a century of inertia and gerrymandering. But one could not fail to become aware that there were strong elements of psychology also; and all the more potent, of course, because unconscious and irrational.

Freud himself pointed to the number of the clergy who are fascinated by railways; by the concept, as he said, of "keeping on the rails". When our Member, Mr. Owen Prosser, first spoke to me of founding a society to "save the railways" as the Association had been founded to "save the waterways", I remarked that the much wider social relevance of the railways should bring him at least a hundred members to every one or ours. I was quite wrong (regrettably for civilised transport in Britain): the railway movement, such as it is, is crippled by the temperamental limitations that Freud divined. They manifest mainly in obsession with detail, in inability to perceive the whole wood as being in any way as real as the separate trees, even the separate, intricate, fascinating leaves, all so different from one another. The railway-possessed man (it is always a man) tends to be a Freudian obsessional walking. The railways movement has now to some extent risen above its specialists and experts, but, alas, it is now considerably too late.

The waterway-possessed man or woman is more likely to be hallucinatory than obsessional. Water winding and twisting between banks; rising and falling by locks and weirs; cataracting or quiescent beneath the arches of bridges; much hidden from the common world; secretive and initiatory; decked by beautiful buildings as by bountiful botany: water either sparkling and glinting or sullen and boding; at once tended and untendable – and ultimately uncontrollable; always a little mysterious, with a life of its own, like a cat; water is of all sex symbols the superlative, and where the sea is sadistic, as Swinburne divined, the river or canal is sweetly seductive. Conflict, and bitter, inexpressible, often unthinkable, feelings are certain. The water-possessed are likely to be inwardly driven; to cling to their separate, private dreams with the desperation of the drowning; to beset with strange ferocity all conceived of as rivals. Equally, a wary, protective, unmoving, unmovable establishment is likely to emerge, as it usually does where men and women come into contact with passion and mystery. No doubt society could not continue if it did not. The concept of abandonment appeals to opposed attitudes: for the establishment it represents end of risk and temptation; for the campaigners it can unknowingly represent end of restraint. The official dislike of the very word abandonment (described as "melodramatic") was significant . . . How strange, the questioning outsiders used to exclaim (and some insiders too), that those pretty, peaceful waterways should apparently generate so much heat and aggression! (But if only the railways could have generated a little more!)

Bulletin 7 announced the opening of our campaign for the Derby Canal. This waterway, a 'wide' one too, which nationalisation had "managed to miss", linked Derby with the wide Trent & Mersey Canal in one direction, and with the wide Erewash Canal in the other; and at its opening the ancient water route to Derby by the Derbyshire River Derwent was allowed to fall to pieces. The Derby Canal Company, finding other uses, more profitable than navigation, for land occupied by the canal, were assisted by a peculiarly antique Act, which made it impracticable to insist upon passage of the waterway by a working boat, as could at that time be required of most other navigation authorities. The company also played its cards slowly, astutely, and without unnecessary publicity. It was prepared to wait forty years or more for the ruin of the navigation to be consummated.

At the outset of the Association's campaign, the prime mover was the late Mr. B.A. Mallender, Managing Director of the Derby Gas Light and Coke Company (since nationalised, of course, unlike the canal), who had aforetime been a director of the canal company also, but had resigned on the adoption of the closure policy; a rare sacrifice, which few have followed. The original list of objectors to the closure included the Derbyshire County Council, the Derby Corporation, the Derby Chamber of Commerce, the River Trent Catchment Board, the Derbyshire and Nottinghamshire Electric Power Company (since nationalised also), and I.C.I. Not unreasonably, we thought the prospect good; but over the years that followed, all these fellow-objectors proved susceptible to negotiation, and we alone were left. The final discussions, with civil servants waiting for us to finish what we had to say, as General de Gaulle waited for Laval's advocate to finish (though, no doubt, more politely, and with cups of tea), were in the mid-1960's. By that time, Michael Macfarlane, one of the movement's heroes, had mounted a really strong local campaign, but I do not think it could ever have been strong enough to defeat the Derby Canal Company. I used often to reflect what a good thing it was that over most of the field for most of our time we had the ill-equipped British Transport Commission to deal with, and not an efficient private enterprise inspired by profit and a philosophy. On the other hand, I am quite certain that, at the end, a free vote of the Derby electorate would have come down on our side. Nor is the smallness of the poll in such cases very material; it is no bad thing for a vote to be exercised mainly by those who know a little of what it is about.

But then there can be no doubt at all that, after the Association's first four or five years (probably after the Market Harborough Festival in 1950), a national poll on the nation's waterway policy would have brought the same result by a far larger proportionate majority. Democracy is a curious matter: capable, like the New Testament, of an almost infinite breadth, depth, and originality of commentary and interpretation. The Derby Canal Company were what is known as realists: long before the final Act of abandonment, large industrial constructions had appeared over lengthy filled-in sections of waterway; so that much was at stake. "You must be realistic," we used frequently to be told by anxious well-wishers: not only in the context of the Derby Canal. I fear that I have often found the realists, to be as much enemies of promise as the expert.

To Bulletin 7, Tom Rolt contributed the following: "Nantwich Basin affords a remarkable example of the disintegration of regional economy (and hence, of course, the accompanying collapse of civilisation as a whole). *Stage 1* Cheshire Cheeses are brought in carts from surrounding farms to the Basin; where they are loaded direct into boats for shipment to Manchester. Boats are specially fitted with racks for carrying cheeses so that they do not touch each other. Cheeses arrive at destination in prime condition owing to coolness and lack of vibration of water transport. *Stage 2* Cheeses are stored in warehouses at Basin, whence they are despatched by road transport without special stowing. Cheese never arrives fresh and seldom undamaged. Meanwhile, Basin fills with mud. *Stage 3* Warehouses have become a buffer depot for Canadian and New Zealand cheese. Cheshire cheese is seldom or never seen in Nantwich. One factory is making Cheshire cheese for export; but in the canteen there the workers are served with Canadian or New Zealand cheese."

Sometimes we received encouragement. Bulletin 9 recorded the following from our Member, Mr. Humphries, Managing Director of the company which operated Coxes Lock Mill on the River Wey: "Here is an example taken from our regular traffic between London Docks and this mill. If a ship berths in London by 6 a.m. on Monday, our barge can load 80 tons of wheat in bulk and get away by midday, reaching Kingston behind a tug, normally with two other barges, by Monday night. On Tuesday morning, the barge continues by tug to the mouth of the Wey and then is taken over by two horses, arriving at the mill, two miles up, by midday. The barge is then unloaded by 3 p.m., and the wheat can be turned into flour and feeding stuffs by teatime. The barge crew can spend the night at home and can load 1000 ten-stone bags of flour next morning, Wednesday, in time to catch the midday tug at the mouth of the Wey. With ordinary luck with the tide, the barge will reach the flour-wharf at London Bridge in the evening, and will be unloaded by 11 a.m. next day, Thursday. On Friday, it can reload with wheat in the Docks and be back at the mill by Saturday midday. By these methods, handling wheat in bulk by water, we are far ahead of transport by lorry or railway. Not only do we save repeated handling, shunting, sack-hire, and time wasted in railway marshalling yards, but we are also able to suck the wheat out of the barges by mechanical means at our convenience at any time of the day or night."

It is difficult not to believe that the continuing transfer of traffics such as that to the roads is the product of positive policy rather than of natural forces. The Budget, it is claimed, cannot be balanced without big automobile exports. Big automobile exports, it is said, are impracticable without an ever-expanding home market. If too many people are willing to live without cars, we may, in fact, not all be able to live at all. In such theorems as these can be found explanations for much in British Transport and British life (or death).

IX

Letters and Lecturers

The fact is that humanity's interests in things truly material has very quickly exhausted itself, the material world being particularly limited and narrow compared with the potentialities of the human soul. Hence universal boredom supervenes, which nothing can relieve save sensationalism, a series of revelations each more startling and violent than the last. Humanity in the cage of mechanism is like a child with a toy of which the normal interest has long been exhausted. In desperation he tries what can be done with the toy upside down, whether any fresh possibilities are revealed by turning it inside out. Finally, there is nothing left but to smash it to bits.

PHILIP HESELTINE

By now, we had appointed two more Vice-Presidents. The first was the Earl of Portsmouth. A pioneer in calling attention to the near possibility of world starvation, he advocated a humanistic agriculture, in place of a mechanistic, as the best means of meeting the threat. His works give a prominent place to rivers and canals as providing the mode of transport most suited to a living agricultural community. When, as Lord Lymington, a Member of the House of Commons, he had played a leading part in the defeat of a measure known as the Canal Barge Bill, which, in accordance with the misnomer in its title, would, in effect, have broken up the family boat system.

The family boat system is undoubtedly open to much improvement (best achieved by enlarging the waterways, and thus making possible bigger boats), but it had brought into being a community devoted to the life, which indeed has important advantages. It is adventurous; it is spent in the open air against a changing background; it is lived as a family. Fascinating details of the family boat system, now nearing extinction (though, all the same, never quite reaching it), will be found in L.T.C. Rolt's "Narrow Boat".

Our second new Vice-President was a painter: Algernon Newton.

Newton's relationship with the waterways was a curious blend of reality and jeu des mots. Not only was the work of Canaletto his main inspiration and ideal, but he painted so many scenes of actual British canals that he was regarded for many years as by far the most important artist in that boundless but neglected field. The character of his art may be summed up in two sentences from the very perceptive obituary of him in "The Times", when he died in 1960, aged 88: "Working in a highly experimental age, he refused to be side-tracked by modern theories. Having decided his course, he kept to it; and produced a body of work consistently high in quality and individual in manner."

Newton proved to be a tall, charming, utterly ageless gentleman, with white pointed beard; also to be the father of the late, demonic actor, Robert Newton, most horrible, most contemporary, as Pinky in Graham Greene's "Brighton Rock". As a Vice-President, Algernon Newton was very conscientious in his duties, regularly attending the Association's meetings and functions. In his studio, near Kensington Church, I met Dod Procter, Ethelbert White, Harold Workman, and other interesting people, and learned much that I had not known before about how pictures were painted when that accomplishment still called for skill, inspiration, and steady self-sacrifice. Also I persuaded these eminent people, and many others, to join the Association. Newton always bubbled with life and interest. He offered impressive proof that youth of heart and love of beauty (to say nothing of hard campaigning) lead to length of years.

At this time also, we added Mr. S.E. Barlow to our Council. His name was to be seen on many working narrow boats, almost all exceptionally well painted; based upon his big yard on the Coventry Canal at Tamworth in Staffordshire. It was understood that at an earlier period he had broken away from the famous Samuel Barlow Coal Company at Braunston, and set up on his own. He was a very small, but well-made man, brisk and spruce, much like a retired jockey. He could be charmingly helpful when one's boat broke down anywhere near Tamworth (I, needless to say, was helpless wherever and whenever this happened, and I have sometimes been accompanied by others less than omnipotent with marine engines): but as a Council Member he made little mark. It was not necessarily a disability that for much of the time he sat in silence. The talkative Council Member is not always the most valuable in the campaign. With S.E. Barlow the trouble was that always in his mind was the official trade argument I have already described, that at the best, very little money was going to be made available for canals so that the great aim was to make sure that all there was of it be spent on the few that were the busiest. Before long, he parted company with us, but honourably and giving his reasons. It was unreservedly right for him to go, but, despite a fundamental conflict in attitude, I was sorry when he left, and sorrier still when, shortly afterwards, he died. It was sad that the trade should still so uniformly take so narrow a view, and sadder when narrowness of view duly brought the trade almost to an end.

In 1947, 1948, and 1949, the Association promoted a travelling exhibition. Most of the assembly and arrangement, largely of objects lent by Members, were done (extremely well) by Angela Rolt. I have prints of "The Times" photographs showing her in the act of positioning a dipper.

Every self-respecting narrow boat is equipped with three cult objects, all under proper circumstances, sparklingly painted with roses and castles, usually on a deep green background. The can, like the half of a milk churn (but where can the reader now see milk churns?), holds the drinking water; not always in those days an easy commodity to come by, unless one had regular places of resort, as did the working boatmen. (Now public taps have been installed at frequent intervals, with, at each, indicators of the whereabouts of the next in both directions; a very useful facility until wrecked by the populace.) The dipper, like a deep frying pan, a very big one, and with a similar long handle, is used for scooping up water from 'the cut' when there is washing to be done, or washing-up, or washing-down. The can and dipper commonly repose on the cabin-top; cynosures, when fresh with paint, of every towpath eye. The third cult object, the stool, hides within. It is a rectangular stool. The top, perhaps eighteen inches long by eight inches wide, is supported not on legs but on a framework of very anthropological or folkish pattern, which gives solidity and stability. No one seems to know whence came the stool or why. A plausible opinion is that it was originally provided for the children to stand on when steering the boat. I suspect that this is akin to accounting for the practice of circumcision by the claim that it is advantageous to health in a hot climate. I feel that the stool entered the boat for less practical reasons, but, once there, came in handy when the children took the tiller, as even an altar can do when one has to dust the tracery at the top of an east window.

Our exhibition undoubtedly offered the finest collection of canal folk material ever displayed until that time; everything from the big painted cratches of working boats to boatwomen's bonnets, boatmen's trousers (those working the "Joshers", the fleet belonging to Fellows, Morton, and Clayton, wore white ones), horse brasses, and Measham teapots. Measham, a village on the Ashby Canal, produced slipware pots and jugs for use by the canal community. They bore affecting mottoes such as "Love at Home" or "Forward the Boat". The most sought after pieces are small teapots with straight sides, like kettles. The Rolts owned (and used) a beautiful example: for which a visitor to the exhibition offered to pay £50 on the spot, but was refused. With the Second World War, the Measham pottery was "directed" to the production of "utility white", and soon disappeared. Now the village is best known as a mart for second-hand cars; the Warren Street of the Midlands. *Corruptic optimi pessimum.*

Everything jingled, jangled, flashed, glittered, moved to wonder and to sentimental tears. No doubt more important was our exhibition's concern for the future: we designed (ourselves) as many wall-posters as the Chinese, and mounted a terrifying battery of horror photographs, scenes of neglect and ruin, sequences of year-by-year destruction, deliberate or at least gratuitous. The worth of a waterways exhibition can still be most rapidly assessed by the prominence it gives to the demonstration of unnecessary or wanton destruction. Wings-against-the-sky themes are still placebos; more to the point remain cries to heaven.

Most of the photographs at that first exhibition, the idylls with the horrors, were taken either by Angela Rolt herself or by my old friend, James Sutherland. For accurate record, tellingly composed, the photographs of these two remain unequalled in the waterways field, and are likely to remain so. It is rather as the portrait photographs of Mrs. Cameron, coming very early in the history of photography, are unlikely ever to be bettered.

Entering the scene at a rather later date, Eric de Maré became the third of the great waterway photographers. His work is less valuable as record, but unsurpassed as poetry. There are no more beautiful waterway photographs than those in his book, "The Canals of England", published by The Architectural Press; none more calculated to move hearts and make converts.

The exhibition originated in an exceedingly generous offer by Heal & Son Ltd., of their fine Mansard Gallery free of charge for its display. Our debt to this firm was great. Both Sir Ambrose Heal and his son, Anthony Heal, became Members of the Association, as did several of their staff. Sir Ambrose, who was famous not only for building up so large a business on a policy of only high quality goods, but also for an enormous collection of antique 'trade cards', met all comers with enormous charm, and the whole firm seemed eager to help.

Our President opened the exhibition on 14th October 1947, with me in the chair beside him. Introducing him to the throng before us, I made some genial though conventional remark about A.P.H. being famous for his voyages with glamorous parties on the Grand Union. When his turn came, he replied very sharply that he did not know what I meant: he had never navigated a canal with anyone but his wife. He seemed quite sincere.

But introducing a more prominent speaker than oneself is often difficult. The customary slow trickle of pale honey can nauseate the audience and be of no help with them to the prominent speaker; but it is what the speaker has come to expect, and he is usually best left to take his chance with it. At the biggest dinner over which I ever presided, at the Alexandra Palace with many hundreds present, I had to introduce Sir Isaac Hayward, long the potent panjandrum of the then London County Council, and after whose connoisseurship of art the Hayward Gallery on the South Bank is named. In doing so, I mentioned how much I had owed when very young to the L.C.C. trams, and especially to the truly immense distances one could then travel in the evenings and on Sundays for twopence. Sir Isaac, like Sir Alan, did not know what I meant: it was terrible that there should have been so many poor people in those dreadful days, and the L.C.C. had felt bound, in determining its fares, to do what it could to help them.

The prominent speaker has his side of the matter. The great faults of the introducer tend to be anticipating what the prominent speaker has to say, and sheer garrulity in doing it. Introducing F.E. Smith, a chairman of a meeting ran on and over. "And now", he concluded, "I have great pleasure in asking Mr. Smith to give his address." Smith rose: "32 Grosvenor Gardens. And I am going there now."

Heals told us that our exhibition broke all records for attendance at their gallery. On many days it attracted more than a thousand people. It was taken up by Art Exhibitions Bureau of Clarges Street, who toured it round the provinces for more than a year and a half. At more than half the galleries it visited it broke the attendance record. 4000 people visited it at Luton (Wardown Park) in three days. Peter Scott formally opened it at Bristol, with the Lord Mayor in the Chair. It was certainly the best small travelling exhibition I have ever seen. I can say this with the more objectivity in that I had little to do with assembling it.

A thing we like in Britain is the 'independent enquiry'. Faced with a difficult decision, authority understandably dodges, and instead of taking it, goes to the antithesis and sets up a Royal Commission or Departmental Committee to bring out more facts. Evidence is taken by supposedly busy people, often serving for years with dust in the air and for little more than the hope of a minor honour after they have been through the investigatory mill perhaps three or four times. (There are experts in serving on public enquiries, as in everything else. There was a Mr. Rowe without whom, for many, many years, no truly independent enquiry was quite sound.) In the end, a Report is published, sometimes in more than one volume, occasionally in double-column, even with scattered illustrations. Since facts of themselves settle nothing (and more facts often, in practice, settle less), little seems to be gained directly, but as major decisions have become almost impossible in any case, each one proving somehow to be still another arrow through the heart, gain can be supposed to result from mere postponement of change, and from keeping so many people happily occupied with taking and giving evidence and counter-evidence, and writing so many tens of thousands of words. In particular, there is a useful and rising profession of Secretary to these enquiries.

The waterways of Britain have been subjected to at least seven such enquiries; which we believe to be a record, though an unwanted one. The first independent public enquiry into the waterways reported in 1880; the seventh and last (so far) in 1958. In addition to these seven, there have been a large number of other enquiries similar in form and method but less independent, because deriving from and confined within the waterways organisation, and thus instituted for the main purpose of apologising for official policy and confirming its basic wisdom. In the second half of my life with the Inland Waterways Association, there was seldom a time when we were not awaiting a report by some investigatory committee, awaiting the official policy statement following such a report, or awaiting the announcement of who would serve on the next committee of enquiry, promised in principle, and what its terms of reference would be. We were handicapped by some of our Members taking seriously each committee, each report, and each policy statement, but the true worth of so much waiting lay in the time it gained for the advancement of our campaign while the opposition was impeded in carrying out closures by the fact that the whole topic was sub judice. The sequence of enquiries also proved, of course, that the Association had Authority on the run, or at least on the shuffle.

Almost the first rule of public campaigning is at all times to fight on ground chosen by oneself and never on ground chosen by the opposition. I always had great difficulty in persuading our Members to apply this rule. It is far more important to assert on all occasions the positive aims for which one is working, however vast and unusual they may be, than to demolish, however convincingly, the contentions of one's opponents. It is better to be dismissed as a visionary than as a niggler and pettifogger. This is partly because visionaries never are quite dismissed.

We delivered memoranda and made oral testimony to many of the public and department enquiries, probably to all of them; but I always tried to prevent too much effort going in that direction. What mattered far more were protest meetings, protest cruises, campaigning publications and statements, the recruitment of influential people with more or less the right temperament, the rescue of individual waterways, the nursing and fostering of all waterway businesses: never missing an opportunity to appear in the press, never allowing ourselves to be unnecessarily overlooked. We advanced (with giant strides) by drama; and the very purpose of a public enquiry is to estimate drama, other, perhaps, than occasional farce. Later evolved the governmental technique of making rebellion not unsuccessful but impossible, by incorporating all rebels into the organisation they are rebelling against. Of this I shall have more to say.

In those first years the report which preoccupied us was the Pick Report. Among Sir Winston Churchill's many enthusiasms was a minor one for canals. During the Second World War, he had appointed the late Frank Pick, regenerator, with Lord Ashfield, of London's public transport, to carry out a one-man investigation into waterways. It was believed by those who had known Pick that he had reported strongly in favour of retaining the canals, of modernising them, and of using them more fully. The difficulty was that the report had never been published. We lost no opportunity of demanding that it should be. When the official rebuffs began to take the form of claiming that the Pick Report was now out of date and had been superseded by "later thinking" (almost all entirely destructive, of course), we became more convinced than ever that Pick would be of help to us. In the end, I did see the Report, and our surmise proved to be true; but I saw it in circumstances which made it impossible to quote from it or make use of it. Since then authority has become very much more skilled in arranging that the public hears only one side of a case while believing that it hears more than ever before of both. As for Churchill's belief in canals, I had a letter from Chartwell during his last premiership. I did my best to reply suitably and sent a small quantity of our best literature. I received an acknowledgement, but heard no more. Churchill himself would have had to be Minister of Transport if any constructive results were to be hoped for in our field.

By now, I was writing forty or fifty long letters each week, including perhaps five or six to editors of newspapers, largely provincial. Among the nationals, we learned that we could count on the support of the "Daily Telegraph" and the "Daily Express"; but on the hostility of "The Times", which either refused us space or gave more space to our opponents. "The Times" used to proclaim a general policy of supporting "the Government of the day" as long as it felt able to; and, needless to say, it is desirable that at least one prominent newspaper should follow that line.

One of my communications to "The Times" resulted in an invitation to talk the matter over with a member of the economics staff. This gentleman entertained me to a single glass of sherry at the Union Club, and, giving me little time to speak (he had another appointment), recounted to me very slowly and distinctly a policy for canals which was entirely indistinguishable from the British Waterways policy. Having thus helped me on my way, he unfortunately had to be off. Not a word of what I had written, appeared in print.

On another wonderful morning, however, though it happened only once, I woke to find that a letter of mine had appeared at the top of "The Times" correspondence column. I actually received several little notes and telephone calls of congratulation. But the most important letter from me ever to appear in "The Times" was one advocating that Vienna, and not Brussels, should be the capital of a united Europe, even of a partly united Europe: Vienna with its strategically dominant situation, universalist tradition, grand and open scale, and numerous, sadly unused palaces. One or two Austrians wrote to me in elderly, illegible internationalese.

Naturally, our letters made more mark in provincial newspapers, though not in all of them. In the provinces too, our campaign was supported in some quarters for years on end; slighted and attacked for years on end in others. It did not depend (either way) upon the proximity to a waterway of the town where the paper was published. It depended entirely upon the imagination of the editor. I acquired a considerable respect for many provincial papers: with them consistency was much less subordinate to novelty than in London. Consistency can be a dull and limiting quality, but in our campaign it was essential, and persistence too. They were the counterpart of drama. The two had to be kept in tension.

For me much of the campaign would have been very dull indeed, if I had lost sight of the distant objects. I was soon speaking on waterways to fifty or sixty audiences a year from outside the movement (I still speak on the subject to an annual thirty or forty); and to most of them I had necessarily to say very much the same thing, for upwards of an hour. In private I sometimes paraphrased Churchill: "There is no subject so large about which so many know so little." After all, the waterways system still extends to three thousand miles, reaching into most parts of the country. There are many comic stories of ignorance; partly consequent upon the occlusion of the waterways for well over a century.

Tom Rolt, seeking an accumulator, was told by the proprietor of a shop in the Midlands that ever since the war, deliveries had been undependable owing to difficulties with the lorry drivers.

"Has anyone ever thought of using the canal?"

"What canal?"

"How long have you worked here?"

"I've worked here all my life, and lived here too."

"Then you must know about the canal under the bridge down the road."

"I always thought that was something to do with the drainage."

If a talk or lecture on waterways is to advance the campaign, the speaker must build up from the foundations, explain what is wrong and how it came about, describe the present situation, and outline what should be done. Above all he must explain why it matters; why all seven of the genuinely independent public enquiries have recommended that, in one way or another, the waterways should be revived. Only when these foundations are laid, should the speaker proceed to extol waterway holidays, or to exalt the achievements of those who have restored individual waterways under the Association's inspiration or auspices. For the speaker it can soon become a monotonous recital; and, if he is to succeed, he must borrow antidotes to staleness from the acting trade. None the less, the speaker on waterways who follows the method I have described, has one great advantage over other lecturers on the subject, or indeed, on most other subjects. New-comers to the topic of speaking on waterways tend to try for popularity by talking almost entirely about recreation and the alleged joys of boating and boat-ownership. They believe that thus they meet the existing interests of their audiences, and avoid the risk of being charged with attempting to educate. It is a mistaken assessment. Many are indeed interested in holidays, and some in boats; but all are interested, and far more deeply, in the realisation of dreams, almost any dreams. The advantage that the campaigning lecturer has over a lecturer without a cause is that the campaigner gives form, however vicariously, to the audience's visions. Total immersion is what tells. Colour films of cygnets and sunsets, though they have their place, must be insipid by comparison with David's account of how he tackled Goliath.

Strange things happen to lecturers, as well as repetitive things. It would make a lecture in itself. As in the theatre, no two audiences are the same; and a prime secret of a successful lecture is the ability to make it a mutual undertaking. George Robey's music hall act was a pattern to any lecturer. He would stand, stage centre, and, often after a long silence, utter a few words, sometimes mock-contemptuous. The audience would respond warmly or less warmly. He would then utter a few more words, and observe what happened. When his act was at what may be called (though not in respect of material) its purest, he would continue in this way for twenty minutes; each motion variable as each audience varied. So works the wary and experienced lecturer.

I was invited to address a newly formed boat club, which, moreover, had become a Corporate Member of the Association in a thoroughly proper way. No fee was offered for the talk, and the date suggested was in December. In a general way, winter lectures suit me best. I maintain a close season in April and May, and another in August and September, in order that I may have scope for fleeing the country and re-establishing anonymity. In June and July I am too hot and have hay fever. During the winter, therefore, I often give several lectures a week. I have seen much of dark, slow travelling; heard whirlwinds of public coughing and sneezing; consumed numberless mugs of refreshment room Bovril; waited countless solitary hours for last trains, the trains that arrive either empty, ghostly, and about to be withdrawn, or packed to the doors with bawling Forty-niners, who have strewn the floors with dead beer bottles and disintegrated sporting editions. The newly formed boat club, however, was not far from London. The Honorary Secretary had said that a car would meet me at an underground station on the line to Hounslow West.

I seem to feel the cold less than most English people, and the heat more. I find it impossible to visit a Mediterranean country in full summer, feel distress at a Whitsun cricket match or flower show, but am seldom other than invigorated and renewed by an English winter. I appear to have a psychological response ten or fifteen degrees below average throughout the scale. But that December night was cold even for me. Even before I had gone below at Russell Square, there had been a fog; by street lights one could see the separate black particles of industrial by-product spinning and coagulating with a germy life of their own.

The motor car was a large one. In the front seat were two men in overcoats and hats. There were few words. I was set down in the back seat. We made off at great speed, stamping our feet, grinding our teeth. Car-heaters were not so common in those days. If that car had one, it had ceased to operate.

There was little to be said. Soon we stopped in a residential thoroughfare off the Great West Road; impossible ever to find again, however urgent the need. In my childhood, I had known orchards in that region. Reference to them will be found in any reputable pre-1930 Guide to Middlesex. Silently, both men left me. Through the gathering smuts I saw them open a small gate and go up a paved path to a semi-detached house. One seemed to have a key, and both disappeared within. I began to reflect upon how little I knew of these people with their large, swift car and taciturn habit. Might I not well be a pawn; a cypher to some account of which I might easily never learn the summation? Lecturers, available on demand to all, are obviously exposed to such chances in exceptional measure.

There was a considerable wait. Nothing stirred in the freezing, faceless street. Then the two men returned down the paved path; one walking backwards; both stumbling beneath the weight and angularity of something borne between them. They let fall their burden on the pavement beside the back door of the car. Impossible, even ludicrous: it was something in a sack. By the manner in which they dropped the sack, one deduced that it was exceptionally weighty or that its contents were of little concern to the two men. My door of the car was opened; one of the men spoke: Did I mind? The sack was shoved in beside me. As it settled, a crunching, creaking noise came from inside it which I could not identify. The men were cursing and complaining; I gathered that the bulb had gone in their hall light. It seemed to be a house without comfort, without women. That is not uncommon among men who go to lectures.

We drove on, again very swiftly, especially considering the murk and atmospheric state of the roads. No explanation was offered, and it was impossible to request one: from first to last a lecturer, like a lion-tamer, must leave no doubt who is master. Silence returned. The two men had stopped swearing and sat like stone. Though I had once known the locality rut by rut, things had changed and I was still lost.

We charged down a back-street and fetched up a few feet from the flooding water of the Thames. It was impossible to see across to the far bank. To the right of the street was a tiny structure in discoloured yellow brick, with a gothic window on either side of a projecting porch, itself lined out in decorative cast iron, now unpainted and defective. I supposed the building to have been a school, but it proved to have been set up by a local nobleman for the recreation of his tenants and to have been given to the newly formed cruising club as a headquarters by the nobleman's successor, now that the tenants all had television.

"Let me lend a hand with the sack."

For better or for worse they declined.

Within the little hall were seven or eight people: my audience. The hall was illuminated by two gas lights on long stems from the ridge of the pitch-pine roof.

"Most of us don't turn out until the fire's going," said one of the men from the car. He spoke as if it were a matter that hardly called for explanation. He gave the sack a push. As it toppled, lumps of coal and rough logs crashed over the grimy wood-block floor.

In one corner stood a circular stove of the "Slow But Sure" or "Happy Tortoise" type often to be found in churches, but smaller. We all settled to lighting it.

The best way to set about a task of that kind is with the aid of large newspaper sheets rolled up tightly into long spills, drawn out to their maximum length and doubly knotted. Six of these, with small pieces of coal packed into the interstices, would have resulted in a reasonable blaze within from five to seven minutes, with all the small coal catching promisingly. When one has mastered this skill, one has lighted upon a main function of the popular newspaper. In a well designed open grate, it can be done by the experienced with no more than three sheets. Unfortunately, I was the visiting speaker, like a king in Old Africa, not to be polluted until the final sacrifice, not a serious force in practical events. The members and friends of the newly formed cruising club set about the work with shop firewood, and, when that failed resorted to various oils, naturally much in evidence where there are boats. The small hall soon filled with different kinds of smoke, and as much as half an hour passed before it had to be decided that no more could be done. There was a fire of a kind. From an unpromising and miscellaneous aggregation smoke continued to rise, not all of it finding its way up the long pipe. Every now and then there was a sharp report. There was very little warmth. No one removed any clothing; but people seldom assume their best to attend lectures, in any case. At least that is my experience.

A few more of my audience had arrived, but there was little sign of rush. Everyone knew how long was allotted to the ritual fire dance. When there were perhaps fifteen, it was time for tea; a matter for a primus stove that had to be lighted too, and then waited for in its turn. Before the end of the evening, I did succeed in speaking for twenty or thirty minutes, and several of the audience kindly said that they would have liked to listen for longer.

Groups that have to attend a monthly talk, let alone a weekly one, as in the case of Rotary Clubs, cannot be expected to have high expectations. Even if all the talks were good, those who listened to so many of them would in the end become lecture-drunk. As very few talks *are* good, that condition

is exceedingly common. The demand for unpaid talks is almost unbeliev-
able in its volume until one has had experience of it. I find that people who
neither give regular talks themselves nor belong to regular audiences have
no idea what an industry it is, and are often sceptical when I tell them. So
great is the demand in England for lecturers of some kind, either unpaid or
paid very little, that a once important art is in danger of being lost, those
qualified in it suffocated beneath the sheer number and woolliness of the
aspiring or conscribed multitude.

I soon found that in self-defence it was essential to charge a lecture fee,
except in special circumstances, such as for talks to boating groups or to
sections of the National Trust; and that female audiences are usually better
than male in almost every way. First of all, there is a connection between
these two things; female audiences are far more often willing to pay a fee.
Male audiences are apt to attempt the irritatingly opposite approach; to
claim or imply that they are conferring an advantage upon the speaker by
being willing to hear (and, of course, assess) what he has to say. But far more
is involved than that. Just as deep culture of any kind normally involves a
private income (not always one's own), so, at a lower level, paying attention
to a lecture requires a certain margin and space in life which, even today,
women are more likely to have than men. And where men are typically
competitive and aggressive, women are typically receptive. Nor is that all.
For a male speaker there is something further which is extremely important. That shady but compelling orator, the late Dr. Goebbels, used to like
there to be even in the biggest audience, a particular attractive woman as
special inspiration: his hypnotic speeches (irrespective of deplorable content) gained in power by being partly addressed to this one woman, and took
strength and flight from her especial presence as admiring conspiratorial
auditor. Even when one is addressing a Women's Institute, it works very
much in that way; or it largely fails to work at all. Extempore speaking has
even more in common with wooing than with acting. If public speaking of
any kind is not extempore but from a previously prepared and written
script, all that matters has failed before the speaker even rises. (There are,
however, "filibustering" speeches, speeches designed to waste time,
perhaps to wear out the audience also; and great fun they can sometimes be.
There are more such speeches on the floor of the House of Commons than
most members of the public have any idea of; speeches designed to *prevent*
some business being attended to or – more commonly – even reached.)

And quite different techniques are, of course, required when the need is
to capture support at a controversial public meeting. Continentals often
have more taste than we have for the major (or would-be major) public
oration; the rhetoric that is intended to inspire to immediate action. That, of
course, is the kind of public speaking that really goes to the speaker's head,
at least when the message finds a response.

X

Mixed Strangers

A modern method of conjuring up the Honest God is to walk three times around the church, and the third time to stand still in front of the church door, and cry "Come out", or whistle through the keyhole.

MARGARET MURRAY

Bulletin 11 chronicles a tour of inspection of the Birmingham Canal Navigations by the three stalwarts of the Docks and Inland Waterways Executive: Sir Reginald Hill, Mr. George Cadbury, Mr. Robert Davidson. The trio put on record that the estimated annual capacity of that fascinating network, which ranges from Birmingham to Wolverhampton, and from Walsall to Dudley, thus covering what used to be called the Black Country but is now known as the Industrial Midlands (perhaps because it has gone rather grey) was twelve million tons. This, observed the Bulletin, was little less than the entire waterways system of the country then actually carried. The B.C.N. now carries perhaps twelve hundred tons each year. Sir Reginald Hill remarked that his tour had given him the impression that Birmingham was the "Venice of the Midlands": a shaft of insight that has since become as much of a convention as Aylesbury Duckling.

Then came the River Boards Bill; under which Catchment Boards were to become River Boards, just as River Boards later bloomed into River Authorities. "The most remarkable characteristic from our point of view of this extremely comprehensive and all-embracing measure is that, while under it existing navigation authorities tend to lose their powers to the River Boards it is proposed newly to establish, the Bill makes no provision whatever to sustain (let alone increase) the rights and interests of navigation users. The Bill appears entirely to overlook the fact that waterways can be navigable, for navigation is the one relevant interest unrepresented by a single member upon the Boards it proposes to set up." And when the Bill was introduced into the House of Lords, only a single peer, Earl de la Warr referred to navigation at all. He complained about the lack of representation for navigation interests, but the answer of the Parliamentary Secretary, the Earl of Huntingdon, was "entirely unsatisfactory".

"In the Bill," continued the Bulletin, "the popular disregard of the possibilities of using British waterways for trade and pleasure boating is again strikingly exemplified. In the whole of our national life, no matter of such size receives so little even of consideration." Though only unnationalised waterways were likely to suffer directly from the omissions in the River Boards Bill, their number included what many would suppose to be among the most important rivers in England, such as the Nene, the Great Ouse, and the Wye. A related problem was that three Ministries were (as they still are) concerned with navigable waterways: the Ministries of Agriculture and of Health, as well as the Ministry of Transport. "Two of these," observed the Bulletin, "have, quite naturally, no interest whatever in navigation, a matter outside their proper functions." Those with experience of the public administrative machine will appreciate the problems connected with the promotion of a national campaign involving three separate Ministries. The Association could not believe there was any answer short of maintaining all navigable waterways "to a fixed standard, like roads," and making them available to all at equally fixed charges. The goal could hardly be more obvious, more promising, or simpler to achieve, but to this day it remains in the distance.

Pressure by the Association resulted in an amendment to the River Boards Bill whereby in cases where a River Board was concerned with a navigable waterway, the Minister of Transport was given power to nominate to the Board a person to represent navigation interests. This power has been very seldom used; and, of course, what was really wanted was an *obligation* that a representative of navigation be appointed whenever a River Board had a navigable waterway in its province.

The reader without experience of the subject may well find the existence of so many authorities, and the determination of their different jurisdictions, a matter of confusion; nor will he be the only one. In Britain, canals have usually been built and rivers made navigable each by a separate private corporation, commonly acting under its own private Act of Parliament; though such Acts almost – though not quite – always contain semi-standard provisions, notably requirements that 'the track' be properly maintained, and that the waterways be available for use by all suitably dimensioned craft for which a toll is offered. Catchment Boards, River Boards and River Authorities have been successively responsible basically for land drainage; but where a navigation authority is lacking, or (more commonly) has lapsed or been bought up and destroyed, then they can become responsible for other functions also. As already stated, my Association believed in a single authority which would exercise all the functions arising, and which would be under a specific duty to exercise all of them fully.

The River Thames provides a notable precedent. During the first half of the nineteenth century, the Thames above London was slowly falling into ruin. The increasing difficulties of navigation had a very damaging influence upon the prosperity of the canals that led into it, notably of the obviously valuable Thames & Severn Canal, which entered it much higher upstream than any of the others. By the reasoning that had prevailed during the last century or so, it might well have been argued that the poor old Thames had been finished as a serious navigation by the advance of the railways and the macadamisation of the roads. Fortunately, it was perceived that the main trouble lay elsewhere. It lay in faulty administration. An eighteenth century Act had vested the upper Thames in a Thames Commission; and had provided that every landowner in the Thames valley to the extent of £100 or more, should have the right to be a Commissioner. The device was sound in principle, and much better than what has followed on most of the country's navigations, but it went too far: with the increase in the population at the time of the Industrial Revolution, there came to be more than ten thousand Commissioners. Administration of the Thames was long not merely inefficient but corrupt: the Commissioners who attended meetings were too commonly those with private axes to grind.

Parliament then had the strength to sweep away the whole system. The Thames Commission was replaced by the Thames Conservancy, which operates to this day (replaced, in fact, by the Thames Water Authority in 1974 – Ed.); not ideally (especially, as usual, in the matter of commercial traffic, which calls for active and positive encouragement), but still better than any other waterway authority in the country, when all the factors are considered, and not least the rapidly increasing problems of the Thames Valley. The Thames Conservancy is based upon two fundamental principles, both vital to the well-being of a navigable waterway. The first is that the governing body is composed of representatives of the many different interests concerned; and representatives nominated (in respect of the great majority) by the interests themselves, not appointed from above to speak for them. The second is that the Conservancy is an all-powered body: there is no separate Thames River Authority, and no separate navigation authority. If similar principles were applied to the entire waterways system of the country, the nation would gain incalculably; in sport, pleasure, and beauty ("recreation and amenity"), as well as in revenue; and not least by providing more scope for responsible self-government. It will be seen how I came to devise the idea of a National Waterways Conservancy.

Bulletins 12 and 13 announce the establishment of the Association's first regional Branch. It was a Midlands Branch. (The appointment of an individual Midland organiser was announced as early as in Bulletin 1.) A local Member made an appointment with me to discuss the matter of a

Branch, one afternoon when he was visiting London. Rain had poured
down all day and showed little sign of abating as the hour agreed drew near.
When the bell rang, our Member proved to be accompanied by a small,
elderly gentleman, whom he introduced as his old father. Both, naturally,
were wet. I gave them tea, and conversation continued for more than an
hour, usefully and constructively. When we had settled everything that
seemed necessary, there was a slight pause while we all tried to think of a
polite generality of some kind. It was the elderly gentleman who spoke.

"I wonder how Mother's getting on?"

I was slightly surprised, this being a new development; but supposed that
Mother was in the British Museum round the corner, at the pictures, or
even buying an umbrella.

"Where is she?" I enquired, entering into the spirit.

"Just outside," said the old gentleman, as if it was the obvious thing.

"If you look out of the window, you can see her."

I rose, walked to the window, and looked. A woman stood alone by a
lamp post on the other side of the street.

"We'd better go, Dad," put in our Member.

We confirmed critical details about the shape of things to come and shook
each others' hands. I noticed that though it was still raining, it was not
raining quite so hard.

The Midlands Branch was launched at a well-attended meeting in the
Market Hotel, Birmingham on St. Valentine's Day 1948. The Market Hotel
was in the street on the south side of New Street Station, the street where
Barry Jackson's Birmingham Repertory Theatre stood. At the meeting, the
Member who was Branch Honorary Secretary designate, rose to his feet on
the platform beside me, turned completely and visibly green, and was
unable to say a word. He had indeed to be replaced as Branch Honorary
Secretary; an important and responsible position, upon which the entire
fate of a Branch can turn, but which involves mainly boring work that
requires to be done meticulously. The Midlands Branch Chairmanship was
accepted by Arthur Goodland, already a friend, and for some years a major
force in the campaign, especially at one life-or-death juncture.

Arthur Goodland, who belonged to a family prominent in Taunton,
was at that time General Manager of the Birmingham Corporation Gas
Department, and could arrange for Branch Committee Meetings to take
place in the Department's extremely handsome, dark-panelled, lustre-
illuminated, soft seated Committee Room. He was wont to assert that
diversity of interests had impeded his advancement in the world. There was
no doubt about the diversity, which continues and ramifies to this day, but
Arthur Goodland's career has consisted in nothing but ascent by long
strides. He became Managing Director of a celebrated and vast industrial

enterprise newly established on the Mersey; and after that a potentate in Guyana, where he entertains visiting Cabinet Ministers from poor old Britain, and probably dines nightly off a table service from Eldorado.

At that inaugural meeting in the Market Hotel, I first encountered Cyril Taplin, long a member (the Association had been operating for almost two years by then), soon an institution. He entered in a heavy overcoat, laid down a visiting card at the receipt of credentials, and said in a loud voice: "Cyril Taplin".

Our Branches, ultimately numbering six (with two others that defected and declared themselves independent), proved of mixed utility. I tried to keep an eye upon appointments to the various Branch Officerships and usually succeeded, but not always. The worst problem by far was, as ever, the sheer shortage of strong candidates. The Branches did, however, meet the popular demand for organised sociabilities, and sometimes met it very well. They performed a major service in taking that task off the hands of the campaigners, except for special occasions, such as the Association's Annual Dinner in London, which became a notable campaigning event in itself. In any case, the formation of regional Branches was an obvious and inevitable development, and, though some proved unsatisfactory, others made important achievements. Everything depended on finding the right individuals to run the Branch. Certainly the Branches added greatly to my knowledge of life in general, and of modern Britain in particular. I harangued them, I went to their parties, I stayed with their officers and their families. I never passed a week without writing them long letters. Many Branch Committee Members became friends as the long struggle wore on.

By now we had appointed an Honorary Consulting Engineer. He was the top man in his field, and known to all as such, and it was his great misfortune that the field of waterway civil engineering had in Britain become so small and sparse. He was Mr. Cyril Boucher, with a line of qualifications as long as a lock-keeper's arm, and all bringing increment to the Association's repute. Mr. Boucher was a charming professional gentleman of the old school; the school of which I had had experience in my father's day. Though no longer young, and with a record of achievement behind him, he was willing to go to much trouble on our behalf and through many muddy ordeals, where he must often have found more eagerness than practicality. My relations with Mr. Boucher were always happy and always courteous, and I hope he lives to be at least 150 in his retirement among the blossoming trees of Abberley.

Bulletin 13 announced that Ninian Hislop had retired from the Association's Honorary Treasurership and been replaced by Robert James Mackay Sutherland; he of the elegant and informative waterway photography, still, as I have said the illustrative mainstay of any rightly directed brochure on the subject. James Sutherland was an old friend of mine. It was good of him to take on the Association's financial mathematics, because he was not an accountant, but like Mr. Boucher, a civil engineer, though of a rarefied kind, concerned with fantasy (the roof of the Commonwealth Institute) and the future. Stowe, where he had been schooled, had made a deep architectural impression on him. Chiswick House was another of his special heavens. He once spent a long time, late at night, explaining to me on the spot what he thought was wrong with Sir Giles Gilbert Scott's new Waterloo Bridge. He also is a man with a remarkable head (if I may so express it): without a word to anyone, he once walked in the dark night across the high narrow catwalk that linked the two tall towers of the former Runcorn Suspension Bridge across the Mersey to Widnes. When we (as in an Edward Lear limerick) exclaimed, he reminded us that there was a handrail (even though – as we could just make out next morning – on one side only). Clearly he was the ideal man to look after the accounts of an organisation which was trying to relate the future to the past, stability to adventure.

Bulletin 13, in announcing the 1948 Annual General Meeting, stated that the proceedings would "be followed by a Dinner for Members, of which the cost will not exceed 5/– per head for food."

Bulletin 12, responding to the many enquiries that we were receiving for hire-cruisers on canals and rivers other than the Thames and the Broadlands nexus, was able to mention two firms on the canals, and one on the rivers of the Fen District. One of the two canal firms had been established before the war, and was therefore a unique pioneer; the other was the first to take advantage of the new atmosphere created by the Association: both should thus be named. The pre-war forerunner was the Wain family's Inland Cruising Association of Christleton, near Chester. The earliest entrant into the new waterways age was the Wyatt family's Canal Cruising Company of Stone in Staffordshire. (The Fen District firm was Appleyard, Lincoln of Ely; long established but newly bought into the hire cruiser business, and generally repolished, by Mr. Harry Lincoln.) Today, there are seventy or eighty hire-cruiser firms on the same waterways.

For most the plunge was no ordinary business initiative (in so far as initiative is ever ordinary), but a desperate gamble taken in the face of every official probability that many of the navigations would shortly be closed, and in the knowledge that, at the best, success must depend upon involving large numbers of the public in a new, seemingly eccentric, and often exacting form of recreation. The exacting element lay largely in the poor state of many of the waterways and in the unpredictable activities of those who administered them. The hirers were required to be almost as idealistic and resolute as the firms doing the hiring. Capital for new businesses could not be easy to raise under such conditions. Often it had to be found from within the Association's Membership, thus making a third, big draft on conviction and courage. Through it all, I never stopped saying that every boat offered for hire, every boat hired, every mile navigated (including, if necessary, by planks tied to oil-drums, or by ancient narrow boats more neglected than converted) contributed to keeping the waterways in existence; that waterway holidays, as well as being, despite all the difficulties, the best that England and Wales had to offer, scenically, physically and historically (which is certainly the truth), contributed also, in their degree, to nothing less than the preservation of human values in an increasingly inhuman world.

Much glory is properly owing to the many who took the risk, especially in the movement's first years. Some were pioneers of the kind Shaw describes: not handsome and bronzed Siegfrieds striding godlike to their destinies, but lean, wary, slow-moving, and unkempt professional survivors, resourceful with second-hand tools and salvaged raw materials, unresponsive to the need for a new television set each year, sometimes a little disordered according to the standards of the sceptical, but envious neighbourhood. They did not make up a host that was easy to regulate, but I fared better with them than with some of their later, glossier successors, because the pioneers had to care more for the waterways than for their own financial and worldly advancement. It is which of these comes *first* that matters, for it is not to be denied that the waterways must humanise in some degree even the smartest Alec, just as even the purest idealist must somehow ward off starvation, and does not at all advance the cause if he goes mad or bankrupt.

There is one more of the pioneers whom name I must: in 1950, Mr. Holt Abbott of Stourport introduced to the world the first powered pleasurecraft ever designed specifically to navigate the entire British inland waterways system.

When time permitted, I began to go on trips myself, to enlarge my empire and my knowledge of it. Having sold *Phosphorus*, I had to hire or cadge a boat. Cadging was never easy. At first, there were simply too few boats; hardly any, in fact. One knew that most men who owned boats would, like Esquimaux, lend their wives sooner. On the other hand, I did benefit from many generous offers of reduced hire-charges. These were by no means to be taken for granted, because at the time most of the firms operated on minute margins; with the force of progress, and almost everyone else and everything else, against them.

The first of these trips (other than the prenatal one – also the sole one – in *Cressy*) was as utterly disastrous as the most realistic and practical-minded could expect. Hire-craft in those days were any existing boats that could be bought (shortly after a long war) and that were dimensionally able to traverse the narrow canals. Usually they were unsuitable in the first place and almost always they were worn out. That first boat I hired after the start of the Association caused so much trouble of so many different kinds that I doubt whether her average cruising distance before coming to a stop, exceeded five miles. All the same, we navigated from near London to Fradley in Staffordshire, where the Coventry Canal joins the Trent & Mersey Canal, and then back to the boat's base on the Thames.

Far worse than the troubles with the boat was the fact that throughout the voyage I found myself quarrelling with a girl friend: on the water a disparity of temperament opened up that on land had been detected by neither of us. This is a common experience, at one level of intensity or another: it behoves one to be very careful indeed when assembling a party for a long trip in a small boat. One finds not only that boon companions on land can become bossy bores afloat, or, alternatively, sheer mudweights of negation; but, more surprisingly, that some who had seemed to lack sparkle at a reception, prove sympathetic and charming (not to say indefatigable) friends on a boat. A good working rule when organising a trip with people with whom one has not travelled the water before, is to make private provision for an escape channel at an early stage: for use by incompatibles or, at the worst, by oneself. For a love affair afloat I have become inclined to recommend an ocean liner . . . The chief cause of trouble among hire-craft crews is individual or mass incapacity for fantasy: an insistence upon treating the transaction as if it were a part of ordinary day-to-day living.

In "The Attempted Rescue" I have described several occasions when I was badly frightened, terrified to the core; as distinct from being merely apprehensive and pessimistic, in the usual way. On that first, disruptive canal voyage, I experienced two more such incidents.

The Association had by then begun to offer for sale, at twopence, a four-page, closely printed, ochre-paper leaflet of navigation hints. Originally written by Rolt, it came to be more and more modified by me, as Rolt's primary concern with introducing pleasure craft peacefully into the working boat community became regrettably less and less important; until in its present form (incorporated into a larger publication, the Association's famous "Pink List") it is almost entirely my work – for better or for worse – with Rolt's pen detectable vestigially by scholars. This document enjoined sternly that pleasure craft should moor on the side of the canal opposite to the towpath. At the time it was written, horse-boats still survived on long runs, and pleasure craft were regarded by the boating community with even less favour than usual when towropes had to be passed intricately over them, often in the early hours of the morning, while the holidaymakers hogged it within until sharply awakened by the rope's rattle and crash, and the hoarse bawling of the steerer.

Obediently, we moored against the edge of a field on the very long, extremely remote, and highly improbable 'summit level' of the Oxford Canal. All went as well as the difference in temperament already referred to, permitted, in the matters of cooking, eating, drinking, washing up, and retiring to rest.

At some vague hour in the middle of the night, I awoke to find the small and lightly built craft rocking wildly and irregularly in the darkness. There was also a variety of loud and frightening but unaccountable noises. I was unable even to imagine what could have happened. It did not seem to be a matter of thieves or hooligans: or, if the onslaught was human, closed mouths must have been agreed upon, which was more frightening than ever, especially when there was so much noise of other kinds. I felt that we were totally unprotected and I thought that in a moment the boat would sink into the cold, night water. For moments, it had been the strangeness that had frightened me most; the conviction, completely real, that there was something on canals, even perhaps in life, that I knew nothing about, and was outside normal existence. There is much about canals and rivers to make one feel like that; and I had read Algernon Blackwood's marvellous Danube story, "The Willows". In the end, there was a special and diagnosable crash. The cabin doors had been forced in. I could see through the darkness that the large white object which had presumably done it, floated in the air within, a few feet from the head of my bunk.

I have described the order of these rapid and confused events exactly as I experienced them. They were inexplicable and appalling. At the point I have reached, there broke in what most might consider to be absurdity, but for me was not absurdity at all but worse alarm even than before. I realised that the large white object was the head of a Hereford bull, and, as described in "The Attempted Rescue", I have a special phobia about bulls (which does not make me condone what men do to them). I had confirmed the emptiness of the field before we had moored, as of other earlier fields; but the bull had been let in during the night. Then I realised that we were surrounded by Herefords, plunging about in the marshy ground, falling over our mooring lines; and understood, of course, that they were but steers.

The nightmare eased, but did not end. Steers though they might be, the animals were becoming enraged by our lines and beginning to bellow and heave. My girl friend pointed out that as they more and more lost control, one of them might break a leg and start a host of new trouble and difficulties. Moreover, we still had two steers actually aboard the extremely fragile boat.

It concluded, as things do, in anti-climax. The intruders were driven ashore quite easily. I went ashore myself among the other beasts in the mud and pulled up our mooring spikes. There was no question of starting that particular engine at that hour: we pushed off with the boathook, and somehow manoeuvred the boat across the canal by manual propulsion. I then towed her a short distance up the waterway, and we settled against the towpath in flat breach of our own yellow leaflet.

That was on the outward voyage. Coming back, we moored one night, not very sensibly, in the cutting at the western end of Newbold Tunnel on the same Oxford Canal. I knew that there was a popular and much better mooring at the other end of the tunnel, but night was upon us, we had had a long and difficult day with the engine, there was cooking to be done, and the cutting was at least peaceful.

During the night, I was awakened from deep sleep by an unmistakable noise. It was the noise made by the two halves of that same door into the boat's saloon closing together. It was a distinctive sound, and we had become very familiar with it. At first I supposed that the doors had been first opened and then blown to by the wind (which had become considerable, even in the cutting). Then I recollected that I had myself bolted the doors at top and bottom. It was another unpleasant moment. I climbed out of my bunk and investigated. The saloon doors were still bolted shut, as I had left them. That was an even more unpleasant moment, as I had no doubt about the nature of the sound that had awakened me; nor had my girl friend, who had been awakened by it also.

There was little to do but go back to bed. Soon after we did so, we began to hear, from our two sides of the boat, a new sound. It terrified both of us so completely that my friend would never thereafter speak of it and I can still recall how I myself felt. And yet it was in a way unremarkable. I should describe it as resembling the sound of a mouse stealing about in straw. My girl friend would never accept that comparison, but could not, or, I felt, would not, produce a nearer one. The sound was not continuous. There were stretches of silence, while we lay tense; but then the sound would begin again. There was no doubt that it was inside the boat, but we had no straw aboard nor anything like it, and I was (and am) convinced that there was no mouse either. It was among the experiences that have terrified me most in all my life, though in the end I merely fell asleep and remained asleep until morning: the noise was certainly not enough to keep one awake by its volume, and I had spent an exhausting day. I believe that the noise related to psychic or mediumistic powers in my girl friend. Probably it was morally innocuous, but it was alarmingly akin to the noises of small animals often described in mediaeval occultism.

The girl in question displayed other psychic gifts during the time I knew her. She could obtain remarkable results working solitarily (though not necessarily alone in the room) with planchette. Narrative would flow steadily in a handwriting that was not hers: much of it descriptive of what purported to be one of her past incarnations, exceedingly vivid and often lurid. Once when I myself was operating planchette with her, we obtained a detailed and embarrassing record of certain recent events in the lives of two friends who were present. They were not close friends. I had known nothing whatever of the matters described, and I was convinced that my girl friend had known nothing either. In the end, she became so alarmed by the alleged revelations of her own previous existence that she gave up planchette altogether and on principle.

A girl whom we both knew, once stayed in my friend's flat, and remarked to me afterwards that the place seemed to be overrun by mice. She had been actually kept awake by their scufflings, she said, and could not think why X had done nothing about it.

On another occasion, this same friend told me that when she had been for some reason alone in the flat, she had heard her name called. She had opened the front door, but found no one. I mentioned this to X, though not the story about the mice (I myself had, of course, heard no sounds of mice in the flat). X replied that several people had reported a similar experience when they had been alone in the flat. It was one story about which I was at first less than convinced: the street outside the building was busy and noisy, and, on the other hand, it is not unusual for people to believe that their name has been called. One day, however, it happened to me. I used to borrow the flat regularly in order to write, as the advance of the Association soon made it impossible for me to write seriously in my own abode. One afternoon, alone in X's flat, I very clearly heard someone call my own name: "Robert!" It was some considerable time after I had mentioned the matter to X, and, though this seems hard to believe, the earlier tales had not even entered my mind before I had gone to the front door and opened it. When I found no one there, I recollected, of course. After that, I no longer doubted.

On a certain occasion, X changed into evening dress in my own spare room or guest's bedchamber. (For years it has no longer mattered much which it is called, as it has been almost put out of commission by the day and night tumult released by the "traffic engineers" in the street outside.) X and I were going to the opera. When I had changed my clothes, I found her sitting in front of the dressing table looking-glass making up her face. I gazed over her shoulder at her reflection. What I saw in the looking glass was an old woman with grey hair; though still undoubtedly X. I had by no means only a glimpse. I was able to stare for a quite appreciable period of time: time enough even to decide to say nothing. Then, indeed, the image dissolved back into X as she then was. I never spoke of what I had seen, but, one day, X spoke of it herself. She told me that one evening when she had been making up in my house, she had thought that in the looking glass she had seen herself as an old woman. It had seemed to last for quite some time, she said; but she had not liked to tell me.

There are a number of reputed phantoms on the waterways of England. Kit Crewbucket is the very epitome of the folk-lore troll, imprecise in aspect but shrivelling to encounter; descended perhaps, as are the fairies, from the Old Believers, who survived among the Christians for so many more centuries than used to be supposed (quite abundantly, as the centenarian

Professor Margaret Murray suggests, until King Charles II's reign; probably in odd corners, until now). There is the Sad Woman of Crick Tunnel. There are the long dead boatmen whose firm steps are heard (sometimes aboard) by those who moor at the far end of the Griff Arm. Everywhere there is the Man Monkey, who rises, like a jack-in-the-box, above the parapets of bridges, poised to spring; and whose likeness, disposition, and aims may be left to speak for themselves. Many of the Association's earlier Members themselves resemble ghosts. Probably some of them were ghosts. It has been often pointed out that no one can tell how many of the multitude in the streets are ghosts. Most frequent among ghosts that are ultimately known to be ghosts are those not initially identified as anything out of the ordinary.

A husband and wife I know were engaged upon a long, slow canal voyage in their own small boat, a main purpose being topographical photography. On a summer evening they moored at a certain spot on the more deserted northern section of James Brindley's Staffordshire & Worcestershire Canal. The husband departed to the village in order to photograph the church and such other structures as might seem suitable. The wife remained on the boat, preparing the evening meal. While she was in the galley, she looked up and, through the porthole, saw a boy standing at a distance on the towpath and staring at the boat. It is not, of course, an unusual occurrence on waterways, and all that happened on that occasion, was that when the boy saw he was being looked at, he ambled off. He might have been ten or twelve years old. All the same, when the husband returned, the wife mentioned the boy. He had looked rather ragged and grimy, she said: outside the pattern required by the Welfare State.

The next morning, the boat went on, but not very far; only four or five miles, I believe. That evening, events repeated themselves. The husband went off in search of the picturesque. The wife started work in the galley. She saw the boy again.

This time there was a difference. The first she saw of him on this second occasion was his yellow, bony face pressed suddenly and without warning against the galley porthole. She says that his hair was especially unpleasant; totally unkempt and matted as in a fight. She also says he had "staring eyes". But perhaps that was to be predicted, and subjective.

She was very alarmed indeed, and made some kind of threatening movement. Perhaps as she was cooking at the time, she even picked up a knife. The boy took several steps back, quite slowly; and then made a gesture, which naturally my informant can imitate better than I can describe. He slowly turned his body sideways to the boat; raised his arm and pointed at the galley with great fixity; and then, turning his head sideways, "sighted" (as my friend puts it) down his outstretched arm, as if down the barrel of a rifle. The boy sustained this attitude for a period of time; his expression being of rigid and horrifying ferocity. Then he dropped his arm, and, as on the evening before, merely ambled away. When the husband returned, he found his wife nearly in a state of collapse.

She re-assembled herself, and the two of them departed, as so often on the canals, to the nearest pub. There they told their tale. All psychic investigators well know how unusual it is to encounter any kind of surprise in the local and immediate vicinity. The response in the pub was one of basic familiarity with the phenomenon. "We know about him," they said. "He's a wild boy."

"What's a wild boy then?"

"He sleeps in haystacks and hedgerows. He lives on roots and birds' eggs and things he can steal. No one can say where he came from. But most of us know about him. He's a wild boy."

Once, of course, there were wild boys in Europe, even in England. A famous one, captured in a forest, was presented to King George II, and having lived to a considerable age, lies buried beside the Grand Union Canal at Northchurch, beneath one of the most striking brasses in the country, bearing both his likeness and his biography. My friends knew these things, but had not expected to encounter a wild boy in the middle of our desperate century and in the British West Midlands. However, they had by then seen enough of canals to know that canals can be very odd; and they left it at that, more or less, and at least for the time being. Moreover, they did not see the boy again.

None the less, they continued to tell their tale, as they advanced by short, daily stages; in other pubs, and in diverse small assemblies. Almost always at least one person present knew all about the wild boy. But, in the end, there was a difference in the response. At one place, a man said: "I know about the wild boy. I heard about him from my father." And then, of course, my friends realised.

This pleasant vagueness about time is still common to the waterways. When I first navigated the Leeds & Liverpool Canal, we began, when still far off, to be told a tale of a cow that had lately swum right through Foulridge Tunnel (nearly a mile long), and, after consuming an entire bottle of brandy, had departed none the worse for the passage. As we neared the tunnel, we heard the story more and more frequently. There seemed every reason to take for granted that it was recent history, and none of our party supposed otherwise. Before ourselves entering the tunnel, we stopped at the portal, whence some of us visited a small nearby inn. They returned to tell us that in a frame on the wall was a yellow newspaper cutting about the cow's exploit. It had happened before the First World War.

XI

Parliament

I have known at least half a dozen Prime Ministers and Presidents who were, in the strict medical sense, insane. I've seen one Prime Minister, whom I knew intimately, who could appear normal when presiding over a conference. But when he was alone and had no such stimulus, a vacant look would come into his eyes, he would say something quite nonsensical, and it was clear to me that he had temporarily lost his mind. It would come back with fresh stimuli, but decreasingly so.

LORD SALTER

Bulletin 13 refers to the first Member of Parliament to interest himself in our cause. Several members of the House of Lords had already done so, especially Lord Methuen, as already related.

Our first M.P. was Mr. Joseph Alfred Sparks, long the Labour Member for Acton. His response came from experience: when working for the Great Western Railway, he had seen for himself what had happened to the Kennet & Avon. Mr. Sparks was one of the most charming and painstaking Members of Parliament I ever dealt with. To every communication he replied promptly in his own beautifully legible handwriting. There was about him none of the patronising attitude that advocates of causes sometimes encounter at Westminster. Mr. Sparks did not make one feel that he was conferring a favour by taking up the waterways cause (or, more commonly, by trying to resist some gross and appalling waterway abuse). On the contrary, he never failed to convey his appreciation of the service rendered to the community by the few who were willing to interest themselves in public matters without immediate personal goals.

During my time, it became possible for a Privy Councillor to state in the House that the Association had the strongest lobby in Parliament. Reflecting upon the strength of certain others, I wondered a little whether the Privy Councillor was not exaggerating, but it was a remarkable compliment, and all the more sincere and convincing because it was not intended as one, but rather as a mild complaint. We came to have a prominent ex-Cabinet Minister as a Vice-President. I even made personal friends among Members of Parliament, and from among supporters of both the major party interests (I cannot recall ever even speaking to a Liberal M.P.). I came very much to like visiting the great Palace of Westminster gingerbread-show or Bartholomew Fair for its own sake. Many Members of Parliament were exceedingly kind to me there, and sometimes remarkably expansive, so that I learned much about prominent people and national affairs, little of which can be written. I can well understand how so many Members of Parliament become so attached to the old place. If Parliament were to move, as has been suggested, from its present, ever gorgeous, ever-fascinating palace to somewhere more modern; to (say) the Shell structure on the other side of the river, quite probably the most efficient in London and quite certainly the most hideous, or to the top of the Post Office Tower, then Parliament would lose a last reason for its continued existence: that so much of beauty attends so much of squalor and boredom. At different times, I have been approached by representatives of (this time) all three parties with apparently serious suggestions that I should consider standing for election myself. I cannot pretend not to have been very pleased and flattered, especially by the occumenical element in the total invitation; but the more I saw of Parliament, the surer I became that its special fantasy was best enjoyed from without. For, on the one hand, I have seen several men enter as idealists and remarkably soon become realists: a civil war would have served their souls better, or a lonely attic with a rusty hand-press; and on the other hand, I could not but become aware that the power of the ordinary M.P., and probably of any M.P., however right honorable, over the fate of the waterways (a small matter or a big one, according to one's aims in life) was a richly costumed nil. Power, I was not the first to perceive, did not lie with Parliament; or probably, even with the Government. Ministers sometimes tell one how much power they have and what a thrill it can be; but there is seldom evidence of it.

In the context of the waterways campaign, Members of Parliament divided into two groups. The majority were, within limits, sincere idealists in the matter (in occasional cases, even visionaries); but, however hard they worked for the cause, they were *never* willing to fight hard *enough* when a critical moment came. They always pleaded that it was not the accepted thing to press the matter further or harder; and that only harm would follow if the convention were ignored. Sometimes this was possibly true, but often the case was that nothing could be worse (within the context), than letting the abuse pass without using Parliamentary machinery against it to the full. There is endless talk in Parliament of the rules, but one can subsist there for years entirely on the conventions; which stand almost exclusively for mutual face-saving in the old Chinese manner, though fractionally also for work-saving. All Members of Parliament are worked to death with the

1. Pencil drawing of Robert Aickman by Peter Scott, dated 1949.

2. 'The Waterways Room' in Robert Aickman's Gower Street house.

3. Robert Aickman's first canal voyage took him to Banbury with the Rolts. This scene at Banbury was typical of the period.

4/5. The first Lifford Lane exploit. The top photograph shows the maintenance boat *Bilster* firmly stuck beneath a bridge whilst Robert Aickman and Tom Rolt look on from the foredeck of *Cressy*. Below: Crowds wait in anticipation as the boats approach the specially raised lift bridge.

6. Opposite: Map reading with 'Roses & Castles'.

7. "We found that a thick rope had been attached to our prow" – Canal Busting on the Huddersfield Canal in 1948.

8. The *Ailsa Craig* stranded disconsolately in Ashton under Lyne after holing itself on a submerged obstruction.

9. Conference at Ashton: Elizabeth Jane Howard, Robert Aickman, Anthea and James Sutherland pose for a press photograph within the narrow confines of *Ailsa Craig's* cabin.

10. 'Ascending into the mountains' – *Ailsa Craig* negotiates a lock on the Huddersfield Narrow Canal.

11. *Ailsa Craig* prepares to enter the western, (Diggle) portal of Standedge Tunnel. Tom Rolt (in cap) stands to the left of Elizabeth Jane Howard whilst Angela Rolt sits to the right of Robert Aickman. 'Wilf' appears to be checking the prop!

12. Smoke from a passing train emits eerily from the eastern (Marsden) portal of Standedge Tunnel.

13. Angela Rolt admires a boatwoman's bonnet with Anthony Heal of the Mansard Gallery during one of the Inland Waterway's Association's travelling exhibitions of the late Forties.

14. On a visit to the Ravenglass & Eskdale Railway Robert Aickman is caught in contemplative mood in the company of his wife and Tom Rolt.

15. The maiden voyage of *Beatrice*, seen here preparing to leave the old Spencer, Abbott & Co boatyard at Salford Junction on the outskirts of Birmingham.

16. During *Beatrice's* Northern voyage of 1950, Peter Scott (at the tiller), Jonathan Balcon and the author are pictured on the river Weaver in Cheshire.

17. Opposite: *Beatrice* passes through Shelton Bar steelworks on the Trent & Mersey Canal near Stoke-on-Trent.

18. A windswept voyage for *Beatrice* up the Shropshire Union Canal.

19. Elizabeth Jane Howard and Robert Aickman wait for Wheaton Aston lock to empty on the Shropshire Union Canal.

20. Opposite: On 20th May, 1950 members of the IWA toured the Regent's Canal from Limehouse to Paddington.

21. Mr & Mrs Aickman at Limehouse with early IWA stalwarts Lewis Edwards and Michael Streat.

22. Chestnuts bloom by Regent's Park as the IWA party pass in a pair of narrowboats hired from Samuel Barlow.

23. Immaculately turned out Samuel Barlow boats at Market Harborough, 19.8.50.

24. The Severn Wildfowl Trust's hostel boat, *Beatrice*, at the Market Harborough Rally.

25. Visitors admire working boats and conversions at Market Harborough basin.

26. Crowds line the Market Harborough arm to see boats passing during the IWA's first rally of boats in August, 1950.

wrong things; with the preposterous and ever-luxuriating "constituency surgery", with the details of legislation without limit, with the degrading preoccupation of holding on to the seat. (And Plato said that only those are qualified for power who do not seek it!)

As a cause advances in public notice and esteem, those linked with it become aware that their contingent of interested legislators includes a noticeably growing proportion from my second group: those who advance the cause because they deem that the cause will advance them. It is very easy for a Member of Parliament to drift into an inconspicuous backwater (by no means necessarily for unworthy reasons), and so to be in the market for taking up and rescue by a prosperous looking vessel passing on the high seas. From this derives the very noticeable phenomenon that the Members of Parliament professing interest in a particular public cause frequently change. The passing vessel may have proved to be less well found than well decorated; or another vessel looms up that is large enough and confident enough to cut across the first vessel's bows. The promoter of a campaign will find M.P.'s quietly disappearing, no longer offering tea or a drink, whom once he had barely needed even to bid welcome to his sheepfold. But bitterness springs from Members who claim to be supporting a cause and an ideal when they are really seeking personal publicity. I have known a Member of Parliament take elaborate steps (unannounced previously to the Association's administration) to persuade all present at a large dinner each to write to at least three Members of Parliament praying resistance to a British Transport Commission Bill; and then when the Bill came up for debate, himself take the lead in recommending to the House that it be passed. It is difficult to explain such things to one's own Membership; but in these ways, a Member of Parliament can prove himself, on his own ground, sound, reasonable, and suitable for advancement of one kind or another.

There are more different kinds of advancement than might be supposed: not merely the Cabinet, with its nowadays almost numberless junior appendages, but a whole wide world of public patronage, stretching from the nationalised industries to a complex of independent enquiries, of which no one person knows the limits; from simple unpaid gobstoppers to seats in the House of Lords, a body which will soon be as sick as the House of Commons, as the hereditary element is steadily replaced by the log-rolling element.

Here I must mention the Association's questionnaire of Members of Parliament. Several hundreds replied that they supported the Association's policy. Only a handful replied that they opposed it. By the rules of the game, the significance of this result from the Association's point of view lay, of course, in the quite exceptionally large number who replied at all: Members of Parliament cannot be expected to make themselves gratuitously unpopular by returning superfluous negatives, and can always plead, with the utmost justice, that they cannot be expected to reply to every mass enquiry in every morning's post. I am not aware that the remarkably satisfactory result of the questionnaire had any admitted effect on the fate of the waterways, but it made excellent material for quotation to the public and in the press, and thus probably had a significance that was not officially admitted. In public affairs, important changes are seldom admitted, and never personally acknowledged, or set to the credit of those really responsible. When a big change is *proclaimed*, it will usually be found to be a change in apparel and presentation only. I do not imply that this is always bad. It should never be forgotten that most change is for the worse. The illusion of change often palliates human restlessness and unease more effectively than the reality.

In a long short story named "My Poor Friend", I wrote about Parliament; a little fancifully but as I had experienced it. I wrote also about that wider, deeper power structure which in the end, and when I felt it would be a waste of my remaining days to contend with it any more, engulfed the Association, as it has engulfed so much else. The narrator of "My Poor Friend" is a slightly seedy character (he cannot even hold on to his University-educated wife) who takes an ill-paid job as promoter of a voluntary organisation (someone else's) concerned with the generation of rural electricity. I quote a few paragraphs from this person's preliminary explanation of how he came to be involved in diverse dubious developments.

"Parliament then.

"Everybody nowadays thinks it is a bad joke that the Member of Parliament can almost never decide how he will vote, but is compelled, none the less, to spend most of his Parliamentary life attending 'debates' based fundamentally on the premise that he can so decide and is, therefore, accessible to argument. A smaller, better informed, number thinks it a bad joke that the 'debates' are, in the event, for the most part hardly attended at all, though almost all M.P.s in default of special personal arrangements, have to hang about while they are going on, in order to pass through the Division Lobbies whenever required, which is often unexpectedly: day after day, week after week, month after month. A still smaller number thinks it a bad joke that we have abandoned the hope, and to some extent the practice, of government by those who are born and trained to power, in favour of government by those who have to struggle, fight, defame, blarney, manipulate, bribe, and conspire to get power, and then to go on struggling, fighting, defaming, blarneying, manipulating, bribing, and conspiring in order to keep it: men and women of one particular kind, in fact, or at least with one particular, not obviously desirable, thing in common. Government, one may say, all Government, must at the best be exceedingly imperfect (so that the less there is of it quantitatively, the better); but the earlier ideal would·still seem to hold more promise than the latter.

"Generalisations such as these are common talk. What upset mc was how it works in practice.

"Government has been carried on less and less visibly for a long time; but the critical thing in Britain has been the swift development of official public relations. Every public authority that knows its business now has what may be termed a paddock for its critics and opponents, not excluding those inside Parliament. Quite rapidly it has become almost impossible to be a rebel. Today the rebels are put in a paddock and then built into the structure. They are patiently listened to, when they have made themselves assertive enough. They are pressed to deliver their ideas in writing. They are invited to serve on Joint Committees. It is implied to them that if they keep their criticisms "constructive", they may even become O.B.E.'s. "Look at our splendid collection of rebels. It proves how strong, important, and on the right lines we are." The Speaker's Corner technique, one may call it: intensely British, brilliantly adaptable, utterly null. Faced with it, Bessemer emerged, quite unawares, as a mere nineteenth-century evangelist; not only incapable of planting his petards deep enough, but incapable of even seeing that he was paddocked, that his ostensibly critical notions were being applied, Judo-wise, to the actual strengthening of his opponents. It is sadly true that only the power to inflict actual damage of some kind holds any hope of surmounting the official techniques.

"Members of Parliament, already persons willing to put up with the conditions I have referred to – fighters, above all, pushers, wheedlers, conspirers – appear today in the hour of their supposed success, merely as front-figures for an impersonal power-machine. The inner conflict, added to the odious daily life, added to the 'constituency surgery', whereat the supposed legislator of peace or war is reduced to the procurer of a supplementary pension and/or surgical apparatus for every elector; all this is too much for any man or woman, any mere human. Degeneration is inevitable, even if it has not largely taken place before adoption as a candidate.

The professional politician's characteristic rejoinder is to multiply his salary and demand that sessions last all day, instead of beginning in the afternoon, so that the shop would be closed in favour of his special – not obviously desirable – type."

The poor fellow does acknowledge that he speaks "with some bitterness"; and it is only fair to add that he concludes the account of his mixed experiences by citing Winston Churchill's remark that "Democracy seems impossible, until you examine the other systems." It may depend, however, upon how far democracy is taken.

My own matured view is that democracy works much better when it is not total. I believe that the vote should be not a right but an acquisition: that, to qualify, the applicant should be able *both* to pass a (simple) general knowledge test *and* to prove that he possesses a certain (very small) amount of personal property; thus showing that he has at least a minimum both of intelligence and of character (as my Great-Aunt used to call it). Under the name of "weighted democracy", a proposal of this general kind was at one time advocated by Winston Churchill himself. I believe that, on balance, the advantages would be very great, and not least to the humblest, whom the contemporary technological meritocracy increasingly penalises. The fact that it is almost impossible to see how the change could now be made, is in itself a criticism of democratic totalitarianism, or majority tyranny. Overt takeover by a political junta is far more likely than reform in the direction of higher quality.

The country in which democracy works best is Switzerland. If one visits Switzerland with an open mind, one can return with a mild, positive belief in democracy, instead of having to fall back upon Churchill's claim that other visible systems are even worse. It is significant, however, that the Swiss, though often envied, are seldom loved: they are thought to lack both passion and great art. Those things do not cohere with native talent for democracy. "Democracy," as H.L. Mencken put it, "with the arts in abeyance . . ." (He was not speaking of Switzerland.) None the less, even as an artist, I admire the success and stability of Swiss democracy. Of course only about half the citizens have the vote: not necessarily the right half. A qualification of *some* kind is required, even though in Switzerland it is not necessarily the best one: the qualification of being a male. More important, I believe, is the reliance placed by the Swiss upon the referendum.

The referendum seems to me by far the most valuable of all democratic devices. I should have thought that to repudiate the referendum principle is to repudiate all that is valuable in the democratic principle, and to hold on to all that is disastrous. I am quite certain Britain would be an incomparably better country if our major legislative proposals were constitutionally required to be submitted to referendum. It is undeniable that it would be a more democratic country. Observing Parliament, I became very much impressed by the volume of legislation that I was certain would never have been approved by popular vote (whether I myself liked the particular measure or not). Naturally, my eyes were first opened by the discovery that while every second fishmonger was eager to press upon me his conviction, surprisingly earnest, that what had happened to the canals was "a shame", yet Government after Government, Minister after Minister, adhered somnambulistically to the same negations, even to the same negative forms of words. At first, I thought that the canals were an odd and special case, having had undoubtedly an odd and special history. In the end I realised that they were representative. Parliament made me more of a democrat than I supposed. The British alternative to government by referendum is government by experts in the use of power.

Most of the Association's Members being British, we never lacked for advocates of the thesis that the way to settle things was by continual fraternisation with the officials on the other side; by "meeting them over a jar of ale", as the recommendation commonly ran. For any campaigning organisation that takes itself seriously, this is the best of all recipes for defeat: it is applying for admission to the official paddock and recommending that the gate be locked behind the entering flock. If the campaign director means business, he will for a long time keep to a minimum all contacts with the opposing officials; he will concentrate all available forces upon building up his own constructive and autonomous alternative to all that the officials have to offer; and, when actually compelled to take note of the other side, he will, I regret to have to add, lose no chance of presenting them in an unfavourable light. A campaign such as ours is more like a war than like a congress: in a war, one knows, unless one is mad, that in most respects one's enemies are indistinguishable from one's own side, but, while the war lasts, it is necessary to treat them as enemies on positively all occasions, if one is to have hope of winning.

It is a hard truth that in a public campaign results accrue mainly from power to do harm. Miss Marghanita Laski once cited the case of the Derby telephone service. A local referendum established that a great majority of Derby telephone subscribers wished not to be involved with Subscriber Trunk Dialling. Needless to say, Subscriber Trunk Dialling was then enforced upon them, as if nothing had happened. What, asked Miss Laski, did this imply for democracy? Only that power to harm was or had become the sole power. The waterways campaign made such big advances not through the wisdom of its philosophy, which few understood or cared about; not through economic arguments, which at all times are so relative and partial as to be quite uninspiring above the firm ground of personal gain; and certainly not through beery or even abstinent concourse with officials.

Our successes derived from continuous, systematic, civilised criticism of the British Waterways organisation in its basic mediocrity and unchangeable lack of imagination; and from the fact that we always offered an alternative that was positive, universal, and simple, and proposed to run that alternative ourselves. When these two policies were largely given up, the Association itself fell into mediocrity. Few really understood the nature of, and reasons for, the strategy which was bringing us results that were envied by most other voluntary organisations with campaigns on their hands.

From first to last, it was for me a race against time with the appeasers among our own Members. From first to last, they were my real foes and the real problem: certainly not the somewhat pathetic, though stubborn, British Waterways organisation; which, indeed, could commonly be depended upon to do the useful, wrong thing, to sustain foolish correspondences in the press, to prohibit the use of some particularly popular navigation, to make wild gaffes in its own house journal.

The race against time, the general problem of timing, was made more desperatre by the familiar circumstance that an increasing number of our appeasers had their own strong business and career reasons to which our opponents had no difficulty in making an appeal. It was what the pioneers had achieved that made the appeasement attitude possible. At the start it would have been merely ludicrous: the epitome of all that had brought the waterways to their century-old plight. Those who created the band-waggon, and started it rolling, were, by normal historical process, pushed off by the business men and career men, as soon as it had rolled far enough.

I became soon aware that such measure of success as I might achieve for the campaign would be the measure of the denigration and obliteration that for me would attend it. It is failure to face, accept, and disregard this fact of life that makes most campaigns of our type so unsuccessful. Victory involves sacrifice in a very deep and wide sense. Those not prepared for sacrifice should not aspire above an organisation that is merely social (and useful enough for lonely people, as I have said). I do not mean by this that I myself made love to sacrifice and went out specifically to meet it. On the contrary, I was at all times full of conflict, having many other interests in life than waterways, and being several different people. In the end, when the most seemed to have been achieved that could be achieved, I took many steps backward and outward to what I hoped might be a wider world.

XII

A Tough Trip

Happiness comes from energy; energy from happiness.

CLIFFORD BAX

In the late summer of 1948, Tom Rolt, James Sutherland, Jane Howard, and I, with others, undertook a six weeks voyage through the waterways of the north; some of the number able to participate only in shifts. We used a hired craft, which, for all the engineering talent aboard, caused us continuous trouble, in what was then the usual way; and we were the last private party to pass through the Huddersfield Narrow Canal.

It was a remarkable voyage, the like of which no one will see again.

The Huddersfield Narrow Canal crossed the Pennines, ascending by many locks to the highest waterway summit level in Great Britain, where it passed through Great Britain's longest canal tunnel. The canal had been abandoned, with many others, by the L.M.S. Railway Company in their mass abandonment Act of 1944. In the case of the famous Welsh Section of the Shropshire Union (which runs from near Nantwich to Llangollen) and of the Huddersfield Narrow Canal, the company had categorically retained the right to admit pleasure craft at its discretion. Only commercial craft were to be excluded absolutely. On the Welsh Section, widely regarded as the most beautiful navigation in England and Wales, pleasure traffic had never entirely ceased; but when it came to the Huddersfield Narrow, with its various navigational fatigues and less fashionable region of the land, my letter of application for a pleasure-craft transit was the first to be received. None the less, consent was forthcoming at once. We were told by the Docks and Inland Waterways Executive, that the canal was in poor condition, but that a gang would await us at the entrance lock, in order to help us with the passage.

We navigated up the Macclesfield Canal, down the Peak Forest Canal, and, rightwards along the Ashton Canal, through Ashton-under-Lyne, the half mile to the start of the Huddersfield Narrow. None of these waterways

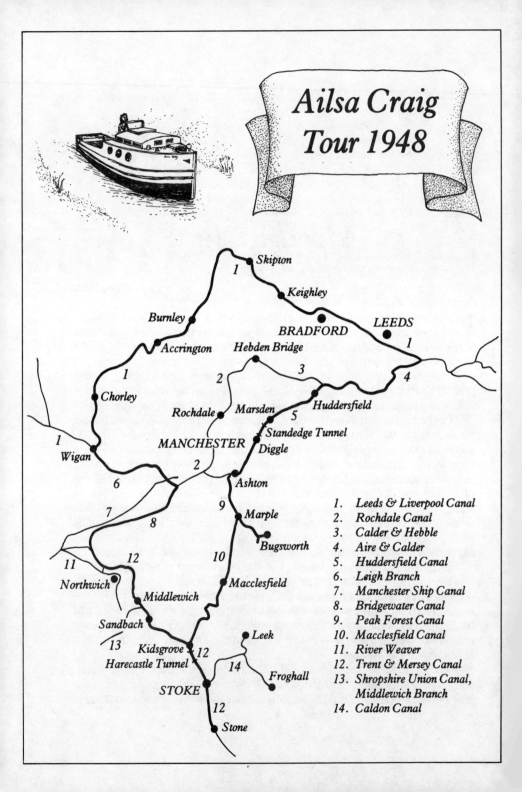

Ailsa Craig Tour 1948

Skipton

Keighley

Burnley

Accrington

Hebden Bridge

BRADFORD

LEEDS

1

Chorley

1

2

3

4

Rochdale

Marsden

Huddersfield

Wigan

MANCHESTER

Standedge Tunnel

Diggle

1

5

6

2

Ashton

7

9

Marple

8

Bugsworth

Northwich

12

11

10

Macclesfield

Middlewich

Sandbach

13

Kidsgrove

Leek

Harecastle Tunnel

12

14

STOKE

Froghall

12

Stone

1. Leeds & Liverpool Canal
2. Rochdale Canal
3. Calder & Hebble
4. Aire & Calder
5. Huddersfield Canal
6. Leigh Branch
7. Manchester Ship Canal
8. Bridgewater Canal
9. Peak Forest Canal
10. Macclesfield Canal
11. River Weaver
12. Trent & Mersey Canal
13. Shropshire Union Canal,
    Middlewich Branch
14. Caldon Canal

were at that date exactly alive with traffic (though the Macclesfield and the Peak Forest are two more that are among the most beautiful in the world); and all the time we had trouble with our engine.

"Nice boat that," said a small boy on the towpath as James Sutherland struggled with the ever-static engine at the eastern end of Marple Aqueduct.

"Up to a point," replied James. "Up to a point."

Moreover, the weather was of the kind to be expected in the region of Manchester. The short stretch of the Ashton Canal proved to be especially alarming. All the other canals we had navigated on the trip had been in desperate need of dredging ("Was the Huddersfield Narrow also the Huddersfield Shallow?" anxiously enquired James Sutherland). The Ashton Canal proved to be very deep (for a British canal); to be peculiarly black; and to be strewn beneath the surface with bulky cast-outs from cotton mills: all, of course, totally invisible and indetectable in the opaque water. We were already very much behind schedule when we entered the canal, and the much deeper water caused us at first to put on a spurt, especially as it was a Saturday morning. After we had struck our first submerged boiler, and been lucky to find ourselves still afloat, we were compelled to navigate as through a minefield. At the same time, rain began to fall; much more thoroughly than on previous days.

Throwing things, or pushing and heaving them, into canals and rivers is a British tradition. It is related to the primitive and exclusive character of our refuse disposal service, as sadism is to masochism, or medal to mould. (Watch the titan garbage squads of Germany: costumed, gloved, proud, vocalising accurately, and bearing all away.) There is a tradition among the working boat community that when a floating or waterlogged corpse is encountered, or perhaps sucked up, it should be disregarded. The life of the narrow boats allows no margin for attending police stations, adjourned inquests, and local press conferences. A boatman well known on the Oxford Canal told me that he had only last week seen a complete pair of boots floating soles upward; and this just after the Second World War when boots were rationed. He had reached for them but had found feet still inside them. He went without the boots rather than risk disruption of his schedule.

All things considered, it was surprising that we were only an hour or so behind our promised time of arrival. None the less, we were too late. Not only was there no sign of the promised "gang", but the entrance gates to the bottom lock of the Huddersfield Narrow had been padlocked. It seemed impossible to moor on that part of the Ashton Canal, which was entirely industrial. We felt compelled to go back on our tracks to some more rural spot on the Peak Forest. As we turned the boat to face the Ashton minefield and the Peak Forest shallows a second time, a minor miracle occurred. A small red door giving straight on to the waterway from the middle of a long brick wall along the water's edge on the side opposite to the towpath, opened, and an elderly figure beckoned to us through the rain.

"You can stop here if you want."

It was the back entry to John Knott's cotton mill, and this was the night, or weekend, watchman. He could not have been kinder or more helpful to us, and on the Sunday morning arranged for us to be shown over the mill, a fascinating and instructive experience which has enabled me to pass among Londoners as an authority on the cotton industry ever since, and to deplore its decline with quite special sincerity. On the Sunday afternoon we all went to Manchester by train for a boat-sized Lancashire meal and a look at the architecture of the railway stations. The rain never stopped.

On the Monday morning, after exchange of tokens with our rescuer, the watchman (I still have the ovoid spool of cotton he gave me), we set forth once more, with caution, for the Huddersfield Narrow. The bottom gates stood open, and, in the heavy rain, we found the promised gang, twelve or fifteen of them, seated within a large tarpaulin structure by the lock side, and frying up. They looked like a landing party from a pirate schooner. We all seemed very willowy by comparison, as well as much wetter. They did not greet our arrival with enthusiasm from any point of view. To start with, they emphasised that they had been there since first thing on Saturday morning, whereas it was now Monday. To continue, they remarked that we would never get up *there*.

This is the usual form of words from the staff of navigations, and, indeed, from waterside dwellers at large, often pronouncing from the bottoms of their gardens as of their hearts. The voyager to slightly remote places hears them so often that they begin to shade in his picture of general human nature: here is tabu. Those strong enough or wild enough to overrule tabu, will seldom find any outstanding difficulty in proceeding whither they planned to proceed; though here the Huddersfield Narrow Canal presented a certain exception: it had become a case for what is known as "canal busting". Moreover, at the junction, that wet and overcast afternoon, there were other factors. Proceeding down the canal to Stratford, which, ten years before the great restoration, was even more a case for canal busting, Arthur Goodland, in his boat *Quest*, was addressed by a professional lock-keeper: "If there are any more ------ boats down here, I shall pack the ------ job in." The lock-keeper had not seen a boat for the past ten years or so, and on the Huddersfield Narrow it had probably been even longer. Earlier on our own voyage, when trying to reach the Peak Forest Canal Terminus in the other direction at Bugsworth (later refined into Buxworth), we ourselves had been admonished by officialdom, "You'll never get down there. I'm the Inspector and I know." We noticed that every morning the maintenance boat with its complement of brewers-up, made a maintenance trip along the rather arbitrary length of waterway that remained easily navigable (from Marple to New Mills), and never attempted to proceed further. These attitudes, however much a part of human nature, are a product also of defeatism and inertia at higher levels. It is at least equally common to encounter waterway staffs who deplore and execrate the weak policy in which they are entangled. None the less, at Ashton we were upsetting routine in a fundamental way; jeopardising security. Herein lies one of the many absurdities (if that word is chosen) of abandonment: most aspects of maintenance have to continue; all that ceases are use, beauty, and revenue. If maintenance did not have to continue, if the canal could just be wished away by Private Bill, abandonment would (oddly enough) be far less popular, because it would imply immediate unemployment.

Negotiations with the gang were further impeded by language difficulties; but, in the end, they emerged from their tent en masse and took thorough charge of us. The boat passed through the first lock (bottom of thirty-two) without anything worse than bashing; but before we knew where we were, we found that a thick rope had been attached to our prow, and that most of the gang were hauling on it, indicating to us from the banks that the "pounds were low". (A pound is any stretch of water, however long or short, between locks. A common cause for a pound failing to keep a proper depth of water is leaking lock gates. But often, through faulty maintenance, there are more serious troubles in the general water supply system from the summit or other reservoirs; a system that basically is simple in the extreme, though highly ingenious in invention.) We passed through a second and a third lock without particular incident, but in the pound that followed, became grimly aware that the boat was grinding and jolting seriously along the bottom of the waterway. Shouts towards the heaving shapes on the sopping and slithery towpath were of no avail.

As the boat rose in the fourth lock, James Sutherland's wife, Anthea (who did much unpaid work for the Association in its early days, and most valuable it was), happened to go below. She found that the cabin floor was deep in water. We had been holed while being dragged through the previous lumpy pound.

On the instant, we had to unload everything in the boat (and it was for some of us a seven weeks voyage, involving books of verse and Chinese dressing gowns) on to the muddy lock-side in pouring rain and in industrial Ashton. Moreover, our arrival was beginning to attract attention: long before we had removed the last weighty or fragile item, there were faces at every cotton mill window within sight, and comment was free, though not always fully intelligible by Southerners. The gang managed somehow to extricate the sinking boat from the lock, and to beach it in the next pound, which they proceeded to empty. (There are always arrangements by which a single pound, or often a shorter stretch, can be drained for repairs or the like; the water being diverted. The flow on a canal is normally very limited; though not non-existent, as many suppose.) As the water slowly fell, the bottom of the canal was revealed; strewn from side to side, from end to end, with decaying, disintegrating rubbish, some of it huge, some of it best described as unimaginable. We were rather occupied trying to resume possession of our gear and to save it as far as possible from ruination by rainfall. Therefore, some time passed before we realised that we were alone. Without a word, the gang had departed. We looked at our watches (those that were waterproof): it was not quite half past one. One learns on canals (as on our Lifford Lane exploit) how much time-discount must be allowed to the personnel for travelling; but no doubt on this occasion the gang had decided we were past their aid. Even the cotton-mill workers had lost interest in us. With so much rain descending, it was a forlorn spot.

The next thing we noticed was that our boat was slowly heeling over in the mud. On the far side of the canal, now almost empty of water, though far from empty otherwise, was a vague and unloved open area stacked or littered with disused aircraft parts that looked unlikely to rise again. James Sutherland and I spent a long time (two or three hours) dragging some of these parts through the rain, mud, and refuse, to constitute both a shore against the side of the boat and a causeway to the bank. Before we had been there another day, there were even planks lashed to the aluminium struts.

It was fortunate that James was a civil engineer, but it is amazing what can be found on the bank and in fields when need arises on a canal voyage. James himself had a habit of climbing over a gate and within only a few minutes coming back with the very object required, even though adaptation and hacking away might be necessary.

A young Member of the Association told me, that with another young man, he had just completed a long tour of the waterways system with the aim of making a film. Knowing little of the subject at the outset, they had consulted maps and reference books, and had decided to start the trip at Preston, descend the River Ribble, and enter the general waterways system at one of its most northerly points by way of the Ribble tributary, the River Douglas. This itinerary presents startling hazards, especially for new-comers; but the two of them coped with the swirling Ribble, and succeeded, a little surprisingly, in entering the Douglas. Here, however, they found the tide falling fast, and the waterway emptying out very completely. One trickle of water continued, none the less, to flow through the wide expanse of newly exposed mud, and it even looked navigable. The trouble was that in the meantime the young men's boat had fetched up and stuck just out of the current on a mudbank.

Our Member told me that his friend had climbed around the stranded hull in gumboots.

"What we need is a shovel."

"No doubt," replied our Member. "But we haven't got one."

Our Member said that his friend had then struggled across the muddy waste, ascended one of the river banks, and disappeared among the scrub. The lower part of the River Douglas flows through a remarkably bleak area: black earth, scratchy bush, and (especially) bog; flat, uncultivated, and uninhabited (thus without possibility of seeking succour). It is not a place recommended to navigational beginners, though Peter Scott's Wildfowl Trust sends parties there for rocket-netting. Still, our Member's friend soon reappeared, and our Member detected that he was indeed bearing a shovel.

Our Member thought it best to say nothing, especially as he had no gumboots. After a little excavation with the shovel, the boat was duly afloat once more, and even on her way southward, toward Tarleton and Burscough.

"I say."

"What?"

"How did you get that shovel?"

"I prayed for it."

The friend belonged to what was then called the Oxford Group.

Late that first afternoon at Ashton, and in time to catch the post, I dictated a letter to Sir Reginald Hill. Fortunately, the ship's typewriter had remained viable; and even the ship's typist (Anthea Sutherland).

We were fascinated by the life of Ashton and enchanted by the kindness of the inhabitants. We received several offers of meals, beds, baths, and facilities for drying ourselves and our possessions; but hesitated to leave the ship. Quite late in the evening, we saw a man standing silently by our boat in the rain. Asked if there was anything he wanted, he replied that he was keeping an eye on us. "They're rough round here," he said, pronouncing the adjective in the Lancashire way. Naturally, we thanked him but said it was not to be thought of. By then we believed we were, in any case, well informed about waterway perils and able to meet most of them. The man would accept no refusal. All he did was withdraw to a certain distance; where we saw him still standing as night fell, still in the rain.

It rained all the time we were in Ashton, and we became aware that the local population simply took no notice of it. On that first evening, I noticed a girl on the towpath, obviously awaiting a boy friend. She wore a light coat, and under it a cotton dress; and she had to wait for thirty or forty minutes. As time passed, we suggested to her that she might like to come aboard and wait in the dry. She politely declined: she seemed so used to the rain that she did not even think to explain that she was used to it. In the end, her friend appeared: he was wearing a jacket, but under it an open-necked shirt. We assumed that they would hasten away; if only to beneath a bridge. Not at all: they walked slowly up and down the towpath amid the downpour in steady, and apparently light-hearted conversation, for at least half an hour, and only when it was finally dark did they slowly walk away, bidding us goodnight. It was then that we saw the solitary figure of our self-appointed watchman.

We saw no sign of anyone being "rough". On the contrary, it is always most noticeable on the waterways (as doubtless elsewhere) that hooliganism grows steadily worse as one proceeds southwards. In a northern city, one can often leave one's boat open and unattended and find it unmolested after two hours' shopping. In the Midlands are severed limbs; and mattresses afloat in the cut that have been thrown from cabins. On the Regent's Canal in London, stones are often hurled at passing boats and even shots fired. John James's famous *Jason* at least once had a trip out to Greenford which resembled that of the *Amethyst* down the Yangtze. Very closely linked with these topographical variations is the attitude of the towpath passer-by to the pleasure-craft, hopefully with pretty girls aboard. In the South come jeers and politically-tinged abuse. In the North, as I have experienced often, come cordial and sincere enquiries: "Having a good time?" "What's for supper?" The northern eye is more commonly hopeful of emulation than envious. But there is one question that the navigator is asked everywhere, by old, young, and very young: "Where are you going?" Often it cannot be answered without a map and a lecture. The navigator should be prepared with two replies. To the more censorious inflections, he should sharply name a town only a short distance ahead on his route and within the experience of all local enquirers. To the more poetical inflections, he should dreamily name the place most distant on his itinerary.

It was not to be expected that we should hear from Sir Reginald Hill the next day, especially as we carried no radio. Rain continued to fall but we had diversions: the most important was that at an early hour, when we were still in pyjamas (woolly ones), we received representations from one of the cotton mills that the emptying of our pound had deprived the mill of essential water supply, so that "hundreds of men were standing idle". We could only suggest immediate complaint to Sir Reginald Hill. The management of the mill behaved very reasonably, all things considered, and acted upon our suggestion. This pressure from industry probably helped to expedite the sensational events that matured on the morrow.

During the day we gave a long interview to the Ashton local papers: local, as distinct from national, journalists are encouraged to report fully and even accurately, and the next issue included column after column of small print about us and about the general situation on the waterways; together with large photographs in which we looked as if we were nearing one of the poles, and also photographs of our plank and aluminium causeway. Naturally, we gave many other less official interviews as the day wore on. We were offered the free loan of a radio, but refused with thanks. We were offered free seats in the front row of the dress circle for that evening's performance at the Ashton music hall (since destroyed, of course, by the said radio). We accepted gratefully and found ourselves matter for reference by at least two of the comedians. It was before the day that flying saucers first landed: I think it sufficed to mention that we were Londoners. The manager shook our hands and said we were already the best known people in Ashton.

And early the next morning, Wilf entered our lives, accompanied by two lusty shipwrights from the Mersey. Mr. Wilfred Donkersley ("call me Wilf", were among his first words) is still concerned with maintenance of the Huddersfield Narrow, dead waterway though it now is. I fear that I cannot remember the exact position he then occupied, if indeed we ever exactly knew. It was certainly a position of authority; including natural authority. Wilf transformed the situation, and remained our indispensable indefatigable guide until we had reached the other end of the waterway. The shipwrights also addressed themselves to the rent in our hull with will and skill. It must be set much to the credit of Sir Reginald Hill that he could and would produce such magic helpers for the instant relief of an expedition of which at bottom he could hardly approve. Always credit where due, as I used to say. (An item under that heading, chronicling and praising constructive achievements by the nationalised authority, appeared regularly – or whenever possible – in the Bulletin.) It never stopped raining, but in the evening, Wilf informed us that by noon the next day, all going well, we should be able to depart. Things went as promised, and there is a final wonderful photograph of the boat casting off, the white hull splashed all over with mud, Wilf at the end of a line (mercifully slack), and Anthea Sutherland at the helm, her face even muddier than the boat. If it were not that the details are much obscured by the rainfall, it might be said that we looked as though we had passed through an ordeal. In reality, I think we should all agree that we had passed through one of the most rewarding experiences in our lives, and certainly one of the most memorable. Of course the singularly happy conclusion contributes to this sanguine assessment. If it had ended in bafflement, we should feel differently. If we were all still there, we might or might not be the happier.

It should not be thought for a moment that our troubles were at an end. Far from it. The Huddersfield Narrow Canal is one furlong less than twenty miles in length, but it took us more than five days to pass through it, even after we had finally cast off from Ashton. This should not be taken as proof that canal transport is slow as a glacier. It is true that the particular twenty miles include no fewer than seventy-four locks, as the waterway crosses the Pennine Chain, and is something of a freak; but 'narrow' locks, as are these, are surprisingly swift to work (and much less laborious than might be supposed), *provided* that they are kept in proper order, which is rare. On the Huddersfield Narrow they could not be expected to be in good order, and they were not. Far more delaying were the hazards of the almost unused pounds; through which only the "maintenance boat" had passed for many years, and that only rarely. If it had not been for Wilf, we might well have taken a fortnight.

Once we had left Ashton and begun to ascend into the mountains, the weather cleared from time to time (it was, after all, still August), and a chilly sun gleamed intermittently. We were much impressed by the fact that as we crawled and juddered through the industrialised purlieus of Ashton, business men began to appear at the waterside and to stand gazing at us thoughtfully. I do not refer to operatives in the various factories, though we greeted many of them too; or even to foremen or floor managers. There were a surprising number of obvious 'executives', in city suits; with whom we felt wrongly dressed to initiate conversation. We suspected that they might be keeping a personal watch to see that we didn't drain their pounds also. We were quite wrong. We received several actual expressions of commiseration that the state of the waterway had involved us in so much trouble; and these led to a quite startling number of close enquiries into the legal position of the navigation (a topic about which no one in England knows anything – largely because care is taken not to tell), and into the chances of trade upon it being resumed, to the advantage of the enquirers' enterprises. When ultimately we delivered a report upon our voyage to Sir Reginald Hill, we pointed out that these enquirers were so numerous and so serious that an official investigation into the support for re-opening the waterway would seem well worth while. But there is as yet no case in British history of a waterway once successfully abandoned, being, so to speak, re-enfolded. Occasionally, pleasure boats may be admitted, strictly upon sufferance, and with no assurance for the future. Legal obligations once shed, have never in the waterways field been resumed. It may be that only when this happens, will the battle be really won.

The Huddersfield Narrow Canal passes for much of its steep ascent and steep descent through northern mountain country, much of which is very fine, though none of it at all equal to the best on the Leeds and Liverpool Canal, or on the third of the navigations across the Pennines, the Rochdale Canal, which was abandoned shortly after the time I am now writing about. By far the most notable event on the Huddersfield Narrow is the passage through the 3 miles and 135 yards of Standedge Tunnel, between Diggle and Marsden; on the canal's summit level of 644 feet.

For our transit we were joined by the Rolts. While awaiting them, I was told by a porter at Diggle station an anecdote upon which (as there now seems no harm in acknowledging) I based my story, "The Trains", which has appeared in many anthologies, and in several languages. As well as the canal tunnel, there is at Standedge a railway tunnel, to which further reference will be made. Out beyond the other end of this tunnel, said the porter, as the line descended towards Huddersfield, stood a house; from an upper window of which engine drivers were aware that someone regularly waved to them. Supposing this person to be a girl, regularly they waved back. It became a well-known feature of the line, indulged and played up to by all the drivers. Time passed, and time passed. In the end, it somehow came to light that the person waving, never distinctly sighted but manifestly female, was not a girl at all, but a very old woman, and (the porter claimed) slightly demented. He told the story jokingly, as if it were the latest thing. Perhaps it was; but perhaps it was as traditional as the Foulridge cow.

The special drama of Standedge Tunnel lies in the fact that long stretches of very small bore lead into large natural caverns in the limestone, comparable in type with the famous limestone caverns of the Peak District. Through these caverns passes the boat and enters the seemingly tiny passages ahead. Much of the man-made bore is unlined through the rock. Also there are at intervals large passages, or "adits", both tall and wide, sloping upwards from the canal tunnel into the railway tunnel at a higher level and to the side. Through the railway tunnel runs the main line of the former Lancashire and Yorkshire Railway. In those days it was still entirely steam operated; so that every time a train tore through the railway tunnel, which, as I say, was frequently, there were not merely the eerie thunder and scream in the canal tunnel, but also dense clouds of smoke and steam blowing completely black. Smoke blew out steadily from both ends of the canal tunnel, as from fumaroles. We stopped the boat at the foot of one of the adits, walked up the slope, and watched several trains roar by.

Our own special drama of Standedge Tunnel lay in the facts that, as in the case of our Lifford Lane voyage, we were preceded through it by a narrow boat, manned by a group of Wilf's henchmen, and that, once more according to precedent, the narrow boat stuck in the very small bore about half way through, so that we had a considerable wait in the noisy, smoky darkness before it was successfully eased and we could proceed. During the latter part of the transit, Wilf regaled us with a sequence of songs. Anthea Sutherland has said to me many times since that she can still hear Wilf singing in Standedge Tunnel. We all emerged so black that there was nothing for us to do but entrain third-class from Marsden to Huddersfield, implying that we had been mining for some unusual mineral; and at Huddersfield manoeuvre and insinuate baths out of the splendidly architectural George Hotel, by showing them press cuttings about ourselves and saying that we should all want large dinners too. Never in my whole life have I made a bath so black as that evening at the George; or on any other occasion really needed three baths, one after the other. It was like early D.H. Lawrence.

At Marsden, the next morning, we went over the splendid canal workshop; little changed at that date since its construction and equipment in the late eighteenth century. On the descent to Huddersfield, even more heavily locked than the rise from Ashton, I fell into the waterway: the only time I have done so in my life. More accurately, I was dragged in; and for the fairly sensational reason that as I was holding the boat on a line while a lock filled, a lower gate of the lock burst, producing such a swirl of water that I was pulled off my feet on the instant. Nor was the canal as shallow at the immediate head of a lock as at most other places. When the three-quarters filled lock had precipitately emptied through the hole in the gate, Wilf and his gang had the hole patched in less than an hour, and we were on our way. In few circumstances is it necessary to fall into a river or canal. I frequently hear tales of people doing so, especially on holiday; often of the same person doing so on several occasions. That gives the clue: falling in is temperamental, as are falling off, and falling out.

At the end of the canal we clubbed together to present Wilf with a watch. I hope it still goes. He transformed our voyage from a slightly anxious obligation to a great adventure. We saw a splendid play, named "Artificial Silk", by a local author, at the Huddersfield Theatre Royal, now no more. The play dealt, of course, with the supersession of cotton by rayon. We followed with another dinner at the architectural George (though it is not quite so distinguished as Huddersfield railway station, which is among the finest in England).

We continued the voyage by way of the Huddersfield Broad Canal, and the Calder & Hebble. I did not then know about Robin Hood's grave ("Bury me where this arrow falls"); hard to find in a thicket on the hills above Cooper Bridge, where these two waterways meet. The Calder & Hebble joins the Aire & Calder at Castleford, and we ascended the latter waterway to Leeds. ("What makes the Castleford girls so fair? They swim in the Calder and dry in the Aire.") From Leeds we recrossed the Pennines by the Leeds & Liverpool, and entered upon the saga of the cow. Industrial traffic was then heavy all the way on from Cooper Bridge, with frequent waits at locks for laden craft to go through first. On the Calder & Hebble and on the Leeds & Liverpool, Angela Rolt was able to take several photographs of vessels still propelled by steam, with masters and crews that would have pleased W.W. Jacobs. At Skipton, Jane Howard and Angela Rolt had a disagreement about fish: unbroken harmony is rare on a long voyage. At Wigan we encountered the hufflers: figures of assorted shapes and sizes that spring from the earth to help the navigator down the long, hard flight of Wigan locks for a consideration – and who manage to convey that the consideration includes an element of protection money. At Wigan Pier, we turned left and crossed the moon-like landscape, with 'flashes' (canal-side lakes, usually a consequence of leakage, seepage, and even breakage, but often useful and even beautiful) seemingly as big as Esthwaite Water or Elterwater; to the Bridgewater Canal, where I made my first direct acquaintanceship with Worsley, the place where the British inland waterways system began, and with its ducal monuments.

One of the best known waterway fairy stories is that of the Duke's stable clock. When building the first Bridgewater Canal, the Duke of Bridgewater would come upon the navigators (*builders* of navigations, this time, rather than holiday-makers on them; commonly known as navvies) lying about in the fields at an early afternoon hour when he considered that they should have been working. He realised that the trouble lay with the striking of his stable clock: like so many clocks, it struck a single misleading note at half past twelve, one o'clock, and half past one; a positive invitation to the navigators to claim that they had made a mistake in the time. The Duke had the clock altered so that at one o'clock it struck thirteen. It was, people say, an excellent example of the pioneering and innovatory spirit in which thousands of watery miles were so quickly and lastingly built. Later, the clock was moved to the tower of Worsley parish church, where it strikes thirteen still; if you are close enough to hear it above the noise of the new motorway.

The voyage ended with my first unforgettable transit of the Potteries, where traffic was then particularly heavy. China clay used to be conveyed from Cornwall by coastal shipping to the Mersey, and thence by narrow boat. The emptied narrow boats were reloaded with the completed pots; which went back to the Mersey for distribution and export: an ideal two-way traffic. The original Josiah Wedgwood had been a notable pioneer of canals. He is famous for his description of the great locks at Runcorn: "The work of Titans, rather than the production of our Pigmy race of beings." Iniquitously, the locks are now destroyed: the inadequacy of the campaign to prevent that occurrence being one of the final reasons for my recession from the waterways world. It was a final proof of values lost.

XIII

The Blue and Yellow

When the Emperor Charles was to make his entry into the town of Dousi, the citizens resolved to do him all the honour imaginable. Thus they made the streets into five bowers, hung out banners, set flags a-streaming, built triumphant arches, and essayed all the magnificence in the world. But in the midst of all this they remembered that at the chief gate of the town, there was a hanged man swinging on a gibbet; and so, to honour the Emperor, they took of his dirty shirt and gave him a clean one..

BEROAL DE VERVILLE

Bulletin 16 records that the working boatman was to receive an extra cheese ration; "a small but not valueless concession to the demand made by us and others that his diet be increased." The boatman who navigated on tidal waters received "seaman's rations", whereas the inland boatman had difficulty in collecting rations at all. "What do we live on?" a boatwoman exclaimed to me at Hawkesbury, where the Oxford Canal joins the Coventry Canal ("Sutton Stop" to the cognoscenti, after the one-time keeper of a general shop). "What do we live on? Kippers and cut water."

At about this time came two campaigns which placed the Association at the centre of the map; and brought in a volume of correspondence from all over the world that only unusual dedication could reply to. All of it was answered fully, with no exceptions and no reliance upon mere formulae.

The first was the campaign for the Basingstoke Canal; about which, as about so many other waterway matters, the full story can as yet by no means be told.

Experience teaches that the Basingstoke Canal may well be the most popular in Britain. Wherever in the land one gives a general lecture on waterways, one can almost depend upon receiving a question about the Basingstoke Canal from the audience. The reason for this is to me obscure; but I imagine it to be linked with the facts that the waterway passes through the military installations of the Aldershot area, where so many have served their time, and earlier through miles of populous Surrey Suburb. In 1949, there was no canal in Britain that seemed to compare with it for appeal.

In the eighteenth century it was hoped that the Basingstoke Canal, constructed under an Act of 1778, and linking Basingstoke with the River Wey (navigable at least since 1653, and often claimed as the site of the first 'pound lock' in England) near Byfleet, would be extended to Southampton Water, so that Southampton would be linked with the Thames, of which the Wey is a tributary. The hope never matured, and the canal which had probably cost more than the income expectations from the length only to Basingstoke justified, floundered financially from the first. In 1869, the company was wound up; and a sequence of events began which in their oddity and obscurity entirely typify the history of a British navigation.

At the winding up, the waterway was acquired by a Mr. St. Aubyn, and then passed through various hands, including those of the late Horatio Bottomley's London and South Western Canal Company, until in 1910 the Surrey County Council served notice on the then owners calling upon them to comply with various maintenance obligations laid down in the 1778 Act, and, upon receiving no satisfaction, took them to Court. The owners produced an ingenious reply. They contended that a statutory company could not be wound up according to the ordinary commercial procedure that had been followed in 1869; so that the original obligation of maintenance could not be enforced against subsequent (including present) owners of the assets, because it was in theory still the responsibility of the dead statutory company. These arguments were accepted by the Court, and the repairs immediately in question, which were to bridges traversing the waterway, were carried out by the County Council itself.

In the end, the waterway was acquired by a Mr. Harmsworth: not one of the newspaper family, but as was understood, a former boatman; under whom reasonable maintenance continued, and the annual tonnage carried was raised from 9,500 in 1921 to 25,000 in 1935.

Mr. Harmsworth operated both a fleet of barges on the canal and a barge-building yard at Ash. The latter establishment was very picturesque; substantial vessels were built in the simplest and most traditional ways, and then simply slid into the adjoining navigation. I have since seen similar boatyards sited with apparent casualness beside waterways in Portugal, and not only operating, but, to all appearances, prospering. It was the death of Mr. Harmsworth that directly involved the Association in what was plainly a tangled history. An announcement was published that the Basingstoke Canal was to be offered for sale by auction.

The history had been *so* tangled that the Association's Council, already involved in an ever-expanding campaign for waterways that seemed more important, and in numberless ancillary struggles, ranging from cheese to tolls, decided by formal Minute to take no action in the matter of the Basingstoke Canal, but merely to watch developments. The decision was entirely vain; within a week so many hundreds of letters had come in, calling for action and occasionally even enclosing fourpence or sixpence (never, I think, more than a pound at that stage) towards the cost of it, that it became obvious that the Association's entire prestige and position turned upon our making a positive response. "What are you going to do about it?" was the usual form of words. Even so, we proceeded with caution: the most compelling reason for which was that the auction was to take place within a matter of weeks, and there was talk of the purchase price being likely to exceed ten thousand pounds, which sum, with our resources, we could see no prospect of raising within the time available. As a start I agreed to address a public meeting in Woking, which had been arranged by our Member Mr. L. A. Edwards, who soon became prominent in the waterways movement, and succeeded Tom Rolt as the Association's Honorary Secretary. He was described by the "Daily Mirror" (in a two-page spread) as having courted his fiancée on the Basingstoke Canal towpath. He had also spent eleven years and more than three pounds purchase price in finding and securing a single copy of the 1778 Basingstoke Canal Act.

The interest in the Basingstoke Canal is most reasonable and the case for it a strong one. There are not many canals of any kind in the Greater London region, and the Basingstoke Canal, though much of it runs through a populous area, is astoundingly remote and rural in atmosphere and immediate environment. Much of it runs through Surrey woodlands that even now are surprisingly unspoiled. It is not always my favourite type of scenery, but on the Basingstoke Canal it is at its best; more like Hansel and Gretel than like the Ideal Home Exhibition. The canal, if efficiently managed to that end, could provide winter moorings for many Thames pleasure craft; much more cheaply than on the Thames and without the Thames flood risk. In addition, there was a small new industrial potential. It is a favourite official argument against canals that the industrial areas they serve have gone into a decline. By or near the Basingstoke Canal were, on the contrary, a number of new enterprises. One, not all that new, was under an actual legal obligation to carry on the canal if boats were made available. But mainly I am sure, it was the trees that called; the trees, and memories of temporary release or truancy from the regions of Aldershot.

The Woking meeting was one of the less enjoyable that have come my way. It took place on 11th December 1948 in the very large Aspro Hall, containing hundreds of seats, and I am sure, very beautiful and exciting under the right conditions. We attracted only fifty or sixty people, and the evening was very cold. Dotted about among the widely scattered audience were three or four solicitors representing different (and sometimes conflicting) interests in the Basingstoke Canal entanglement. They carefully wrote down everything I said as I spoke in December of how lovely the waterway was in summer; skirted round the legal position; became excited about the income possibilities; and asked for large contributions in cash. The atmosphere did not make for oratorial abandon and the audience remained sluggish. There was a certain amount of tepid opposition, mainly from representatives of local authorities, who, reading from vast folios, assured the meeting that they spoke in a personal capacity only. Their main argument was that the canal bred mosquitoes. It was, of course, an argument well chosen for a popular audience. It was also quite untrue. On almost every canal, and certainly on the Basingstoke Canal, there is enough movement of water to make mosquito-breeding impossible. When mosquitoes are found (which on British canals is not as commonly or as inconveniently as might be supposed), they have bred in static pools and puddles on the land. (Gnats and midges breed in vegetation.) As Bulletin 18 observed, "Anyone even walking along the towpath of the exquisitely beautiful Basingstoke Canal, lined for much of its length with woodland and common, and reflecting that its continued existence may be jeopardised by those representing the local residents, may wonder at such lack of imagination. Grants towards the preservation of something so beautiful might rather be expected from those in whose area it lies."

With difficulty I dragged a Basingstoke Canal Committee into being by virtually making every person who rose to his or her feet with a question or comment, a member of it, and then reinforcing this group of strangers with a handful of dependable Association Members who had been more or less directed to be present. It was a twofold technique with which by then I had become fairly familiar. One could rely upon the stalwarts soon to inspire most of the casuals.

At the Aspro Hall, one of these picked Association dependables was Christopher Barnes Grundy, who played an increasingly prominent and indispensable part in the entire national waterways campaign from an even earlier time and for ever afterwards. Then in the Regular Army and for many years subsequently (he later won the Military Cross at Korea), he was at that time conveniently stationed at Aldershot. He used to tear about on a fiery motor-bicycle, and his contribution to the Basingstoke Canal campaign was highly spectacular. Both his father and his mother (the latter had pioneered in the women's army during the First World War) were as interested in waterways as he was; and also his brother, Martin, a solicitor in Liverpool, on the outskirts of which city the family resided in a house occupied in earlier times by the Earl of Derby's Agent. Ultimately, when a Major, 'Crick' Grundy retired from the Army to succeed David Hutchings as Manager of the recovered Stratford Canal. Martin Grundy has held numerous positions within the Association all down the ages. Than the Grundy's there is no family which has given more to the waterways.

Also on the Basingstoke Canal Committee was Cyril Styring. This gentleman was a Sheffield solicitor who, among other things, had built almost the whole of his (very large) residence with his own hands, including the plumbing and wiring, and who cruised the waterways in a Thornycroft steam-operated launch, named *Festina Lente*. He offered two thousand pounds to the Basingstoke Canal purchase. Later, he became first Chairman of the Association's North-East Midlands Branch and held that position until his death. He gave the Association a silver working boat of somewhat fanciful design which, as the Cyril Styring Trophy, is presented each year to the Member, not being a Council Member, who is deemed to have contributed most to the cause. Though the exclusion of Council Members (for a variety of obvious reasons) has reduced the scope of the award as a record of the developing campaign, yet a remarkable list of winners is by now engraved upon the mount.

At the end of the Aspro Hall meeting, I could not believe that the Basingstoke Canal was likely to be saved. Cyril Styring's fine offer having not yet been made, we had in hand, or promised, less than a thousand pounds, including several hundreds offered by a Member in Argentina, who I had never met. The auction was two and a half months ahead. It seemed improbable that nine thousand pounds more could be raised in time to save the Basingstoke Canal; though such was the unique spell of that waterway that even "The Times" made a half-column report of the Woking meeting the principle feature of its Home News, ending with the words: "As the meeting closed, one felt that the Inland Waterways Association had scored a notable triumph."

Interest steadily grew. Teddy Edwards and I spent more and more of our time talking to the press about the Basingstoke Canal. We outlined perfectly sound projects whereby the Canal could be more fully and more variously developed and made more remunerative, and one might have thought that the Basingstoke was the only canal in the country, instead of being by no means at the head of the national list for renovation and imaginative management. To the long-standing and deeply ingrained concern for this particular canal above all others, were, I think, added three new factors. One was the first full entering into public consciousness of the Association's general programme and campaign. The campaign had to be rendered down to the size of a particular well-known waterway in order that its unfamiliar ingredients be digestible. A second factor was that element of boom and bubble which commonly attends for a time a supposedly new phenomenon. At first, everything is presented as pristine and lucid, though those who expect such presentation to continue for long, will find much disillusionment, because it is a commonplace of the press that people normally prefer to hear about trouble than about joy, to read criticism rather than praise. The third factor, and, in the context of the waterways, by far the most important, was that the Basingstoke Canal attracted interest because there seemed a possibility that we could own it, take possession of it, and operate it in our own way. People can hardly be expected to feel much enthusiasm about waterways that have been nationalised: and this applies, for different reasons, whether the people are informed about waterways or not.

With the interest, or even fervour, inevitably came rumours. The general drift of local authority opinion was still in the direction of filling the canal in; or rather, most idiotic of all (though a great favourite in many circles, not all local governmental), of filling in sections, leaving other detached sections for 'local boating' and towpath meandering. On the Basingstoke Canal, this idea recurs to this day. It is a useless idea, on the Basingstoke Canal or anywhere else; for pleasure as for business, the outstanding value of any waterway lies in its being a part of the national system; and any length that has been deliberately cut off, has a forlornness that is exceedingly depressing (though money has still to be spent on maintaining it). On the other side, tales of imaginative investors filled the air. Business men, it was said, had at last realised the potentialities, and were competing with one another to make the Basingstoke Canal the most modern in the country. It was time, people remarked, for a little initiative, now that the war had been over for years. Prominently figuring in the stories of paradise to come was no less a person than Jack Buchanan, glamorous, magnetic, already well known to be as dynamic in the boardroom as on the boards. I was told that "if the price was right", Jack Buchanan had detailed plans for boating stations, a waterside country club, and popular excursions in a new type of craft on the long summit level.

There were also mysteries. Of these the most important was what had happened to the navigation's top six miles. The last edition of Bradshaw's "Canals and Navigable Rivers of England and Wales", the standard and basic reference book, states that "The canal is at present (1928) only open for traffic to Brookwood, but will shortly be opened throughout to Basingstoke". By our time, the situation was that the canal was navigable (more or less) far beyond Brookwood, but that the long tunnel at Greywell, about twenty-four miles further on, had suffered an internal fall of masonry, and that the six miles of canal from its western portal into Basingstoke itself, had been so encroached upon as to have largely disappeared. It was plainly probable that the rot had started when the fall in the tunnel had been left unrepaired. The auction particulars indicated that the property offered for sale extended only from the Wey to Greywell. We never discovered by what legal process, if any, the navigation into Basingstoke had been ended. Moreover, it was of much import in the matter of water supply. The Basingstoke Canal, as built, had drawn much of its water from the River Loddon, which passes through Basingstoke. Without the supply from the Loddon, the canal has had to rely on springs and small lakes (or natural reservoirs), which have never entirely sufficed, though there would be a great improvement if the canal were maintained in first class navigational order. I do not know to this day what happened to those top six miles. It seems remarkable that such information is not readily available, especially in an area so near to London; but it is typical of the British canals situation. There are always public interests eager to smuggle them out of existence and private interests standing by to benefit.

All ended first in drama and wild hope; soon afterwards in tears.

At the Aspro Hall meeting, the most promising of the few strangers who had risen to their feet had seemed to me to be a well-built lady who had announced herself as Mrs. Marshall. Her comments, unlike some, had been precise rather than merely aspiring; and she seemed to have a vivid vision of the canal's possibilities. I should have had no hesitation in pressing her to join the new committee, but, in fact, she seemed eager to do so. After the meeting, I neither saw nor heard from this promising Committee Member until, on the evening before the auction, my telephone rang at about seven o'clock. It was Mrs. Marshall asking whether she could see me immediately. I think it was about nine o'clock when she arrived.

She spoke first and at length about the many advantageous things that could be done to the canal, and again I was impressed by her grasp of the circumstances and by her imagination. After she had delivered an almost complete verbal prospectus, I remarked that while it was a splendid programme, upon which she was to be warmly congratulated, yet the trouble appeared to be that whereas the property was deemed likely to fetch upwards of ten thousand pounds, we had in hand only upwards of three thousand. It seemed that waterway history was being made when Mrs. Marshall replied, "I think I can find the balance."

Soon afterwards she departed, but not before telling me that the Basingstoke Canal Committee had set up a Purchase Committee, which had nominated her to do the actual bidding on the morrow. She provided no further information about where "the balance" was to come from. I supposed that she had been referring, at least in the main, to her own resources.

The auction took place at Aldershot on 1st March 1949. So great was the throng that at the last moment the proceedings had to be transferred to a larger hall. The town was placarded with notices reading simply "To the Sale". Every significant national and local newspaper was represented, and the sale was constantly punctuated by the taking of photographs. Mrs. Marshall's winning bids were six thousand pounds for the waterway itself and a total of three thousand pounds for various essential ancillaries, such as lock cottages. The fact that the total expended was thus less than had been predicted, was almost certainly a result of various commercial bidders having held back in order that the waterway could be acquired, as was supposed, by a public and charitable organisation. The purchase was greeted with scenes of popular enthusiasm most unusual at an auction. Even the auctioneer made a congratulatory speech, saying how pleased he was that the waterway would henceforth belong to a body exclusively concerned with the public well-being. These scenes of rejoicing continued through the evening in the town of Aldershot, where several firms declared the rest of the day a holiday when the result of the auction was announced. The purchase was announced in all the BBC news services, and, that evening, and next morning, the press references throughout the country were lavish and enthusiastic.

All this quaint detail is true, but of course, it was also too good to be true. It was like the singing in the streets, the linking of arms with strangers, on the first day or two of the Bolshevik Revolution. On the evening of the auction my only slight concern had been as to whether the money could really be forthcoming in support of the Association's name and legal liability; but on the very next morning, my telephone rang out again, it was again Mrs. Marshall speaking, and more precise trouble began, though of a quite different and quite unforeshadowed kind. "You mustn't think that your Association has bought the canal," said Mrs. Marshall.

The next four or six weeks are difficult to write about. I shall merely quote the brief report in Bulletin 19, which I still find a temperate and statesmanlike declaration. "At a meeting, held prior to the Auction, of our Basingstoke Canal Committee, was established a Basingstoke Canal Purchase Committee, composed mainly of Members of the Association who had kindly offered comparatively large contributions towards the purchase. It was the view of many concerned, and certainly of the Council of the Association, that this purchasing Committee was to be regarded as subordinate to the Basingstoke Canal Committee which established it (and, therefore, to the Association itself); its establishment (according to this view) being required merely to meet the present constitutional inability of the Association as a whole to acquire and hold an actual waterway or other similar real property. Immediately after the sale, however, it transpired that a majority of those forming the Purchase Committee (and thus a majority of those contributing to the purchase) deemed the Purchasing Committee to be an autonomous organisation not so linked with the Association as to be under the Association's control. It being clear that it is, in fact, impossible for the Association to exercise over the major contributors (without whom the Canal could never have been saved) a control to which those contributors are unwilling to submit, and it being repeatedly and earnestly insisted by the contributors that their sole aim will be to run the Basingstoke Canal along the best lines advocated by our Association, our Council has decided, after protracted negotiations with the contributors, to accept the independence of the Purchasing Committee while offering it all support as long as a satisfactorily constructive policy is adhered to, aimed at the fullest possible use of the waterway for navigational purposes."

Most of the "protracted negotiations", to which even Peter Scott gave much time, were with Mrs. Marshall; and it would be hard to find a more resolute or more adroit negotiator than she, then and later. The position to this day remains obscure. It seems clear that most or all of Mrs. Marshall's "balance" came from individuals outside the Association and whom none of us even met. Cyril Styring, dissatisfied with the course of events, soon withdrew his offer of two thousand pounds, which presumably (but I do not know) increased the draft upon the unknown outsiders. Whenever thereafter the Council of the Association felt compelled to have a talk with Mrs. Marshall about the state of the waterway, we were regularly told that it was these outside interests, in fact controlling the canal, that resisted ("could not find the money for") developments of the kind we believed in. No doubt it was true, because in the end (years later) Mrs. Marshall herself departed from the Basingstoke Canal scene, and not, one gathered, in the friendliest circumstances.

As will be perceived, and as many readers will know themselves (the appeal and popularity of the Basingstoke Canal continue still), the central tragedy has been that none of the hopes that rose so high at the time of the auction, have been fulfilled. Since 1949, it has been very difficult to take a boat on the canal at all: instead of the matter-of-fact, matter-of-course access (to every navigation) in which the Association believed, special negotiations were required in every case; very special and often very protracted – quite beyond the scope of the ordinary boat-owner or the time he was prepared to afford. Trading craft there have been none, though Mr. Harmsworth had operated regularly. On balance, and despite spurts of constructive activity, the condition of the navigation has gone down and down, until at the time of writing it is low indeed. Of course there have always been difficulties and explanations, but the course of events compares ill with the recovery of the Lower Avon, the Stratford Canal, and even the Chesterfield Canal. With that carefully worded judgement, I shall draw away from the Basingstoke Canal. It is proper to say that at many moments of difficulty in the national waterways situation and in the Association's own often turbulent history, Mrs. Marshall stoutly and eloquently supported the right, the constructive, and the imaginative cause. The main moral of the Basingstoke Canal case lies in the fact that it was the filling-in proposals of the local authorities, and the total absence of a national waterways policy, which compelled us (and the public) to rely upon rescue arrangements so plainly less than ideal. At the time of the auction (as, probably, once more now), the official threat to the survival of the waterway as a through navigation was desperate. When Mrs. Marshall ceased to manage the canal, a Council Member of the Association, Mr. David Cooper (who later left the Council when I did), prepared with others an admirable and detailed scheme for the transfer of the waterway to the Surrey and Hampshire

County Councils; in default of the National Waterways Conservancy, which has never been established.

The second of the two campaigns which greatly advanced the Association's cause with the public was the fight against the 'blue and yellow'.

In the chaos of nationalisation, the narrow boat carrying fleets had in principle been left in private ownership, but a large number of narrow boats had in fact come into the hands of the Docks and Inland Waterways Executive, because they had formerly been the property of navigation-owning companies that had been nationalised. The boats went with the company's lock cottages and offices. By far the largest such group was the fleet of the former Grand Union Canal Carrying Company. Many of the boats had been built by Harland and Wolff when the famous Leslie Morton had been running the carrying company, and were less than fifteen years old. (These were steel boats; but even wooden narrow boats will last more or less indefinitely, certainly forty to sixty years, if they are properly maintained according to known rules, and if the waterways they trade on are reasonably maintained too, so that the boats do not drag along the bottom.)

Whatever the Docks and Inland Waterways Executive failed to do, there was one thing they did promptly and spectacularly. They ordered that all their haphazardly acquired craft, narrow boats and others, were to be painted blue and yellow. The order appeared in practice to apply to the outsides and insides of the boats, and to all the furnishings. On the narrow boats it was the end of the roses and castles. One began to see even blue and yellow cans, dippers, and stools.

The volume of correspondence about the Basingstoke Canal, heavy enough for an organisation of volunteers with only one paid assistant (even though it was Jane Howard) was as nothing to the torrent that poured in about the destruction of the traditional boat painting; but, on this topic inevitably, the writers felt even less compulsion to enclose fourpences and sixpences. I was particularly impressed by the almost world-wide distribution of the protests. It was plain that wherever the British flag (then) flew, and in many places where it did not, there were nostalgic people in whose dream of home the castles towered beside the narrow waters and roses flowered improbably. We had no difficulty in finding for the alternative a name from popular mythology: the yellow peril.

It was a particularly horrible yellow, known officially, we were given to understand, as 'gold', and a particularly horrible blue. Neither colour had any part on the waterways, where the commonest colour masses had been red and green, white and black; and blue is well known to be the last colour to choose for open-air application, because of a special perishability. In no time at all, the blue and yellow, inappropriate at the start, looked faded and jaded. We discovered that the choice of these colours had been made by Mr. Robert Davidson, in many ways the Executive's most respected member, as I have said, at least in old waterway circles. It was something to find that any single decision had been achieved by any single individual. We surmised that Mr. Davidson had been impelled by a very Yorkshire desire (as Yorkshire sees things) to "eliminate sentiment"; of which the roses and castles were, of course, the essence. It was also perhaps the very first thrust in the campaign to eliminate the Association as idealistically conceived; to bring things down to earth.

Many people since Mr. Davidson, especially among the Association's own Members, have claimed that the campaign for the roses and castles was a waste of time and effort. The world, and especially the Anglo-Saxon world, will never lack for puritans. A few words of answer are possibly worth while.

In the first place, we had little choice. The demand for action was so vast and expressed in such strong terms, that had we ignored or opposed it, we should, as in the case of the Basingstoke Canal, have lost all credit.

In the second place, the campaign was a marvellous propaganda opportunity, for those with an eye and an instinct for such things. Within that context, its relative and practical importance in the working waterways scheme was almost immaterial; unlike the absolutely vital arguments for a National Waterways Conservancy, a new rates structure for carriers, and a properly constructive national waterways policy, it was something that the wide, indifferent public both cared about and could understand. It was only through such means that a wide waterways scheme would have any hope at all of accomplishment. The Association had been founded many years too late, and was struggling desperately against time. The campaign for the roses and castles had the same publicity importance as the campaign for the working boats themselves. There is a sense in which both (and many other big things that we did in the times to come) were mere means towards, mere summons to, the far wider purposes of keeping and properly maintaining the entire existing (or then existing) system of inland waterways, and building new and better ones.

The third answer to the puritans is that the roses and castles were among the most beautiful and heart-warming things to be seen in the whole of Britain; and the last large-scale and authentic survival of popular folk art. They were supremely worth fighting for in themselves. They symbolised excellently the philosophy that the Association had been founded to uphold.

"The Times" published a letter from Peter Scott; and another from Barbara Jones, who wrote a detailed and illustrated account of the boat painter's art in her book, "The Unsophisticated Arts". The proprietors of "Time and Tide", then still in the Lady Rhondda era, offered free reprints to all applicants of a statement on the subject by me. As not one single defender of the new colours ever emerged from outside the Executive,

Bulletin 19 was able to speculate upon what the newly inaugurated "public ownership" amounted to.

The numerous Members of the Association and others who thought it worth while to write directly to the Executive, received (naturally) a standard statement; and a second standard statement if they wrote again rejecting the first. The first statement took the curious line (well calculated, however, to confuse and deter objectors) that only a small part of the total narrow boat fleet on the canals was affected: "the other five-sixths of the carrying craft are owned by independent carriers, who will, no doubt, continue to paint their barges in the present colours." Bulletin 19 did not fail to call attention to the incorrect description of the boats as "barges", the most elementary blunder in the entire waterways world; but the main rejoinder was, of course, that the state-owned vessels should presumably set an example to all the rest, and not be (automatically, as it were) the mere squalid bobtail of the fleet. It was hard to see, when one came to think about it, how nationalisation could be justified otherwise. Moreover, at this very moment, the proportions defined in the Executive's statement were seriously upset: the biggest of the surviving narrow boat carrying companies, the famous firm of Fellows, Morton, and Clayton, gave up in discouragement, and the Executive bought their fleet. (These were the boats known colloquially as "Joshers", after the Christian name of a former Chairman, and these were the boats of which the crews wore white trousers.)

The Executive's second standard statement took the line that the number of boat painters available was insufficient for the full decoration of the entire flotilla; but that "Nevertheless, the Executive have no intention of suppressing a decorative art or its practise in brightening entrances and interiors of cabins". To meet the first of these claims, we assembled a nation wide list of persons willing to paint roses and castles, and able to do so up to a standard acceptable by us. The list proved to be considerably longer than we had expected, but a notable feature of it was the number of painters perfectly able to carry out the traditional scheme, who had been prevented from doing so either by orders to paint in blue and yellow, or by being directed by the Executive to other work than painting. We then set about launching an apprenticeship scheme, whereby the supply of boat painters would be assured in the future. We did this in alliance with the Rural Industries Bureau, whose Director, the late Cosmo Clark R.A., made a brilliant and abiding contribution to the problem of conserving human skills and satisfactions in a mechanised world, and played a prominent part from first to last in the campaign for the roses and castles. Bulletin 19 remarked mildly that it was "perhaps surprising what tasks devolve upon our voluntary organisation". To seek acceptance of the apprenticeship scheme and of its products, Peter Scott had a wings-against-the-sky luncheon with Lord Hurcomb; who, inevitably, made "significant reservations". However, the Executive did announce that the blue and yellow was only "experimental". Bulletin 20 offered confirmation: "On some boats a brighter blue and a richer yellow are being employed. Wavy lines are appearing, instead of straight; and a rather better lettering than the original etiolated design". But Tom Rolt reported that at the Executive's Ellesmere yard, even the weather vane had been painted blue and yellow.

"Those who are interested in the survival of the last of our traditional popular arts are asked to keep the campaign alive," wrote "The Architect and Building News". We succeeded in doing so for the better part of a year. The most important success was a broadcast on 2 July 1949 at the peak listening hour of 8.30 p.m. The BBC had the usual difficulty in finding any independent defender of the official policy: not a single boatman, not a single designer or decorator, not a single business man could be lured forth in support. At first, Sir Reginald Hill said he would appear personally; but in the event the case for the blue and yellow was stated by the Executive's Public Relations Officer, Mr. L.A. Goss, and by one of its Engineers, Mr. C.A. Wilson. A most unfairly strong aggregation clamoured for the roses and castles: Sonia Smith on behalf of the working boat community; Barbara Jones, for the design profession; Captain Patterson, a Director of Samuel Barlows, a big carrying firm; and, perhaps most weighty of all, Frank Nurser himself, then the best known exponent of the art that was threatened. The proceedings terminated in an unscripted free-for-all debate between Messrs. Goss and Wilson on the one side and me on the other. We were told that the broadcast was heard by at least fourteen million people. It was one of the broadcasts that I have thoroughly enjoyed; mainly because I was not required to keep to an agreed script, an obligation that makes me sound like a zombie. The broadcasting authority always kindly assures me of this resemblance at the rehearsal or run-through, and always I cordially agree.

After the big broadcast, we naturally received more letters than ever. We shouted, wheedled, exemplified, derided; though serious debate continued to be impossible, for none would argue against us. Barbara Jones and Cosmo Clark produced balsa wood models of the sterns of a motor and a butty memorably, but practically, adorned; and the models were delivered on a handcart to the Executive's headquarters. We never entirely ceased to protest as long as I was in charge of the Association.

There was nothing more to show for it. Neither the Docks and Inland Waterways Executive nor any of its plus-ça-change successors budged further. It was agreed that the cabin interiors and the furnishings might revert to tradition ("Canal Boats to Stay Gay" ran the idiot headline in the "Sunday Times" – though at least they were not called barges); but the exteriors remained blue and yellow. Commercially, it was "bad packaging", as Captain Patterson expounded in the broadcast. Domestically it was tyranny; bureaucratic intrusion into the ancient floating homes of the boat people. Artistically, it was mass destruction by a state authority; as in the case of the waterside structures. As publicity for a struggling new authority in charge of a struggling old industry it was disastrous. But perhaps it was not seriously meant to be otherwise.

It was a transaction that set the tone of official waterways policy for many years to come.

Both the Basingstoke Canal campaign and the campaign for the roses and castles have to be deemed failures in respect of their very important immediate objectives; but for the fame and prosperity of the Association they were successes exceeded by few of the far more important achievements in later years. One saw so clearly how strongly in favour of the Basingstoke Canal and the roses and castles was all public opinion; and how little public opinion amounts to when opposed by experts. Once again: public opinion is only heeded when it has power to do harm. For example, little can be attained by saying that one's opponent, Zero, is a splendid chap who is only doing his job. Zero's private splendours are immaterial if his job is to be a philistine. What a different world it would be if every individual was required to accept responsibility for his individual actions! As once when there was belief in another reality than this.

XIV

North with Beatrice

Life has no value except the inestimable value of a few immortal hours, and one must endure the rest for their sake.

HUGH KINGSMILL

Not that only the nationalised waterways authority was unsatisfactory. 1949 saw the closure of the Rochdale Canal, which was another waterway that the Transport Act had "managed to miss". Thirty-three miles long, with 'wide' locks, it ran from the Bridgewater Canal in Manchester to the Calder & Hebble Canal near Halifax, crossing the Pennines by a route of often superb beauty. Commercially, it had never recovered from a period of railway domination; and my Association was not yet strong enough or rich enough to do anything effective to save it. Here its very size and grandeur were difficulties. It must also be added that the Association had influential Members in the district who did not believe that the effort should be made. This was, I think, my first serious encounter with an internal problem which at times thereafter caused much organisational upset, and also, in my opinion, lost for the nation at least one other waterway of major importance, fifteen or sixteen years later. Any person of sensibility who today walks the towpath along the uplands of the Rochdale Canal, must weep at the destructive folly of the past.

By now we had launched, as well as our original Midlands Branch, a Kennet & Avon Branch (never satisfactory, and later to break away from us), a North Eastern Branch, and a Fenlands Branch. The second of these scored an early success. It was one of the usual curious stories.

The Linton Lock Navigation, established by Act of Parliament in 1767, consists of nine miles of the Yorkshire River Ouse, which, upwards of these nine miles, becomes the River Ure. The Ure was nationalised by the Transport Act, but the nine miles remained under their ancient jurisdiction, that of the Linton Lock Commissioners, mainly citizens of York, and self-renewing as in the case of the Suffolk and Essex River Stour

Commissioners. Below the Linton Lock Navigation, the Ouse is controlled by a Committee of the York Corporation.

In 1936 heavy repairs were effected to Linton Lock itself, the only lock on the nine miles of river. It was believed that the repairs would be effective for many years, during which a reserve fund for future repairs could be built up from revenues which in pre-war days amounted to about £400 per annum. When the war came in 1939, traffic ceased almost completely, and the repairs fund could no longer be augmented. In 1943, most of what there was, had to be spent on the repair of flood-damaged banks. In 1947 came a far worse flood, which completely submerged the lock and compelled the evacuation of the lock-keeper's house. Probably as a consequence of this flood, a leak developed in 1948 through the floor of the lock, which sucked out cavities under the bottom and then behind a side wall. The collapse of one side of the lock seemed imminent.

Repairs were estimated to cost £2,000, and the Commission had almost no funds at all. There was enough, it was generally rumoured, to pay for their annual dinner in York, but for little else. The Commissioners pointed out informally that if their legal obligation to keep the lock in repair was insisted upon, they would have no alternative to declaring the Commission bankrupt.

The matter was dealt with by Cyril Boucher devising a method of repair much less costly than the official proposal; by our North Eastern Branch appointing two representatives to the Commission; and by the Association's Membership finding most of the money for the work to be done. It was a great success for our Branch and for Cyril Boucher in particular.

An interesting case that began seriously to torment us at about this time was that of the Bridgwater & Taunton Canal in Somerset. This navigation, about fourteen miles long, from the port of Bridgwater to the county town, follows the course of the River Tone, which had been made navigable under an Act of 1699. The canal, more convenient to work than the original river, was purchased during the nineteenth century by the Great Western Railway; and night began to fall. During the Second World War, a number of "temporary fixed bridges" were constructed across the waterway at towpath level, supposedly for the passage of tanks, though local people were very strong in the assertion that no tank had ever used a single one of them. Perhaps the bridges were for recourse in the event of invasion. It was well known that the silted and overgrown Kennet & Avon was Britain's "Blue Defence Line" against that occurrence. At nationalisation, the Bridgwater & Taunton was one of several waterways that remained under the direct control of the Railway Executive (though they were transferred to the nationalised waterways administration years later). It was hard to say whether this made negotiations easier or more difficult. I should say it was as broad as it was long; as shallow as it was deep. The only thing that mattered about the waterway itself was that it was impassable.

"As it is virtually impracticable," the Railways Executive wrote to me in January 1950, "to work traffic on the Canal owing to the limited headroom of certain temporary fixed bridges spanning the waterway, the provision of which arose through circumstances beyond the control of the Railway Executive, the question of the prohibition upon the use of locks is unimportant . . . The manipulation of locks generally by occupants of boats has been discountenanced as, apart from the possibility of damage, there would be some risk to the users."

This was a waterway which, with most others, the boatman had a legal right to use and the navigation authority a legal obligation to keep up. (These conditions no longer obtain: lately, on most navigable waterways, the user has lost all his rights and the authorities have shed all their obligations.) The (then) Ministry of War was under a defined liability to remove the "temporary" bridges whenever called upon after the end of the conflict. The Railway Executive had not sounded the call, nor has British Waterways (successors to the Docks and Inland Waterways Executive) ever sounded it since. From the viewpoint of national waterways non-policy, it is an almost ideal state of affairs that the canal should be conclusively blocked by barriers "beyond the control" of any navigation authority. The fight has fluctuation like a fever. A West of England Branch of the Association was formed to forward it; fell in one of the Association's three major internal tumults; rose again as a South Western Branch – with the Bridgwater & Taunton rather too far from the centre of its concern. Through strife, through weariness, the "temporary fixed bridges" stand. One day they will no doubt be annexed to the Imperial War Museum, and scheduled as monuments.

That was our existence: each case that I have briefly cited involving scores of letters, some involving hundreds; with constant visits and excursions to all parts of the country added, and endless administrative ingenuities. The few cases I have mentioned may be amplified and multiplied by reference to the many back numbers of the Bulletin. Some people said that such "far-out, borderline cases" as the Bridgwater & Taunton (and others that I have not named) were a waste of our time. Those who spoke thus, were, naturally, often Members who did not live or operate near the waterways in question. It was the old argument again that we used to hear from the trade (which even by now had far less of a voice to speak with). The rest of us believed that if the far-out waterways could be saved, then the more obvious ones need not even be feared for. In the end, this was proved to be true: the recovery of the Stourbridge Canal led the way to a perceptibly better (though no more than that) governmental policy for much of the system. And always we pointed out that the current condition of a waterway gave little idea of its modern potential, but reflected only the accidents and mishaps of history, the destructiveness of interests that competed with water transport.

The recurrences of turmoil within the Association, to which I have several times referred, and which remain so vividly patterned on my life and thoughts, were made almost inevitable by the conflict between the floodtide of our advance, in respect both of our own numbers and of our influence with public opinion, and the utterly frustrating destructiveness and stolidity of the officials resisting us. That many of our Members should favour a bargain with authority was only to be expected. The suggested deal usually included three items in varying proportions of emphasis: that some waterways should be kept at the cost of letting other waterways quietly slide (known, at one time, as a "policy of priorities"); that talk of a National Conservancy and a national waterways policy should cease, and the officials be left more or less quietly in possession "to do the best they could with the limited resources available"; and that suggestions of enlargement, modernisation, and new building be accepted as the moonshine of extremists: not the concern of the common man chugging with his growing family along the pound to a boat club rally. By me the boat club member was told that every mile he or she navigated contributed to a securer present and an infinite future: for some it was a truth long sought; but for others, an imposition. The grand aims could not but narrow with time. There was always the race to achieve as much as possible before the world's more worldly-wise citizens democratically took over. Every success, by making the cause more of a band-waggon, brought failure nearer. With every success, I had to run the faster.

As early as Bulletin 20 appear the first hints of the second campaign for restoring a waterway by voluntary effort; and where the Basingstoke Canal campaign failed, the campaign for the Lower Avon succeeded so triumphantly under Douglas Barwell as to constitute, with certain of its successors, the greatest social adventure, as we may term it, in Britain since 1945. The Lower Avon Navigation Trust, of which Douglas Barwell has been chairman (and I am a Council Member) since the start, has raised more than £70,000 by public subscription and donation. It has purchased that part of Shakespeare's Avon which runs from Evesham to a confluence with the Severn at Tewkesbury, and which was crippled by the Great Western Railway (almost needless to say) buying the rest of the navigable river, from Evesham to Stratford. It has restored the collapsing installations, and begun to make the Avon for Birmingham what the Thames is for London. It is possibly even within sight of working at an annual profit. It has transformed many people's lives and philosophies. It has been achieved with only half a river; and none of it would have been possible if the navigation had belonged to the state. If the Avon had been nationalised with the Severn, its navigation works would now lie dead and decaying, as on the Yorkshire

River Derwent. It is small wonder that the man mainly responsible for the achievement has been excluded from the fountain of honour which regularly besprinkles those responsible for waterways that are half-usable or closed. Twenty years of unpaid, highly skilled, dedicated, day-and-night toil and drive and leadership to *restore* a waterway are hardly matter for official gratitude.

The first phase of the waterway campaign concluded in splendour with the Market Harborough Festival of Boats and Arts in 1950, first glimpsed in Bulletin 22; but that same year, when, as Chairman of the Festival Committee, I was already in the thick of the struggle to create the joys ahead (against bitter opposition, needless to say), came earlier the long voyage on *Beatrice*, episodes which will live always in the memories of those who participated.

Peter Scott had created the Severn Wildfowl Trust between the Gloucester & Berkeley Ship Canal and the river. From early times, thousands of wild geese and ducks have settled every winter on the flat grasslands known as The Dumbles; and the Trust began at once to assemble a captive and permanent collection also. In no time, there were thousands of visitors as well as birds; and many people wished to spend periods of time in the area, where boarding houses are far from abundant. Now, a generation later, the Trust is a vast establishment; but its first effort to provide its own simple accommodation for visiting ornithologists took the form of a converted narrow boat, ingeniously adapted to sleep as many as sixteen people at a time, though not with unlimited space to roll around, and to feed them as well. The vessel, at the time it was purchased, was named *Beatrice*, and it was agreed that to change the name of a ship was unlucky (a belief widely disregarded in later years on the canals). It was on her maiden voyage after conversion by Spencer, Abbotts of Birmingham that the second, and crucial, lifting of the Lifford Lane obstruction took place, as already chronicled. It was on this first voyage too, that Philippa Talbot-Ponsonby, later Peter's wife, stopped a wildly runaway horse in the quiet village of Upton Snodsbury near the Worcester & Birmingham Canal, by merely extending her arms and breathing magic words. *Beatrice* reached the Trust's terrain at Slimbridge in good order and was moored on the Ship Canal in the area pleasantly known as The Patch. A female factotum was installed to run her as a hostel.

Beatrice proved a great object of interest to many Trust members, as well as to every passer-by at The Patch bridge. One thing led to another: in the end, Peter Scott undertook a long lecture tour to distant waterside communities, using the boat as transport and as a mobile, floating base. I was responsible for the itinerary, and accompanied the entire trip. It was in April and May of 1950. We traversed 450 miles of waterway, from as far south as Slimbridge (between Gloucester and Bristol) to as far north as

Wigan. We passed through 273 locks. We had many anxieties and many adventures. It was a period when the number of living individuals who had made such extended trips through the waterways system at large, could be counted on one man's fingers and toes, and possibly on his toes alone.

The worst of our anxieties was, as usual, the engine. The Trust had fitted a model recommended (or at least suggested) by Tom Rolt, and indeed installed by him on *Cressy*. What had not been realised was that whereas this type of engine worked adequately (and very cheaply) in the hands of so dedicated an engineer as Rolt, it was less suited to more dégagés navigators. It had caused difficulty on the maiden voyage down from Birmingham; and, though on the lecture tour we always had several able amateur mechanics aboard, we had engine trouble from first to last. So much time was lost even on the short run from Slimbridge to Tewkesbury, that an heroic decision was made, and the engine was replaced by an engine of a different type at Bathurst's yard, working far into the night. Tom Rolt might well have laughed, had he been there: the new engine proved little better than its predecessor. It was a most curious business. This was no case of a hire craft laden with inexperienced beginners. Though I myself was not, nor am, even a beginner when it comes to engines, we always had several people aboard to whom in infancy flywheels had been of more interest than windmills. They could at least take everything to pieces, and put much of it back again: given time, of course. Time was the worst problem. There was a fairly stringent schedule of lectures to be maintained. Thus we found ourselves navigating the oddest places at the oddest hours; compelled to seek professional aid in almost impossible circumstances (but seldom seeking it in vain). Peter Scott was obliged too frequently to have recourse to long distance taxis. This had to be hushed up for the sake of the waterways cause. Boat engines, other than the pounding Swedish Bolinders in working narrow boats, were, I repeat, always like that in those days; and I am not sure that they are much better even now. There are splendidly reliable boat engines in the United States, I am sometimes told.

Nor was the weather commonly clement. It was on Thomas Telford's long, wide, and very shallow Shropshire Union Main Line that it did its worst. On the Shropshire Union a vessel must keep meticulously to 'the channel' (the invisible track ground out under water through the accumulated silt, by the regular passage of boats carefully taking this one course – especially loaded working boats); and on the Shropshire Union the channel is (or was then) difficult to discover and hold to at the best of times. *Beatrice* encountered for several consecutive days a gale reported by the wireless to exceed fifty miles per hour. The same wireless reported that in our near neighbourhood the wind had completely overturned a motor car. The only way of keeping on course so outstanding a target for the wind as a seventy-foot long converted narrow boat drawing little more than two feet,

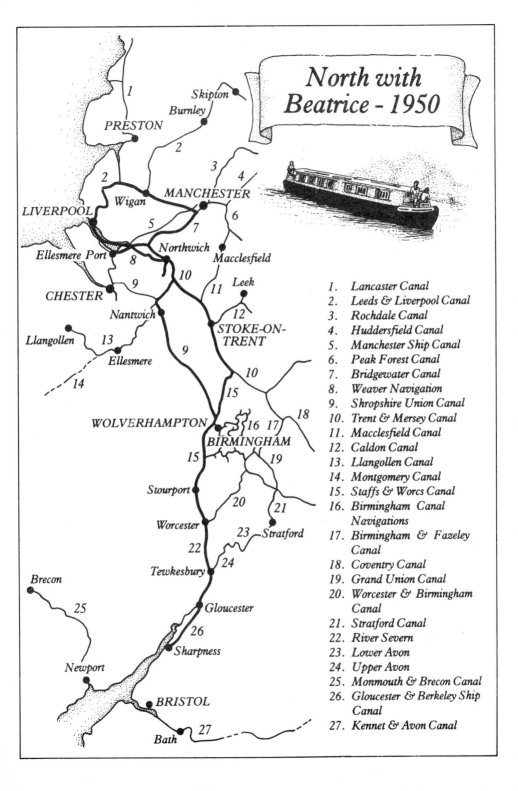

North with Beatrice - 1950

1. Lancaster Canal
2. Leeds & Liverpool Canal
3. Rochdale Canal
4. Huddersfield Canal
5. Manchester Ship Canal
6. Peak Forest Canal
7. Bridgewater Canal
8. Weaver Navigation
9. Shropshire Union Canal
10. Trent & Mersey Canal
11. Macclesfield Canal
12. Caldon Canal
13. Llangollen Canal
14. Montgomery Canal
15. Staffs & Worcs Canal
16. Birmingham Canal Navigations
17. Birmingham & Fazeley Canal
18. Coventry Canal
19. Grand Union Canal
20. Worcester & Birmingham Canal
21. Stratford Canal
22. River Severn
23. Lower Avon
24. Upper Avon
25. Monmouth & Brecon Canal
26. Gloucester & Berkeley Ship Canal
27. Kennet & Avon Canal

was to land a hauling party on a line at the bow and a similar party at the stern, while a single person remained on board to steer, as far as this was possible, and try to make the engine go. Progress was incredibly slow and continually interrupted by the boat sticking. In addition, it rained continually. The photograph taken (somehow) by James Sutherland of our party toiling as described, is, I modestly claim, one of the most remarkable in the British inland waterways field.

There were many other adventures. Almost as soon as we had emerged from the Gloucester & Berkeley Ship Canal on to the Severn, and traversed the winding passage through Gloucester, we found that the river was emptying out. In reference books, the Severn is described as tidal up to Tewkesbury, but there is a weir at Gloucester, and it had not previously occurred to me to take the tide as a serious navigational factor above the northern entry to the Ship Canal. Nor normally is it: we were unusually unlucky. What happened to us was that we found ourselves stuck fast on an emerging mudbank in midstream almost as soon as it had occurred to us that something out of the ordinary was developing. We remained stranded there for hours. Another exceptional circumstance was that the sun was shining. A remarkable lady named Mary Byng produced a guitar (not then the instrument of hardship it now too commonly is) and sang us songs in five or six languages most convincingly, while we lay about on the vessel's long top. Much of the Severn runs between high muddy banks. Where we were, there was also a wide current of shallow water on each side of our mudbank. As we grew more and more anxious about the delay, Lord Geoffrey Percy, then the Trust's pyrotechnologist (directing the rocket-netting of birds for ringing), said he would try to wade and scramble ashore, with a view to seeking for us a tow from a vessel with a stronger engine. This he valiantly did; but when he had clambered up the high bank of yellow mud, found that in the previously invisible meadow at the summit was that familiar waterside amenity, a bull. He had to make a very swift transit of the field, but in the end, he managed, astonishingly, to raise for us a stoutly powered little craft that dragged us off the mud and towed us to Tewkesbury.

Even with the new engine, long delays continued, as I have said, and, in consequence I covered myself with glory one night by navigating the boat, or at least holding on to the helm, from Holt Lock to Lincomb Lock (still on the Severn) in total darkness without even running into the branch of a tree, though many of them dropped out into the river. (Narrow boats do not normally carry navigation lights; and the traditional aid even to traversing a long canal tunnel is a small and weak hurricane lamp. "You want only a faint beam on the peak of the roof," the tale goes – or then went. Certainly *Beatrice* had no lights at that point. It had not been proposed that she should move after dark.)

This feat was, I think, the main reason for Peter Scott later making a favourable reference in actual, published print to my navigational prowess. It made me resolve thereafter to specialise in strictly pitch-dark nightwork: preferably, as between Holt and Lincomb, with little cut-glass measures of gin handed up, and a pretty girl in a windcheater and thick trousers to express continual admiration through the murk.

Ascending the Staffordshire & Worcestershire Canal from Stourport, at a village where we moored for the night, we encountered an episode. We were told that earlier that day the body of a woman had been recovered from the waterway: almost certainly a suicide.

In the pub that evening, Geoffrey Percy encountered a working boatman.

"Did you hear about the woman who fell in?"

"'Ear about 'er!" rejoined the boatman. "I got 'er round me blades."

Geoffrey had at an earlier date been involved in a related incident. While birdwatching at some almost non-existently early hour on the banks of Virginia Water, he observed on the other side of the lake a constable in uniform who was obviously having difficulty with some task. The man's struggles made birdwatching difficult, and before long Geoffrey wended his way round the lake in order to offer assistance. As he drew near, he realised that in the water was the body of a woman; at which the constable was poking with a long pole.

"Let me help. The two of us will soon get her out."

"Get her out! I'm trying to work her into the next county."

Very odd things indeed can happen during early morning birdwatching. One ornithologist was occupied in that way by the shore of a Scottish loch. He became aware of an inexplicable entity that had somehow appeared on the (generally rather open and bleak) opposite shore. It looked like a man and yet not like a man: and, what was more, it appeared to be entirely black. The ornithologist was alarmed from the start, but as he stared at the entity, it began to move along the side of the loch. It seemed to be doing so with extraordinary swiftness. The loch was fairly large, but it was not long before the idea came to the ornithologist that the entity might be making for him in particular. He departed at a quick walk. After he had managed to look over his shoulder, the walk became a very fast run. But the situation was hopeless: the black entity was gaining upon him at a rate entirely beyond common experience; and he could see now that as well as being black, it was huge. Beside that part of the loch stretched a rough road, down which the ornithologist was fleeing. When the entity had all but caught up with him, the ornithologist threw himself over a five-barred gate into an adjoining large meadow or waste-land. There was little point in doing so. It was sheer, unthinking, desperation. As he landed on the ground, he fainted. There, hours later, he was found by a shepherd; still unconscious, but otherwise alive and without physical injury. Possibly he had seen what is known as an "elemental": perhaps the earliest and most primitive form of surviving organism, natural or supernatural. It was understood that he gave up birdwatching thereafter.

On the windswept Shropshire Union, the engine (old or new seemed hardly to matter) sickened so badly that, local talent having proved insufficient to restore it, we were compelled to summon a mechanic from Bathurst's. Two Bathurst mechanics joined us at Nantwich, states the log, "one of them travelling with us to see the trouble for himself, while the other drove the car that conveyed them. When the mechanic on board had realised the state of the engine, he realised also that the other mechanic had motored off with their tools . . . In the end, they stayed with us working all through the night and getting only what food we could provide for them. They were still working when we woke up the next morning." I suspect that engines in small boats have never been very satisfactory since the days of steam (especially the later days of steam, when steam, briefly, was as dreamy to use as high speed gas). Marine internal combustion engines seem to be "created sick", as Fulke Greville remarked of man.

In and around Liverpool, we had much entertainment. It was the first time that I (or anyone else aboard) had descended the Leeds & Liverpool Canal below Wigan. The first part of this section, going down the Douglas valley, is beautiful; the second part, insipidly suburban (though it includes the half-circuit of Aintree race course, with its famous "Canal Turn"); the last part, parallel with the Liverpool Docks, wild and Irish in the extreme. I do not think there are many places like it (or as it was then) on the entire waterways system. Our hearts sank lower and lower as we forged on through an unmistakably hostile population, most unlike the usual waterside inhabitants of the north; knowing that soon we should have to moor, as Peter Scott had a lecture that very night. It was a Sunday, and our advance was in the end stopped by the fact that the lifting bridge at Litherland was lifted only on weekdays. The immediate environment was totally unpromising for a night's rest; or even for leaving the boat unoccupied while we attended the lecture and dinner after it at the Adelphi until no one could say what hour.

The sequel recalled our first night at Ashton-under-Lyne in 1948. Some way back, I had happened to notice a long brick wall not unlike the one at Ashton, rising similarly from the waterside on the bank of the canal opposite to the towpath. It was in a comparatively quiet spot, and, what was more, there was in the wall a door; a green one, battered and faded, not a red one, as at Ashton. I proposed that we retreat and moor against the wall. Not unnaturally, there was a certain scepticism and even testiness. Would such a very faded door be likely to open, let alone on a Sunday? How *far* back was it? Narrow boats are not easy to navigate for long distances in reverse, especially through a jeering populace; and there was no "winding hole" in which to "wind" it at Litherland. (Turning a narrow boat can normally be done only at special wide places, and is known as winding, because a clever boatman can make the wind do the work.) Was I quite certain that I had seen the door at all, and was not merely dreaming of 1948? No one else seemed to have seen it, or even the wall. The truth was that the marked absence of local sympathy with our pilgrimage had begun to rattle us.

Still there was nothing else to do but withdraw, and we zigzagged away amid many jests. Probably it was fortunate that the distance was as great as it was, because the critical elements on the towpath soon tired of following us. In the end, I plunged ashore, heavy with responsibility, and tried the rusty handle. It was like H.G. Wells's story: not only did the battered door open at once, but it gave on to a green lawn, surrounded with trimmed bushes and weeded flower beds. I cannot recall the "huge velvety beasts" mentioned by Wells, even though Peter Scott was leading the party. Beyond the big lawn was a pleasant, late Georgian house. The place proved to be the demesne of the Seaforth and Litherland Constitutional Club; and Peter Scott had at that time only lately retired from being President of the Home Counties Young Conservatives. (He contested a seat in the 1945 election at very short notice, and lost it by only 435 votes, despite the nationwide Labour slide. "It was only a few weeks after the election that the narrowness of my escape began to dawn upon me", he writes in "The Eye of the Wind".) "The Steward made us welcome," says the log, "and was most helpful in every way. The mooring, in a somewhat unattractive district, turned out to be one of our best."

It had long been planned that on the next day we should emerge through Stanley Dock on to the Mersey and ascend the big river to Weston Point; a trip never recorded as having previously been performed by narrow boat (let alone by converted narrow boat) and embodying obvious elements of frisson and mild risk. James Sutherland, already an Associate Member of the Institute of Civil Engineers, had, during recent days, spent time with his steel tape, slide rule, and calculating block; and had just emerged with conclusion that *Beatrice's* metacentric height made it probable that she would roll over upon encountering a wave of a height that she seemed very likely to encounter. At the least, her seams would open.

We all duly attended Peter's talk in the crowded-out Picton Hall. "Wild Birds of the Severn Estuary" was, I see, the subject. At the start the audience had an unexpected wait, because, as we gathered, the Lord Mayor of Liverpool, who was in the chair, had attended chapel in his usual way, where the service had been a long one. "Outside the Hall," states the log "a well-spoken man made a demonstration against the evening's talk, the Lord Mayor, and the previous Lord Mayor." It was not the sort of thing we were accustomed to, but it contributed to the unexpectedness of Liverpool. "We don't want that man here," I remember the demonstrator proclaiming in loud but earnest tones, through the cold dark drizzle; reference being to the evening's lecturer. I imagine that the demonstrator was both a Roman Catholic (the Lord Mayor being a nonconformist) and a Socialist (the lecturer being a Conservative).

Before dinner, several of our party were driven through the Mersey Tunnel (then almost new) and back by the Merseyside Naturalists' Association, which had sponsored the talk; so that it was quite late when finally we reached the Adelphi. None the less, we secured one of the noted corner tables in the French Restaurant; where before the evening was over, we were sighted by Sir Malcolm Sargent, one of the Association's very first Members (he remained one until his death), who, as the log puts it, "stood us two rounds of drinks and most kindly offered us free seats for a performance of Beethoven's Mass in D, inviting us also to dine with him after it." As the performance was to be on the next night but one, when we expected to be exceptionally far away, we felt compelled to refuse the tickets; but Sargent would not take No for an answer, as the saying used to go (Sargent was seldom one to do such a thing), and we departed with the pieces of pasteboard, lamenting that we could never use them.

Of course things matured quite differently. By the time we reached Litherland again, it was very late and raining harder than ever. The next morning we had to cast off at seven o'clock: it was a matter of "catching the tide". When, at about dawn, the rain appeared to be descending much as on the night before, and a noticeable breeze to have sprung up as well, those responsible for our leadership turned over in their bunks (in so far as that was possible in the *Beatrice* bunks) and gave more detailed thought to what was involved. The consequence was that "we did not leave our excellent mooring at Litherland but we devoted much of the day to purchasing various marine items: an anchor, a good pump, new lines, a chart, etc.; driving about for the purpose, six in a taxi, from place to place in Liverpool." It was astonishing how difficult it was to find "marine items" on sale in Britain's second seaport. It would have been far easier in, say, Stoke-on-Trent; where they would have been all obtainable in one place. "We ended by taking the taxi to Fazakerly Royal Southern Hospital, where P. Scott visited a young admirer of his, afflicted with poliomyelitis . . . It rained continuously all day."

The weather was only a little better the next morning, but a schedule stretched ahead and we could wait no longer. We cast off at half-past-seven and stopped for breakfast at the top of the Stanley Dock Branch Locks. The possibility in some minds that the breakfast might be our last, was startlingly confirmed, after we had descended the locks, by the appearance on the dock wall, of a well-known local member, her hair streaming (as often) in the high wind, and crying, "Don't go. I beg you not to go. I beg you." Peter Scott said something gallant, and we moved ahead into the final lock to the Mersey. Just before the river gates opened, Martin Grundy leaped down on us. Having already assisted us on the canal, he had taken the day off to challenge death with us. He had to cross a large coastal steamer, lying between *Beatrice* and the wall of the huge lock; and come down the steamer's side on to our roof.

"A memorable day", says the log for 18th April . . . "just as we emerged through the lock gates into the river, the sun began to shine to our great surprise and joy; and, despite some heavy rolling at the outset, a consequence largely of washes left by vessels vastly bigger than ours, the whole passage passed off smoothly, delightfully, and according to plan. As we entered the river, a Cunard White Star liner passed the entrance to our dock going downstream to the Atlantic. Ours was the first occasion on which a converted narrow boat had entered the Mersey; and we travelled all the way up to Weston Mersey Lock, about fifteen miles or so, all virtually by sea." (The Mersey widens above the Liverpool-Birkenhead straits, very much as, above the Lisbon straits, the Tagus widens into the Straw Sea.) "The narrow boat displayed qualities which surprised us; and all of us found the trip most memorable and enjoyable, especially in the sunny weather which obtained almost throughout. We clung in the main to the northern shore, much merriment being caused aboard by our evasion of the Garston and the Seldom Seen Rocks. The keeper of the Hale Point Lighthouse waved to us as we passed" (the massed commuters at Liverpool Pier Head had done so earlier). "We went up on a spring tide and our engine fortunately behaved well, only stopping once." We reached Weston shortly after three o'clock. The log further records that the Member who had feared for our safety (or sanity) appeared at Weston and "seemed most surprised by our survival."

We passed through the short Runcorn and Weston Canal and ascended the massive Runcorn Locks (Josiah Wedgwood's "work of Titans"); both now iniquitously destroyed; as already stated. Sir Malcolm Sargent's concert was well in view. It was a matter of our catching the 5.49 train back to Liverpool from Runcorn. But going up the locks, we were delayed by a large fleet of lighters that was descending them. Certain of the lighter crew members were disputing among themselves quite savagely as to whether it was Wednesday or Thursday. We were able to settle the argument by telling them it was Tuesday. When we reached the top of the locks, we flung ourselves into what we regarded as our best clothes, and ran hard towards Runcorn station. We were just too late. We saw our train steam out. The road bridge across the Widnes-Runcorn straits had not then been built, and there was not time to be saved by taking a hired car across the splendid but leisurely transporter. We had to await the next train. We entered our box only just before the interval, and looking not unlike a collective of Flying Dutchmen.

At the end of the concert, which was a splendid one, we went to seek out Sargent. The Philharmonic Hall had a genuine Green Room. There we found him; seated at a small table in the middle and dealing with a very long, very slow queue of autograph-hunters. In those days, it reminded one of a queue for ration-books.

At dinner in the Adelphi we were joined by Joan Cross and Gladys Ripley, who had been among the soloists. Sargent, while feasting us, himself ate and drank almost nothing, as, in my observation, was his wont; but reminisced continually, including first-hand anecdotes of Chaliapin and Pachmann. The pianist, Mathilde Verne, when a girl (and a very beautiful one), wished to enrol as a pupil of Pachmann, then still in more or less full possession of his faculties. Pachmann indicated very conclusively that his wife would not approve. Mathilde Verne suggested that she disguise herself as a boy. "Alas," said Pachmann sadly, "it has been tried." It was at this gay meal in the Adelphi that Sargent made a comment on canal-cruising that soon became famous: "After all," he said, "it's an elderly man's sport." Joan Cross made an extremely witty rejoinder: "*He* prefers bird-watching". None of the obituary notices that I saw, gave any idea at all of Sargent's extraordinary character; and it is right that more time should pass before an attempt is made to depict and analyse it. Typically, the evening ended with Sargent's departure to the airport, whence he was to fly to South America (not, I suppose, directly). At the Adelphi that same night, we also met Eric Portman, whose current play, "His Excellency", we had all visited during the downpour the previous evening. An actor who never gave a bad performance, and who gave many great ones (expecially as Byron in a brilliant play named "Bitter Harvest"), Mr. Portman proved as charming to meet as he was inspiring to watch. This cannot be said of all eminent actors.

After we had resumed our voyage, came, on the very next day, the odd sequence of events at the town I can only name Y. By this time, we had all become rather accustomed to some kind of official, or at least ornithological, welcome at our various landfalls; to at least some scattered sprigs of red carpet. At Y, where, for once, we actually arrived punctually, there was no one at all. When we had made fast, and were wondering whether a party should go forth in search of the hall in which Peter was committed to lecture ("Wild Birds of the Arctic"), a small boy sauntered up with an oral message: the Mayor hoped we would join him for tea in the Parlour. "What, all of us?" The small boy supposed so.

We were placed round a single enormous table: seven or eight of our party, each with an elected or appointed guardian of the community on either hand. I sat on the left hand of the Mayoress. In the centre of the table was a masterwork from the municipal treasure: a fabulous silver tureen. It proved to contain a massive bounty of fried eggs, sausages, bacon, black pudding, and lights. Helpings outstretched the liberality for which the North is famous. While we munched, a servitor made the round, filling every tumbler from a huge jug. I supposed the fluid to be water, but it proved to be neat gin; and, what was more, every tumbler was charged to the brim. None of the people entertaining us made any reference to the matter. All seemed to take this refreshment for granted, and to be downing it as casually as if it had been daily fare. None of the *Beatrice* party felt disposed to fall short of the example set. There was no refill from the jug. Next came strong tea: again in Northern torrents.

The lecture hall was at once makeshift in construction, crowded to the doors (persons were even squatting among the roof trusses), and exceedingly warm. Not all of the *Beatrice* party were feeling at their best. The Mayor rose to introduce the speaker; and to this wide effect he spoke: "Ladies and Gentlemen, we are honoured to have with us tonight the man who brought to England the imperishable glory of being the first to reach the North Pole. Tonight he is going to speak to us about the birds he saw on the way." The error was not unusual; earlier on the same voyage, a boy had shouted an enquiry from the towpath: "That the boat that went to the North Pole, mister?"

We descended the Anderton Lift, which conveys boats between the Trent & Mersey Canal and the River Weaver, fifty perpendicular feet, in caissons. James Sutherland, naturally, climbed to the vertiginous summit of the structure; and returned with reports that, as a civil engineer, he could not at all advise us to rely on it. We navigated the Manchester Ship Canal from Runcorn to Ellesmere Port. This has since been made impossible in more ways than one, at least for a boat such as ours on an itinerary such as ours. None the less, there is no way of seeing and appreciating the Manchester Ship Canal that is to be remotely compared with a passage along it in a comparatively small, powered boat. We continued to explore the waterways of this north-west frontier of the network: crossing the Barton Swing Aqueduct; mooring at Wigan Pier. A woman at Rode Heath, on being told, in answer to her question, that for some of us the voyage was their annual holiday, observed that the people in question must be crazy.

We ascended the Cheshire Locks to Harecastle Tunnel; more than a mile and a half long, and so layered with legend that a first passage of it has been compared with a first crossing of the line. It was not my first passage. I had gone through in the opposite direction, south to north, at the beginning of the 1948 voyage already described. The tunnel had proved very wet (there are 'dry' tunnels, completely or comparatively; and 'wet' tunnels), and we had observed that the dimensions of the bore varied considerably at different periods of the transit, but our boat had been small, and our minds had been concentrated upon the fearful independability of her engine.

This time we reached the northern portal at early fall of eve. As always, a lecture engagement lay ahead: "What are we waiting for?" asked someone. "Let's go through now." But a number of working boats lay at moorings round the tunnel mouth, and their crews proved critical, even hostile. The rule was that boats were not allowed through after a certain hour. We knew the rule, but had been given special authority to disregard it, in view of our schedule. The demonstration by the working boat crews, normally paid by the run or trip and not by the week, persuaded Peter that it would be diplomatic for *Beatrice* to wait until next morning.

When we awoke, all the working boats had gone, because working boats, like tented Arabs, commonly disappear at sunrise. Coming up the locks, we had damaged *Beatrice's* bow-strip, so that we began the day with a telephone call to the Anderton Company at the far end of the tunnel, telling them that we should probably arrive for repairs at about 10.30 a.m. After a careful breakfast, we entered the tunnel at 9 a.m., almost precisely.

The tunnel was at that time normally worked by an electric tug, which drew power, by a bow of tramway type, from a wire overhead, and also picked up a chain from the bottom of the waterway. A voyage behind this vessel could be a strain on the nerves: the noise of the links in the chain grinding over the cogs in the drum on the tug made spoken communication impossible; the wavery dimensions of the long tunnel were lit up but not defined by almost continuous blue flashes; the tug was incredibly slow. But now the tug was out of action for repairs; and boats had authority to go through the tunnel under their own power. The reason for the installation of the tug had been fear lest the smoke from the early powered craft lead to suffocation. The tunnel had been built, and its ventilation surmised, upon the assumption that boats would be 'legged' through by direct human effort. When *Beatrice* entered the tunnel, we perceived at once that the diesel oil fumes left by the early morning narrow boats (and by others during the previous few days) could be quite as unaesthetic and quite as promisingly lethal as any smoke.

We chugged ahead into the thick blackness; our handkerchiefs held to our faces. In the case of many canal tunnels, including several long ones, the far end is visible (during daylight) from the moment one enters: a remote, greeny-yellow circle, as before the child at birth. Here there was nothing; until, after perhaps seven or eight minutes, suddenly we saw before us that the bore of the tunnel was about to become much smaller, the roof much lower. It did not happen gradually. What we saw was a perpendicular wall filling the upper part of the comparatively spacious tunnel through which we were passing. The historical explanation of this curiosity is typical: the tunnel (itself Telford's successor to the original, parallel tunnel by Brindley) suffered so much from subsidence caused by mining operations in the hill above, that it was decided to renew and enlarge the bore; the work started at the northern end but came to an end (few could be relied upon to say why) many years earlier, at the point which now lay before us.

We edged through the murk into the small aperture ahead. The steersman, at the stern, had to crouch so low that it was impossible for him to keep much grip on the situation, but that mattered little as *Beatrice* was now crawling tightly down the neck of a bottle. A much more serious problem was presented by the remains of the towpath to the steersman's left. Few British canal tunnels are provided with towpaths. The Harecastle towpath was, and is, broken away and under water at several places, and so cannot reasonably be used for a transit of the tunnel on foot, but none the less forces boats out of the tunnel centre and against the far wall. This is a serious matter along the length where the top of the bore has subsided, and we soon realised that if *Beatrice* was going to jam, the point of stoppage was going to be the top right hand edge of her conversion structure, for the passage of which the spring of the tunnel arch had become what might hopefully be called marginal.

Theory was converted into practice almost immediately. *Beatrice* came to a gentle but total stop: wedged between the tunnel arch on the steersman's right, and Telford's immense wooden rubbing strakes, vast planks edging (and designed to protect) the collapsed and soggy towpath, on his left. The steersman shut off the engine; partly to prevent us being asphyxiated. There was very little air and not much light, but a certain amount of romantic noise, caused by the cataracts of water from within the hill that Brindley, amid many, well-deserved, congratulations, had arranged to flow through the tunnel walls and thus reduce the need for reservoirs (the tunnel being on the summit level of the canal). After thought, we restarted the engine and attempted to retreat a short distance. We were wedged tightly enough to make this difficult, but we achieved it in the end, with some pushing and hauling from the wet and muddy towpath, upon which it was difficult, in that section, even to stand erect. James Sutherland returned to the point where we had stuck, and set about sawing through and removing a portion of the stout and heavy towpath planking: a task faintly comparable with a minor labour of Hercules.

After he had succeeded, we tried again, and this time advanced considerably further. I was aware that the very low section extended for a comparatively short distance, and our spirits were rising, when, on an instant, we stuck once more. This time we proved to be stuck so tightly that we could not even retreat. It would therefore be impossible, with the equipment we had, to remove a further section of the towpath planking. There was no space in which to operate the saw. The only hope lay in the piles of slimy bricks which the Docks and Inland Waterways Executive had thoughtfully placed at intervals along the even slimier towpath, for (as we belatedly realised) this very purpose. The wedged navigator loaded these bricks on to his vessel until her hull went down far enough into the water for the superstructure to clear the arch of the tunnel roof. Fortunately the water in canal tunnels is usually far deeper than in the silted-up, rubbish-choked open reaches. Ours was a large vessel to lower, but there was nothing else to be done. Peter organised the whole party into a human chain through the near-darkness, and we started transferring the nearest pile of bricks to *Beatrice's* floor, where much care had to be given to their even and effective distribution.

It was discouraging work, especially as there was just enough light for us to see *Beatrice's* gracious interior becoming ever more filthy and slithery; and soon a youthful member of the party lost his head, and began screaming that he could stand no more and must get out, a bad case of claustrophobia. It was fascinating to see how Peter dealt with him; an impressive demonstration of natural leadership and moral force. He reminded the lad that he was going to a good school (alas, it would be wrong for me to specify which); a place where one just couldn't behave like that; he even spoke of the Empire (the term still being occasionally in use), and of the conduct expected of an Englishman. The effect was astonishing. The boy quietened at once, resumed work on the bricks, and gave no more trouble, as the saying goes. I have often wondered since what could be done in like circumstances today.

We loaded more than two hundred bricks before *Beatrice* could be made to budge; even though James Sutherland had been sawing off the corners of the main entrance hatch runners that were jammed against the tunnel brickwork. By that time, she looked as if she had been long under water, and lately raised, like the *Gustavus Vasa* in Stockholm harbour. As we crept ahead once more, woodwork and ironwork screeching and ripping off from time to time, we quaffed packet soup salted with black mud, and cowered beneath the streams of water from overhead. We emerged from the tunnel at 3.40 p.m.

It was snowing. There was an assembly of working boats hideously delayed by our misadventures. There was an official of the Docks and Inland Waterways Executive: his task was to bid us unload the Executive's bricks immediately; which we immediately did under his stern eye, piling them up in the snow on the towpath at the tunnel entrance, while the working boat crews cursed us as they entered. We understood that the bricks would be restored to their original site by the Executive's staff: a ploy we would be excused. No doubt, all kinds of dirt money, danger money, and overtime would have to be paid. Once again we had been a charge upon the taxpayer. We were relieved when a call upon us late that night by the same official of the Executive proved merely to be on behalf of his daughter, who wanted *all* our autographs.

Snow fell for most of the next two days. Descending from Stone to Great Haywood, we followed a pair of working boats laden with cheese, which smelt cheesily. We found the Clifford Arms at Great Haywood stuffed with rustics singing folk songs. It was only on the canals that one still came upon such things. We were nearing the region of the Wild Boy.

On the last night of all, at the splendidly architectural Queen's Hotel in Birmingham, now demolished, I see from the log that "we discussed exhaustively the wonderful work of the Midlands Branch in attempting to save the River Avon": as hereinbefore proclaimed. When I first knew the Queen's Hotel it was, in great part, a pleasant family establishment, where at teatime in the lounge one might suppose oneself at Sidmouth, or even Torquay, rather than in an industrial city, and where, moreover, one might sometimes remark, sotto voce, that it was surprising so magnificent a place did not cost more. During the Association's 1951 troubles, the first of our civil wars, I recall running races with Eric de Maré along the Queen's bedroom corridors, stretching to the horizon, splendidly carpeted, casually soundproof. Conditions such as I describe were to be found in many of the other railway hotels that so often came my way in the path of duty. They were pleasant, relaxed places to stay in; with women sewing in the loggias, and children fighting in the bathrooms. Today they are populated almost entirely by men with brief cases: hommes sans femmes, hommes sans faces, hommes sans âmes. The great hotels have become too stratospherically expensive for anyone else.

XV

The Festival I

. . . the aloe, which blooms but once in a hundred years, and then bursts into blossom with a clap of thunder.

THÉOPHILE GAUTIER

Towards the end of 1949, we felt that it was time we did something for the Members.

When people rang me up and enquired, as they commonly did, what they would "get out of" becoming a Member, I replied, sometimes sharply, that although there were certain possible advantages to Membership, such as receipt of a Bulletin unequalled by any other organisation, occasional dinners and the like, yet the only reason why anyone should even consider joining, was a deep conviction not only that the waterways of Britain should have a future, but that the future we proposed, and our general method of promoting it, were the right future and the right method. By this austere procedure (while it was still followed), we achieved a Membership of higher calibre than most, and avoided clogging our campaign with a numerically excess force, all demanding advantages, welfare, and endless administration. Another matter to be borne in mind was, that after the Association became a "charity", and thus able to operate a "covenant scheme", the Department of Inland Revenue became very rabid about our providing no "benefits of membership", in their sense of the term, no knitted boat-socks for every Member at Christmas, no clubhouse with a bar.

We thought that a small rally of boats would best meet the case: undeniably a contribution to the Association's campaign, and at the same time an established method of promoting competitive enjoyment among boatowners. An important point, however, was that only a small minority of our Members owned boats: we were neither a boat club nor a trade association. The need to provide supplementary attractions for the majority led to conflict and to astonishment.

The first and blameless announcements appeared, as already stated, in

Bulletin 22: " If available labour and resources permit, we hope to organise at a town in the Midlands (to be announced later) a Rally of Members' boats from all parts of the country, with prizes offered, and, it is hoped, shore festivities at the town selected." Tom Rolt expressed the view that we might get twenty or thirty boats; and no one on the Council, myself included, could see reason to question the estimate.

The town we had in mind was Market Harborough; which virtually selected itself by reference to the waterways map. Movement between north and south of boats exceeding seven feet in beam is prevented by alternative narrow-lock bottlenecks, which should long ago have been widened: one consisting of the narrow locks between Gayton and Northampton; the other the flights of narrow locks, encountered one after the other, twenty miles apart, at Watford (Northamptonshire) and Foxton. Market Harborough, while reasonably near to the centre of England, is the most southerly town accessible by wider craft from the north. It also stands at the end of a canal 'arm', so that our projected rally could not be accused of obstructing working boats; in those days a significant consideration. Furthermore, Market Harborough was, and is, a pleasant and ancient town, of much the right size for our purpose: neither so small that it might be unable to do us justice, nor so large that our Rally might disappear among conflicting attractions. I was aware, also, that at Market Harborough was John Fothergill's Three Swans Hotel; of which I had great expectations. At the time the announcement went into Bulletin 22, the only doubt was whether Market Harborough would want *us*.

A deputation of us set forth to meet a deputation from the Market Harborough Urban District Council. We entered the Council Chamber quite expecting that an invasion of the town by water gypsies would be dexterously but decisively discouraged. We departed with the offer of financial help from the proceeds of a special rate; with the free loan of a handsome building (already appropriately named Welland House) in the centre of the town for use as a Rally Office; with the nomination of the District Council Engineer to represent the Council on the Rally Committee; with every possible expression of cordiality, and every possible proposal for practical help. Beyond doubt, this almost incredibly happy upshot was largely brought about by the Chairman of the Council, Councillor Allsop. This gentleman, understood to be by trade a manufacturer of gravestones, showed an immediate and imaginative grasp of what we had to offer to his community. His positive attitude was all the more notable in that no proposals such as ours had ever been submitted to a British inland town before. Councillor Allsop seemed positively to welcome this dangerous element of innovation. His support for all that we did never flagged: as our edifice rose higher and higher, he rose with it, and cheered us on. Having been critical of Members of Parliament, it is a pleasure to say, that again and again, in many different places, I have been much impressed by the quality of local government leaders, especially in the smaller communities. Expecting to encounter cautiousness and preoccupation, one is repeatedly surprised to find that the man or woman in Councillor Allsop's position far outdistances the average of the citizenry in vision and enterprise on behalf of the locality.

We settled upon the week of 13th August in the following year, 1950.

It was already becoming apparent to me that much more was possible than a small rally of boats, with perhaps a hoopla stand on the bank; and that much more, being possible, had become essential. The threat to the waterways, and the public ignorance not only of the threat, but even of the fact that three thousand miles of waterways still existed, were so desperate that every practicable, available, conceivable bugle should be blown, drum beaten, tambourine rattled, and sword drawn on the waterways' behalf. We were the only serious campaigners in the field: if we did not shake the world now that (thanks to Councillor Allsop and his colleagues) we had such a wonderful chance, then all, or almost all, would very probably be lost, and our own hands justly forfeit.

It could not be expected that everyone would share this view.

In January 1950, Tom Rolt asked me to spend a night aboard *Cressy*, then moored at Gayton, just off the Grand Union Main Line. It was, I recall, astonishingly cold; with the canal under ice that one could walk across. Rolt had indicated that he had "something to say to me". This something proved to be that he wished to retire from the position of Honorary Secretary. He informed me of this in the pleasantest and most hospitable way; giving the reason mainly that he thought four years service was enough for any one person. I was aghast. I argued strongly; persuaded or over-persuaded him to reconsider; and thereby unwittingly put myself in a false position. Though little or no mention was made of "Association policy" or of the impending event at Market Harborough, I have since realised that by resisting so strongly I entered into some degree of moral liability to modify any views of mine on policy that might conflict with Rolt's views. At that moment, I was not conscious of any such thing: I believe that I was mostly alarmed by the prospect of having to carry the responsibility for the Market Harborough event (as well as for the whole Association and its campaigns) almost alone. Therefore, I handled the situation wrongly. I have often since been heard to say that when one is offered a resignation, one should always accept it. Steady increase in experience has confirmed this view.

For relations between Rolt and me progressively deteriorated. There were a variety of non-waterway difficulties: one was connected with a book of (splendid) ghost stories by him that I had sold on his behalf to Constables, and even found a title for ("Sleep No More"); another arose when he suddenly accused me of having owed him nine and fourpence for, I believe, something like two years. Further development of these and related themes would be inappropriate. My summary, for what it is worth, based on Rolt's career in voluntary organisations (as distinct from his notable career as an author), was, and is, that while he has much to contribute at the primeval, pioneering stage, when the organisation is completely new and fresh, he is, by temperament, less qualified to meet the demands that arise when the organisation is well off the ground, beginning to look prosperous, and required to do battle for twenty-four hours (or more) each day. I suspect that there are three types of temperament associated with three stages in the development and advance of a voluntary organisation: the grass-root prophets, symbolised by Tom Rolt (than "High Horse Riderless" nothing could be more prophetic); the organising and militant idealists, represented by me (let the 71 issues of the Bulletin speak); and, later, the business and political 'realists' and consolidators, reflcted by my successors. Catching the right winged bird at the right moment is the problem for such as care about the particular campaign's success.

Tom Rolt ended that year by putting his name to a Memorandum calling for a policy of "priorities" (as I saw it, keeping some waterways and letting others go), and proposing in effect that the Association become more of a discussion group and less set upon a single aim. This led to the events that I have described as the Association's first civil war. At the end, Rolt and his fellow signatori (few of them, as usual in such cases, persons of his stature) found very little support among the general membership; or, in my opinion (obviously in my opinion), there would be few waterways left now! But the troubles, coming immediately afterwards, lost much of the immense good that accrued at Market Harborough. I was so preoccupied with keeping the Association on what I regarded as the only practicable course in the desperate situation around it, that I was largely unable to follow up the new opportunities and expanding good will in the outer world which the Festival brought into being.

Soon after our meeting with the District Council, it was agreed that the Rally should expand, or at least try to expand, into a Festival of Boats and Arts. The word 'Festival' was then much less flyblown than it is now; Bayreuth, Salzburg, perhaps Edinburgh came first to the mind, rather than Shrimphaven and Sandalford. Some might say, I perceive, that it was we who began the decline. In any case, I have to acknowledge that the expansion of the Rally into a Festival was strongly urged by me.

I have already stated my main reason. I had two other reasons. The first was that I had separate links with Gerald Barry, the Director-General of the Festival of Britain planned for the following year; with Leonard Crainford, his principal adjutant, especially (at that time) in the context of the Festival Gardens at Battersea; and with Hugh Casson, the Festival's overall artistic director. I had hopes that if the display at Market Harborough could be made big enough and bright enough to persuade some of these people to attend it at such a relevant period of their lives, then, to say the least, the waterways cause and the Association could not but gain.

My other reason was that I wanted to run a Festival.

Tom Rolt did not deny that "land attractions" were desirable; or even dispute that, if possible, they should include some kind of dramatic presentation in the Market Harborough Assembly Rooms. Where we differed was that while I had in mind to organise this histrionic landmark myself, Rolt proposed that we should seek to engage the Young Vic on contract. I do not think that Rolt would nowadays deny that he thought, among other things, that I was seriously outgrowing the proper size of my boots, and should be cut down thereto. The matter almost settled itself when the sum asked by the Young Vic proved to be far higher than the sum for which I thought I could mount a production on my own: not a lesser-known piece of Sophocles in the original tongue (as was – more or less – apprehended by a few), but some little light comedy suited to the gay holiday atmosphere we were all working for, however bleak the early committee meetings were proving. I had no idea what this light comedy would be, but I knew as well as anyone else that light comedies are the thing for holiday audiences, or were then. Indeed, I was able to turn the tables by pointing out that the piece offered by the Young Vic (alas, I have forgotten what it was) seemed perilously intellectual and problematical. Rolt responded by resigning from the Committee, of which I was Chairman, taking Angela with him. He, and others, had already pointed out that, in any case, we seemed to have nothing like enough money to pay for a production of any kind.

One divined that for Tom Rolt the repudiation of the Young Vic had been but the final outrage. Earlier, even on the Festival Committee, there had been other, more aquatic disagreements. At one point the Festival had been saved only by the charm and relaxedness of the lady ('girl' might give a more exact impression) who represented amongst us the British Travel and Holidays Association (as it then was): another organisation which appeared to take a thoroughly sound view of the Festival's possibilities from the outset. Again and again, waterway troubles have been eased by the non-expert; and the non-expert eased by the even less expert.

As there were twenty-six persons on the Committee, and as the meetings took place in my house (the Association then having no other office and very little money), the room could become very crowded when there was a majority attendance. It often took more than an hour to move out the larger furniture before a meeting began, and little less to bring it back again long after midnight (though by then the workers were normally fortified with a good meal at the Blue Cockatoo). None the less, the meetings, as always, achieved far more at far greater speed than can be expected of the more formal gatherings to which the Association ascended later; meetings with a sheet of plain paper and a spotless blotter before every upright chair. Also the Market Harborough Festival Committee Meetings were more enjoyable (after the early storms had blown over, which they soon did).

We appointed Mr. Arthur Thornley as Rally Harbourmaster, and at no subsequent event of the kind has there been a better one, because no better one would be possible. Mr. Thornley well reflected the ideal of virtuosity and versatility upon which I set such store in the campaign's early days. By trade a printer in a big way of business, he had succeeded Sir Malcolm Sargent as conductor of the Leicester Symphony Orchestra, and was now the inspirer and grand factotum of the Leicester Opera Club.

The representative of the Market Harborough local authority, their Engineer, Mr. J.G. Barlow, proved to be such a source of quiet strength that he was later invited to join the Association's Council, on which he ultimately served for a number of years. He spoke so quietly and so closely to the immediate point that one only stumbled upon his accessory talents by accident. These varied from an unusual grasp of the Association's aims and philosophy (something that was always unusual) to an astonishing, hidden-under-a-bushel gift for humorous and fantastic writing. At our Festival, too much of Mr. Barlow's duty lay in the direction of providing what are tactfully called 'disposal points' at more or less sufficiently frequent intervals down the long – and ever lengthening – line of projected moorings. He had also much scope for conjuring such elemental things as water and light, in volume unprecedented at Market Harborough, from the equally elemental air. Nor must I omit to acclaim Mr. Barlow's colleague, Mr. Hudson, the Clerk to the Council. Though he felt that, as he put it, he would be of more help off the Committee than on it, his contribution was memorable, and none the less so because always as unobtrusive as it was perfectly timed. One of the tasks with which he was associated was the compilation of a list of those prepared to offer Festival accommodation to supplement the town's four or five, mostly small, hotels. This tricky enterprise was brilliantly successful. Doors long sealed against the outer world opened without a creak. Unknown beds turned down to receive unknown sleepers. There was a new call for doormats proclaiming Welcome.

We persuaded the Lord Lieutenant of Leicestershire, Lord Cromwell, of Misterton Hall, to be Patron of the Festival. Peter Scott and Barbara Jones agreed to be Joint Treasurers of the enterprise; and the Committee further included such picturesque figures as Elizabeth Jane Howard and Cyril Taplin. Bill Christie (Mr. E.W.H. Christie, author of "The Political History of the Antarctic") joined the party in order to keep us within the law. Before being called to the Bar, he had owned a converted narrow boat, named *Dorothy*, in which he had crossed The Wash, being, I believe, the first to do so in such a craft. After his call, he rapidly became, as he still speciously remains, the leading authority on the complex, little known law of waterways: of which eminence the main employment is the provision of endless advice (Opinions and interviews) upon how best to essay resistance to the slights and encroachments of the officials; and thereafter, often, attempting to implement that advice in the Courts. No one could have advised more skilfully or more stoutly or more subtly than did Bill Christie. For a number of years, it might have been rewarding work, though exacting (and almost unremunerated), but in the end, inevitably, the officials infiltrated among the campaigners, and turned the force's flank, no blame to him.

Barbara Jones designed a Festival poster for reproduction on shocking pink and bitter lemon and arsenic green papers. I wrote most of the Festival handbook, touching life at many points between the two covers, but admitting only to the authorship of the "Short Guide to Places of Interest" in the Market Harborough area. Wicksteed Park, in Kettering, offered tea in cups that children could not break, Stamford's many attractions included "the grave of Daniel Lambert, a former officer of the prison service who weighed more than 52 stone". Wing, in Rutland, retained "a good example of an ancient turf-cut maze; relic of the Old Religion". It was unfortunate that when the time came, no one could find a moment to go anywhere.

We made provision for a Waterways Exhibition in the town's mediaeval Grammar School, of which Sir William Bragg had been a distinguished alumnus. It is a timbery structure on legs, between which the good wives once sold butter and herbs, while those with a vocation pursued scholarship over their heads. Paintings by Peter Scott would be on view (and on sale) in the Art Gallery. At our behest, the Arts Council, then a pleasantly un-assuming and amateurish body, made available a small collection of master-pieces which had to be accommodated in the cinema foyers, so fast were all normal spaces filling.

In the cinema itself we arranged for "Painted Boats" to be shown: an Ealing Studios film about the narrow working boats. Several personages more noted on the waterways than before the cameras give personal performances in it. Jenny Laird, not yet espoused to the Principal of the Royal Academy of Dramatic Art, looks touching in overalls. Sometimes a boat is going in one direction and then (but only for the knowing) is going in the opposite direction while still on the same journey. There are some unexpected verses by the late Louis MacNiece (specially written). The making of the film was accompanied by many ground-staff groans about "a slow-moving subject", and by lengthy towpath waits for the shiny sun. "Painted Boats" has remained a popular film ever since, and, considering the physical difficulties and policy controversies, it is amazing that it is as good as it is. It is, however, on the short side; of something less than full feature length. To accompany it at Market Harborough, we selected an early film of the Marx Brothers; merely because we wanted the best of everything, as far as might be practicable. It had struck me on a number of occasions, however, that the Marx Brothers could have made an excellent film about the waterways themselves: with Groucho as the Chairman of the Official Board; Chico as a typical working boatman; and Harpo as director of the public campaign (ours). Harpo's genius on his instrument was itself a powerful qualification. One has to harp and harp and harp.

We also gave the first public showing of the British Transport Commission film "Inland Waterways". This item had an amusing background. Sometime before the Festival, I had been sent a snowy card of invitation to a British Transport Commission film show at the Odeon in Leicester Square. The audience had proved to be almost as distinguished as the invitation card. Five films had been shown, of which the tasselled programme indicated that four would be available for hire free of charge by the public, while the fifth was for the Commission's staff only. Needless to say, the fifth was "Inland Waterways". As, rather unexpectedly, it proved to be a very fair piece of work, I immediately wrote to Sir Brian Robertson, then Chairman of the Commission, petitioning that it be made publicly available with the rest. Sir Brian, always, in my experience, courteous, reasonable, and imaginative, almost at once agreed that this should be done; so that we in return were able to offer a distinguished public premiere. The waterways section of Sir Brian's huge empire soon hit back, however. "Inland Waterways" is informative and modestly optimistic in approach, doubtless because intended for internal consumption only. A second official film was produced; dismally defeatist as far as the greater part of the waterways system was concerned, and providing many photographs of broken down locks and general dereliction (all, it was to be supposed by the unknowing, past possibility of repair). This film was significantly entitled "There Go the Boats"; and I had evidence that it was thereafter the film regularly recommended to the uninformed enquirer. "Inland Waterways" contains some charming background music; difficult, indeed, to expel from the mind. I was told by the composer, Edward Williams, that he had been commissioned to base his score upon canal folk-songs. He had travelled up and down the waterways with his recording apparatus, soliciting all the very eldest boatmen, some hardly able to speak, let alone to sing, but had found nothing significant until at the very end of his search he had come upon a gnarled ex-navigator in a public house in Acton, who had welled forth again and again, like any Cecil Sharp.

George and Sonia Smith undertook to take people for trips during the festival in their working boats, *Cairo* and *Warwick*. They would pick up in the Market Harborough Basin, and 'wind' at the Bone Mill, about two miles up. This establishment, which (at least in those days) smelt every bit as vitally as could be hoped for, became a familiar landmark or watermark. "Come for a trip as far as the Bone Mill before tea?" people would say; and I later heard of a Member from afar who actually took a job at the Mill, where he was sighted through the gates lugging bloodsmeared carcasses.

Cairo and *Warwick* also provided longer trips to Foxton, where tea was offered both by the Black Horse and by the Shoulder of Mutton. This place was and is famous for the Inclined Plane; a typical example of British canal muddling. The plane conveyed boats in caissons running on many rails up and down a hillside, and substituted for a slow flight of ten locks. It functioned for only twelve or fifteen years. It was then decided that the volume of traffic did not justify the cost of keeping in steam the engine that moved the caissons. The plane was abandoned and the ten locks reinstated. If the plane had been kept for only a few more years, electrical power would have solved the operational problem. Out of action, the plane vanished from the face of the earth. By the time of our Festival, there was very little to be seen, except a photograph in the Black Horse of the Babylonian installation in full service.

The corset factory of Messrs. R. and W.H. Symington and Co. Ltd., another major enterprise of Market Harborough industrialism, and placed at the very centre of the town, kindly offered a tour of inspection (with refreshments) to Festival visitors. The demand was, of course, enormous, though sometimes shame-faced. I joined the party myself, but it was not quite the same thing (as I hope Symingtons will not mind my saying) as attending a show by a fashionable corsetière in Paris. Production was on too large a scale (though not, of course, for the business prospect); too uniformly pink (at that date). "I *cannot* see why women *want* to tie themselves up in this way," exclaimed Barbara Jones. With so many around to whom one was expected to set an example, it was difficult to say much in reply. There was a Symington cousin, Noel Symington, with whom both the Rolts and I were in communication; independently, of course, by that time. He was understood to have crossed the Sahara Desert solitarily on a motor bicycle. Now he lived in a nice house near Market Harborough, and every now and then stood for Parliament as an Independent; alas, without success. Eight years later, he very kindly sent me a copy of his book, "Return to Responsibility". Noel Symington was one of those who felt that something was basically wrong wth things, and who worried about it. The Symington family is (or was) of course, also "in" soup.

We arranged for the manufacture of "Small commemorative plaques in metal, specially designed for mounting in boats". Our purpose was to present one to each arrival by water. They proved one of the most popular features of the Festival; and at subsequent jaunts of the kind have been imitated competitively in wood, plastic, cast iron, and even glass. One encounters cockpits as bespattered with plaques as the jacket of an ex-serviceman turned tramp. At Market Harborough, the plaques were made of mere tin, and were positively intended to be unobtrusive. Had we foreseen how highly esteemed they would be, we should have gone in for something flashier.

We set about assembling the Trophies.

A.P. Herbert, Peter Scott, and I presented large silver fantasies from Postons off Cannon Street for annual competition. (By now, we had no doubt that the event would recur annually for years to come; and, up to a point, as James Sutherland might have put it, we were quite right.) The A.P. Herbert Market Harborough Challenge Trophy was, and is, presented to the craft that has covered the greatest number of toiling miles to the Festival (or, subsequently, on most occasions, Rally). Peter Scott's Challenge Trophy is for the vessel that on the way accomplishes the greatest distance on salt water. He and we hoped for many entrants from abroad, but there were none at Market Harborough, and I have since heard of none elsewhere. My own Challenge Trophy is for the entrant who en route slays the greatest number of dragons, and rescues the highest total of maidens – (more mundanely, for the most enterprising and meritorious voyage). From time to time it has tempted novices into achieving the impossible, which, of course, is all that matters in this life, and especially on the waterways.

We also managed to cadge silver objects for five "concours d'élégance" awards; for boats that were thought to look nice, for boat engines that seemed actually to go, for galleys in which proper meals could be prepared. These concours d'élégance offerings have since proliferated to excess. Boat owners always tend to claim that their vessel is in a quite different category from other vessels lumped in with it by the perspiring judges; so that a clutter of small sub-divisions soon burgeons and spreads, each with its own award, equal in every possible way to every other award. In later years, the Association has regularly offered prizes for "the best flower arrangement by a Junior Member", and "for the best cake cooked on a boat during the course of the Rally". Here may perhaps be detected a trace of male status anxiety. As if a woman on a boat at a Rally should want to spend hours of time making, baking, jamming, and icing a competitive cake! At Market Harborough, participants were sternly assured that all awards were entirely incidental (not to say, accidental) and that the only true reason for attendance was a determination to forward the campaign for the waterways. This was both objectively true and psychologically potent. I also emphasised that participants should see themselves in the lights of hosts to the public and not as guests seeking diversions. I pointed out (among other things) that thus they would enjoy themselves more.

I have said that prominent among the attractions of Market Harborough at that time was John Fothergill's Three Swans Hotel. I find that Fothergill is being forgotten; nor was his stance through the greater part of his life calculated to assure his immortality. Even then, he was written off as a hotel-keeper who wrote quaint books about his trade. John Fothergill was, in reality, one of the most stimulating and admirable people it would have been possible to meet.

He began life as a painter. He knew Oscar Wilde and many of the Nineties' circle. In partnership with Robert Ross (a much lauded man who was, in the main, an odious man: but that is matter for another book than this, and a longish one), Fothergill ran an art gallery which is famous for having given the Post-impressionists their first London exhibition. He parted company with Ross and, for reasons that I do not know (maybe there was nothing particular about them), embarked upon a career of hotel ownership. First, he acquired the Spread Eagle at Thame which he proceeded to run on highly individual, highly civilised lines, becoming a famous figure in the process, especially among persons linked with the University of Oxford; though as everything he did, he did with style, he could not expect to be universally popular or loved. Later, he moved to the Royal Ascot Hotel; and later still to our own Three Swans of glowing memory. Fothergill originated the cult of the personal hotel, now encountered in many different places, usually in a late stage of decadence.

Fothergill's books about his hotels (which he tended to call inns, not without reason) do not sound likely to be good. Those who read them, will find that they are irresistible, impossible to lay down before the last page. (His anthologised or digest compendium of 1949, "My Three Inns", may be found to provide the best starting point.) The daily spectacle of odd human behaviour is observed and chronicled by an artist. Fothergill swerved from gaiety to scorn and back again, like a full human being; and he wrote beautifully, had a true, personal, idiom. The reader soon notices also an innocence about him, for all the worldliness he had witnessed, in the worst sense of the word. He seems always surprised by what the world mainly is; in particular, astonished and taken aback by its extremely slender concern with loveliness. I can confirm that as, in these matters, he wrote, so was he.

Even when I first knew him, he was already nearer to eighty than to seventy, and his life was saddened by the fact that his wife, Kate, who figures much in the books, was, like my own mother, almost immobilised by arthritis. Without announcing ourselves, we went one winter evening to dine at the Three Swans, in order to have a look around. Throughout the establishment, the decor was of that splendidly individual kind that can in no way be characterised, that would probably break up for almost nothing at a forced sale, but that reflects a soul caring first for beauty (that which is always strange) and not at all for fashion. Here there would be a bright oriental print of a sagacious Monstrosity; there a faded Andalusian shawl dangling through the dimness; and there again merely a black corner: or was it a black cabinet – even a motionless black man? With the sturdily British main course, lark pie or the like, came, on each plate, three prunes; and with the coffee, as we sat before the dining room fire, entered Fothergill himself. He dressed in the style of a Cromwellian officer: black, white; breeches, and huge buckled shoes; but it never struck one as affectation, or as anything but natural and inevitable. He had received a report of our conversation, and said at once that our Festival would be the best thing that had ever happened to Market Harborough, or ever could happen.

Had we noticed the long and elaborate iron bracket which carried the inn sign out over the High Street? Fothergill told us that he had designed it himself and had arranged for it to be cast by a Leicestershire blacksmith. He said that he had offered a prize of fifty pounds for the best newly decorated shop front. Not a single shop had even been entered. From hints dropped in the Council Chamber, we had already gathered that Market Harborough regarded John Fothergill with many reservations. Market Harborough, said Fothergill, could do with a shaking-up. As I have already indicated, he was still able to deliver such discourses as these far more in surprise than in anger.

He took us down to the big, stone-floored kitchen; where, on every day in the week but one, he himself did all the cooking. ("John Fothergill's Cookery Book" is the only work in its field that I am able actually to recommend). There stood the barrel of prunes: a full-sized wooden cask of the period before aluminium and plastic. A few prunes came with virtually every meal at the Three Swans.

We ended by provisionally reserving most of the hotel for the "distinguished visitors" we hoped for. With more conviction I booked a small, upper garret for myself. I sensed already what years of subsequent boat rallies confirmed; that if one finds oneself prominently placed at such functions, pleasant though they can often be, the most fatal abode is a boat, the most desirable a nearby attic to which one can at moments fly for a session of sweet silent thought.

XVI

The Festival II

A ball is almost a short lifetime in itself. Everything that happened beforehand retreats, for the time being, into a kind of pre-natal oblivion, and the world waiting for you when you wake up next day, seems as vague and shadowy as the eternity that waits beyond the tomb. Like somebody's life, the ball goes on and on, and the incidents stand out in retrospect like a life's milestones against a flux of time whose miniature years are measured out in dance tunes.

PATRICK LEIGH-FERMOR

There remained the tricky but hypnotic question of the play. Peter Scott, with mad impulsiveness, guaranteed the escapade against loss for a substantial sum. As we could hope to run for only five performances, but aimed at making almost everything professional, it is with the sincerest possible sigh of reminiscent relief and with warmest congratulations to all my friends who helped, that I record the upshot; in the end we did not have to call upon the *whole* of the guarantee.

I thought a suitable piece might be Benn Levy's "Springtime for Henry": a farcical comedy, and thus eligible under the fundamental law of the time; but genuinely and brilliantly witty from first to last; also a great business success when first offered. I believe that Mr. Levy was eighteen when he wrote it! His later productivity, interrupted – or at least interfered with – by a longish term in Parliament, has been erratic. His total opus seems to me to vary from the dazzling to the leaden, according to the piece; from the groundling parsonical to the most sparkling empyrean. No doubt Mr. Levy is several different people, like the rest of us. "Springtime for Henry" manifests a flair for the stage which is most exciting. It also has one set and a very small cast – four, in fact. For the Market Harborough Festival, these things were material. Of course I was criticised for not presenting something "solider". The guiding light of the local amateurs was especially sharp with me in this context. It was only to be expected.

A real difficulty was that "Springtime for Henry", like "Painted Boats", was not quite long enough to fill an evening, except perhaps an evening between the Berkeley and Ciro's. I resorted to the outmoded but excellent device of a 'curtain raiser'; and selected for the purpose Alfred Sutro's "A Marriage Has Been Arranged". This charming little piece has a cast of two, with an Edwardian dance orchestra offstage, and the girl in a period ball-dress. As it also offers a touch of de Musset-like poetry, it seemed perfect.

I recruited the first three of my four players by the simple device of tracking down people whose work I had liked, and asking if they would care to join the party, with more promise of fun than hope of cash. None of the three had I ever previously met; nor had any of the three ever previously heard of me. All three were extremely prominent in their profession: all three accepted my invitation. They were Barry Morse, Carla Lehmann, and Nicolette Bernard. In each case, I became certain at first meeting (which in the case of Barry Morse was at the Margate Hippodrome, now demolished) that I had chosen well; and so it proved to be. What is more, all three became close personal friends.

I was speculating upon whom to invite for the remaining part, when I began to observe a ruminative mist in the eyes of our guarantor, Peter Scott. "You know," he said, "I should rather like to have a try at John Jelliwell myself." As Peter, according to himself, had never acted before, though he undoubtedly excelled at reciting "The Hunting of the Snark" and at singing American railroad ballads, I was slightly concerned about his impact upon the distinguished professionals we had engaged. There was no cause for concern: Peter's extraordinary capacity for excelling almost immediately at everything he undertakes, emerged even in this unusual context; and I think that many, in the audiences and in the cast, would agree that, when the time came, his was the performance that made the greatest impact, and by a purely histrionic criterion. I very seriously regretted that I had not invited at least one talent scout from the film industry to see him. Peter Scott might easily have had at least the offer of a still further career; somewhat of the kind that had been offered only a little earlier to his friend, James Robertson Justice.

We had a little more trouble in the matter of a producer. A well known lady, now deceased, had been recommended to me, and I engaged her, but we failed to become friends (I think that may be the best way of putting it) and in the interests of the divine harmony that was now beginning to permeate our little group, I had to ask her to depart, though with a gratuity. Immediately, I acquired experience of a very important and recurring item in the life of a modern impresario: a complaint from the union, in this case, Equity. I succeeded in dissuading the union from actually bringing our project to a stop, which is more than every impresario has done; and clutched, panting slightly, at Barry Morse's suggestion that he produce

"Springtime for Henry" himself. This he did with great robustness. I offered the production of the Sutro piece to Elizabeth Jane Howard, whose career, it will be remembered, had begun at Michel St Denis's London Theatre School; and she rose very beautifully to the occasion.

Peter and Jane and Barry and I motored great distances in Peter's car, borrowing things and wheedling people.

The main contributors were, of course, Members of the Association. Within this category, no less a person than Sir Ambrose Heal lent us furniture for the stage (and especially beautiful pieces for the Sutro); and no less a person than Hardy Amies lent us the most ravishing dresses. I was astonishingly proud that I had already come so near to the league of talents that I wanted the Association to be. Through another Member, Anthony Quayle, then the Director of the Shakespeare Memorial Theatre at Stratford, we borrowed more square yards of night-coloured puma-textured velvet than I had supposed the modern world to hold in any one place. We used it for 'backing' and, indeed, for fronting too, as will be explained in a moment. I remember our motoring to borrow a set of 'stage weights' from still another Member, Derek Salberg of the Alexandra Theatre in Birmingham, member also of a long-established stage family. We entered Birmingham by the astonishing rural route that even now exists, from Studley through Beoley and Forhill to King's Norton, the straight, up-and-down road which the Romans built along an even more ancient track; and we picnicked in a quiet field that was probably within the city limits. It was pleasant to be with people who did not insist upon the A45 (the M1 being still unthought of).

Barry Morse persuaded Alan Miles of the Richmond Theatre (where my great aunt had formerly conducted me to the pantomime) to lend us scenery; and I arranged for it to be painted at the Northampton Repertory Theatre, to designs by the remarkable scenic Director and general inspirer of that establishment, Mr. T. Osborne Robinson. The Northampton Theatre is most unusual in having still a fully-equipped (and perfectly delightful) scene-painting workshop.

I had first met Tom Robinson when I had been invited to attend a production by the Northampton Drama Club at their beautiful little Masque Theatre, of a play set on a canal boat. This visit had a variety of other consequences. I was elected a Vice- President of the club, and myself made several appearances (of a sort) on their stage, on one occasion with a ghosts programme, on another with a poetry reading, in a third with a general talk about the Theatre and what I thought wrong with it (even then). I also formed a close friendship with a gifted lady who appeared with great distinction in a number of the pieces presented. Tom Robinson loves and is knowledgeable about the theatre and about Venice almost equally; and only slightly less knowledgeable about Gordon Craig and St. Petersburg. Later, he illustrated in colour several of my stories upon their first appearance in silky Christmas Numbers of "The Tatler".

Not the least of the tasks before The Inland Waterways Association Festival Theatre Committee (Jane Howard and me, with my dear friends, Mary George, now Director of the Electrical Association for Women, and Ann Pym) was the adaptation of the Market Harborough Assembly Rooms. This structure, though large and provided with a substantial Dress Circle, Balcony, or Gallery, had a flat floor, and a stage which, though again large (surprisingly so), was no more than an open platform. Within the resources and time available, we could hardly provide a ramp for the auditorium, but James Sutherland designed and superintended the erection of a complete built-in proscenium, assembled from numberless, clanking parts hired from S.G.B., auxiliaries to dramaturgy throughout Britain. It was typical of James's dedication and devotion that he spent night after night (as well as day after day, of course) enlarging and improving his giant construction, often clinging like a gibbon to the topmost strands in a not very good light, until hours so late or early that his wife came to me in serious protest that he faced utter breakdown. It was this proscenium framework that on the last day or two we fronted with swathes of the night-coloured velvet. Some anxiety also arose from the substantial stage-lighting equipment hired from Strand Electric. Its demand upon the power supply of the Assembly Rooms left little margin, and we had to meet representatives from the Board of Directors. None the less, the Assembly Rooms was convenience itself, in my opinion, compared with most of the 'multi-purpose' halls, built with public money, that are the current fashion, and that often replace far more attractive structures. At least the Assembly Rooms were open, spacious, uncluttered, and malleable. The only thing really wrong was the flat floor for the audience; but I know of no hall anywhere that has installed the tilting floor that used to be hopefully recommended by the Arts Council: level for dances, raked for plays.

An exquisitely beautiful poster for the plays was painted by Joanna Dowling. This girl walked in here one day, dazzled all of us by the subtlety and poetry of her work, agreed to modify her name along lines suggested by me, illustrated a few books, met a few French noblemen, wore delightful garments, but in the end settled for British matrimony and domesticity. She will never be forgotten by those who knew her in her brief flowering. She was almost the only young British painter whose work has really moved me; but it was of a kind that was unlikely to have much of a future with a wider public of today. An illustration by her to Lin Yutang's "Importance of Living", which I bought the very first time I met her, hangs to my left as I write; and, on the landing outside, the original of her poster for the Market Harborough plays.

It is worth adding that the Assistant Stage Manager at Market

Harborough was Prudence Balchin, daughter of Nigel Balchin. She was very young for the work and was very, very good at it. If I were about to produce "The Miracle" or "White Horse Inn" or "The Ring of the Bibelungs", she would be the first person I should seek for.

And, in the meantime, the boats were arriving. Before we had finished there were 120 of them; filling Market Harborough Canal Basin and winding far out into the country.

In the Basin we placed the converted narrow boats, and arranged for them to be floodlighted every evening; the Severn Wildfowl Trust's *Beatrice* was moored in a small inlet of her own, where her blithe complement dispensed joy at all times. Every day the Festival lasted, the crowds on the towpath grew. The District Council's estimate of the final attendance was more than 50,000 persons. Unfortunately, no arrangement could be arrived at, whereby we, who did not own the towpath, could charge for the spectacle; and the spectacle was not of the kind for which more can be extracted from voluntary collecting boxes than from a fixed payment, as is the case, for example, with a cathedral; though, of course, we did what we could in that way. The weather remained generally fair, despite some very heavy showers; or the towpath would have become impassable, as happened at several subsequent Rallies.

Morale seemed to remain high; with a large number in an appropriate condition of continuously advanced euphoria. *Cressy* was, inevitably, a centre of disaffection (Rolt invited Sacheverell Sitwell to the Festival and did not introduce him to me); but, every now and then, Angela would descend from the waterway to Welland House, where many of us were toiling away, and say something kind. The only other trouble that I can recall, other than a comic incident on the last day, to which I shall refer in due course, was a matter that made a considerable impression on me: few of the general Membership seemed to think Rolt's attitude was anything out of the way, whereas the hostility and loathing aroused by a Member who posted a notice to the effect that his converted narrow boat was open to inspection at a 'cost of one shilling', had to be experienced to be believed. Complaints were brought by individuals and by deputations. One could hardly speak to a Member without his grumbling about the fellow Member's demand for a shilling; and often in tones of quite astonishing venom. Nor did these complaints come, even mainly, from Members who were willing to admit the public to their boats free of charge. Alas, it was not the principle that most rankled; it was the shilling. As my own feeling was that the Member complained of was perfectly entitled to try for his shilling if he felt like it, and that his notice contributed to the diversification of the Festival, rather as the gypsies contribute to the success of the Derby, I seemed to become more clearly aware than before of a gulf between me and the majority; a difference primarily of scale, in that Rolt's activities might well effect (for better or for worse) the entire future of the supposedly common cause. It was evident that most people did not even appreciate this; it was the notice demanding a shilling that worried them.

None the less, and as far as I was concerned, it was my happiest week. My objective of a grand affirmation of life, with the renewal of the waterways at the centre of the affirmation, was on course for achievement. Peter Scott was painting signs bearing legends such as "To the Basin" or "Coffee" or "Children Only". Mr. John Baldock, the local Member of Parliament, had looked the very image of a young naval officer when he had officially opened the Trade Exhibition in the Market Hall; Mrs Baldock had looked the image of a young naval officer's wife; and just the right amount of breeze had aerated just the right amount of sunshine. There was even a queue, all day and for much of the night, at the exhibition in the Old Grammar School. Mary George and Ann Pym were working devotedly at the theatre box office (never an easy job in any particular); and were to be relied upon to fill a circus maximus. Every morning at eight o'clock, the day's rejoicing was inaugurated by the discharge of a maroon up at the Basin. (It will be realised by now that, at Market Harborough, the canal, not being a river, is at the *top* of the town.) Daily, the fuse was lit by Cyril Taplin, who was Assistant Harbourmaster; daily, Mr. Taplin's subsequent withdrawal was a matter of rejoicing to early risers; and daily the discharge left no citizen in doubt that the fleet was in, together with King Riot.

There were fringe attractions almost beyond cataloguing; and commonly concurrent. There were displays of Polish National Dancing. There was the Rutland Police Band (and very good it was, as is everything that comes from or remains in Rutland.) There was the Kibworth Silver Prize Band, with community singing (though not for me). There was Model Car Racing (not that I can recall it). There was a Fancy Dress Dance for children (I remember that well). There was a cricket match: Market Harborough Town versus Bedford. There was the election of the Festival Queen, her coronation behind the Leicester Caledonian Pipe Band; the "Display of Dancing in her Honour" by the Market Harborough Scottish and Square Dancing Society. There were alfresco nocturnal oscillations for all, to the Rogues of Rhythm Dance Band. And there was everything else that could be thought of, including a chess tournament. We had smoked out all the talent which hides away, insufficiently vitaminised, in every English country town. And now our Patron, the Lord Lieutenant, was on his way.

We had notified him that most boating people set great, sometimes aggressive, store upon being "informal", and often array themselves very carefully to that end. The six or eight of us who awaited him had thought it best to follow tradition, and had confined themselves to washing the tar off our hands and roughly combing our hair. Great, therefore, was our perturbation when we first heard and then saw the Lord Lieutenant's procession.

We had expected a comparatively casual arrival and a pale grey suit. Lord Cromwell arrived in full-dress uniform, and with outriders. I myself was so stunned that my memory must have suffered. I can recall nothing of what happened during the rest of that morning. During the afternoon, however, I gave a strenuous lecture on waterways in the Assembly Room, with our Members scattered like pirates among the thronging townsmen. On the next afternoon, it was Peter Scott who spoke: "Lapland Adventure", described as "Illustrated by colour films, shown to the public for the first time".

But undoubtedly it was the Three Swans that was at the centre of the excitement. Every evening, at about eleven o'clock, a crowd of more or less exhausted workers would assemble round a big table; from the theatre, from the Basin, from Welland House, from many other busy corners. Every night, Fothergill would provide not merely dinner, which itself would have been remarkable at that hour in a small English country town (let alone nightly); but a John Fothergill dinner, a repast idiosyncratic and distinguished by any standard. Life was renewed in everyone; and, afterwards, the festivity, of one kind and another, seemed never to end. Not that it was commonly a matter of uproar. Rather was it a matter of that communal intimacy, between twos and threes, ultimately among all, that feast of soul, which is perhaps the most valuable of all human experiences, and assuredly one of the rarest. By the end of the week I reflected, first, that on no night had I slept for more than four hours (on odd nights it had been three); and, second, that I seemed entirely the better for it. As remarked in "The Attempted Rescue", I am one to whom wretchedness brings not insomnia but slumber. Who (I feel) wants to sleep when he is happy? . . . At Market Harborough, the actresses apparently did. True to their trade, they were never visible before midday. But for an actress, sleep is a particular professional necessity.

During the last three days, our visitors from the outside world were assembling at the Three Swans: among them, Gerald Barry and his wife, Hugh Casson and his, James Robertson Justice, Michael Ayrton, Cecil Day Lewis, and Jill Balcon. I remember Gerald Barry coming down to breakfast one day and announcing the Corporeal Assumption of the Blessed Virgin. I am not really sure that the dogma was first promulgated at the exact time, but I know that it was the first I heard of it (having been very busy). On one morning, Fothergill came upon me entering the almost empty "inn" to collect some aquatic documents. He drew me into his office, and, in a voice of confidential urgency, asked me an agreeable question: "*Where* did you find *so many* beautiful women? How did you *do* it?" He added that he had never seen anything like it. Since he clearly wanted an answer, I murmured something about the magic of the waterways.

As each day we all sat round the big table at luncheon, autograph books used to be brought in, piled up on salvers, and all of us were required to contribute signatures and, if possible, messages. The messages had soon to be omitted, because novelty was impossible, when quantity was so pressing. Never since have I seen so many autograph books at any one time. On the penultimate evening, the public attractions ended with the Grand Display of Fireworks. It took place on the Cricket Field (by courtesy of the Club), but it proved impossible to confine the attendance to "the outfield", as had been planned. The attendance swarmed over everything, 20,000 of them, it was estimated; and it was a climax of my life up to that point, when, with Gerald Barry and others, I sat at the front of the throng on a podium (a collection of boxes might possibly be more accurate) watching the vast discharge while the cheering and excitement rose and rose until the final patriotic scene. Such moments seldom recur in a single life.

A less agreeable moment that has never again come my way, arose when a Member who had agreed to serve as Medical Officer to the Festival, having asked if he could see me in private, told me that he had been invited, as a physician, to look at a girl on one of the boats who felt off colour, and that he had suspected poliomyelitis. It was arranged that the girl be moved to hospital with a minimum of disturbance. I believe that the diagnosis proved correct, but that, fortunately, the girl made a rapid and complete recovery. Nor, I am glad to report, were there any ill consequences to the Festival, or, as far as I ever learned, to anyone else who attended it. It is no more than the truth to say that, had it been otherwise, the state of the waterways of Britain might now be very much less satisfactory even than it is.

But there were many separate and distinct moments of excitement. On the first night of the plays, Nicolette Bernard in "A Marriage Has Been Arranged" gave a performance which was one of the most beautiful and moving I have ever seen on any stage at any time. She came off at the end, fell into my arms and said "Was I good?" I am not sure that I can recall any single moment in my life that excels that one. The two productions, with their magnificent furnishings and glittering costumes (the distinguished purveyors must accept these epithets from the pomping trade), looked noticeably more elegant than the West End average of the time. This circumstance, added to the varied eminences of the players, and the oddity of the entire venture led to our efforts being heard of outside the enchanted area of the Market Harborough Urban District Council.

On the Thursday of Festival week, we received an invitation to take the two productions to no less august an establishment than Sir Barry Jackson's Birmingham Repertory Theatre; at that time, as for many years before and for some years after, the place where the true *art* of the theatre was more consistently upheld, as I have written elsewhere, than in any other theatre in Britain. Though we were invited merely to fill a week when the theatre would otherwise have been closed for a summer vacation, it remained a considerable distinction to be asked at all. Very late at night, at the end of John Fothergill's dinner (or supper), all concerned held a curious meeting in a large hall at the back of the Three Swans; very high, rather crumbly (Fothergill had told me it would not be safe to mount any of the Festival events in it), hung with vast and vague and Far Eastern draperies, ill-lighted, dusty, and rather chilly. Someone recalled the Sadler's Wells ballet named "The Haunted Ballroom" and said this was the Haunted Board Meeting. Alas, we were compelled to say No to Birmingham. Not surprisingly, none of the cast had a further week available, and Peter Scott perhaps least of all. Had things been a little different, I daresay our group would be on the road still. But things seldom are different in that kind of romantic, helpful way.

It is worth remembering that six years later, in 1956, a group of Association Members, dwelling at that time on boats in Little Venice (a way of life then and now inevitably frowned upon by every kind of democratic public authority), mounted a musical comedy, of which they wrote the words, composed the music, and comprised the cast. The piece won the first prize in a "Sunday Times" amateur theatre competition and was then booked for a week at the Richmond Theatre (which seems to recur in this narrative). Having seen the entertainment there, I was not surprised to learn that at least one offer had been received of a fairly lengthy tour; but the offer had to be declined, for similar reasons to those that weighed at Market Harborough. None the less, it was a pleasing landmark in the Association's campaign of affirmation. I myself, needless to say, am convinced that it would have been in accordance with the true will of all, if the decision, both at Market Harborough and at Little Venice, had been affirmative, however reasonable the apparent obstacles. Only by seizing (or embracing) such moments can life's clinging ivy (or death's) be thrust back. But only when the tree has died, does the tree know.

At the Market Harborough Festival, Mr. Holt Abbott's pioneering holiday cruiser "specially designed for use throughout the British inland waterways system", made its first (and triumphant) advent; and at the Festival too the "holiday liner" made a very early appearance in the history of these specialised craft.

I had for some time realised the public demand for boats that would offer holidays afloat by the week or fortnight, with all provided ('laid on', as they said in the Women's Institutes), after the style of a Caribbean Cruise, or as near to that as could be compassed. One obvious difficulty was that most of the more interesting wider waterways (wide enough for the cruising craft to be of reasonable proportions) are in the North, where it is well known that few of those seeking such a holiday ever wish to go. Ever the dream of the lady who sits next to one at a banquet in Yorkshire or Lancaster, is to reside in Bournemouth; but the lady in Coulsdon has no notion of the North other than that it is cold and unmodish.

Some time before the Market Harborough Festival, I received a call from a Mr. Alan Smallwood. As I recollect, he told me that he had operated an inland liner service on the waterways of France, but had lost the vessel through some Act of God. He wondered whether there would be any possibility of a similar service in England? I explained the circumstances. Mr. Smallwood, undeterred by the national attitude of Eyes South, took the risk of adapting to it. He converted a pair of working narrow boats with such ingenuity that between them they would more or less fulfil the various human needs and functions arising. He set up New Way Holidays (a great pioneering moment) and he brought the boats to the Festival, with a charming girl in yellow trousers as crew, first of many other charming girls on these and similar bâteaux de joie. Mr. Smallwood told me that in earlier life he had been one of that nationally noted group, the Ovaltineys, and offered his help with our problems of the stage, which we were very glad to accept. Subsequently, there have been other entrants to the waterway liner business, still mostly, though not entirely, on the narrow canals, and therefore with craft but seven feet wide. It is the ultimate form of lazy holiday ("peaceful" might be a more polite word). One need do nothing but eat, sleep, and watch the (incomparable) scenery pass. I have found that this is what a very large number seek. Though the attitude is inconsistent with strenuous campaigning, all navigators, however quiescent, make grist for the water mill. "Is there dancing aboard?" a lady once asked me at a Townswomen's Guild. "My son will never go, if there isn't."

Despite the discouraging incident of the man who charged a shilling, private enterprise flourished at the Festival. Inevitably, there was a small but alert group offering commemorative pottery. Frank Jones of Leighton Buzzard, one of the best of the boat painters, attended: "Visitors", stated the Programme of Attractions, "will be able to watch Mr. Jones working at his colourful and unusual trade." There were headscarves depicting, within thirty-six square inches, almost everything that could be thought of: portraits of Brindley and Telford; the Seven Wonders of the Waterways; painted boats; swans; cans, stools, and dippers; together with four lines of closely instructional narrative in black script round the border. Maid Line Cruisers, a name of more than maiden power in the years thereafter, but then still germinating at Halliford Bend, offered "Special Attention to Members of the Inland Waterways Association".

For the last night, the Saturday, we planned a Grand Festival Ball, during which the Awards would be presented. Our plays were handicapped by the circumstance that no Saturday performance could be offered, as the Assembly Rooms was, beyond doubt, the only building large enough for the ball. We proposed to precede the choreambies with a fairly ceremonial dinner at the Three Swans for Lord and Lady Cromwell and our sparkling miscellany of distinguished visitors. John Fothergill had kindly offered us the exclusive use of the dining room for this purpose. Other diners would be accommodated in an apartment at the back.

After an exceedingly busy day, I came back to the Three Swans at about 6.45 p.m. As the Lord Lieutenant's party was asked for 7.30, I was aware that I had by no means unlimited time to change and to look over the final dispositions. Immediately I entered, I became aware of a subdued murmur of voices from the dining room. I pushed open the door. The room was full of stout parties at high tea; a coach tour, as I could not but discern. My next idea was that it must be the day before I thought it was. But it was not. I found Fothergill, not without difficulty. The answer was simple: Fothergill had forgotten all about the Lord Lieutenant; that the Three Swans was called upon to provide us with a meal before the usual hour of 10.30 or 11.00. He had simply overlooked it.

Our conversation was overheard by Vera Barry. This lady had made a considerable mark as a statuesque actress, first under the name of Vera Poliskoff, and then under that of Vera Lindsay; and especially in the fastidious productions of Michel St. Denis. Her extraordinary beauty was (I am sure, still is) of the grand, Venus de Milo, regularly featured, perfectly proportioned order that is less common than once it was. "I will help," she said. "We will lay the tables together." As she was in trousers and rather muddy, it was obvious that she too had no time to spare, but, with the selfishness of crisis, I accepted her offer at once.

Fothergill shooed out the stout parties, the Three Swans people cleared the tables, and Vera and I set to work in their wake. By about 7.20 the job seemed done; or at least able to be left to the Three Swans staff for the final touches. I looked at Vera. "Don't worry about me," she said, as she departed.

A man can always change in five minutes, if he really has to (my Father had a habit of changing into evening dress – 'full' evening dress, in those days – while in the taxi); but Vera Lindsay was down before me, transformed and radiant. It was a feat that I shall always remember. The Lord Lieutenant was a little late, as was, of course, inevitable in all the circumstances; but the circumstances must have overcome me more than I realised, because I find that I can recall not one single thing he said during the semi-banquet that followed.

But I can remember now the rumpus, the shining faces, the Chinese lanterns, in the Assembly Rooms; also the slight dustiness of the atmosphere. All our guests participated in the distribution of awards, each handing over a different trophy and shaking a different hand, while the Market Harborough Advertiser took photograph after photograph. But the thing I later came to remember best of all was that when I rose to read the list of winners, with the Lord Lieutenant at my side, the actor, Hugh Griffith, who was staying on the Rolt's boat, emitted a loud, though solitary, hiss; unquestionably the hiss of an experienced professional. It was easy to foresee what would happen next to the waterways campaign; and when, long afterwards, the clash of civil war finally subsided for the time being, Mr. Griffith's sibilance retained in my ears a significance no doubt far exceeding his uninformed intention. It is hard to know, for I have never met Mr. Griffith.

Apart from the proportion of Peter Scott's guarantee for the plays, the total deficit on the Market Harborough Festival was only £70.

It seemed incredible that there would never be another one; though no doubt in accord with a fundamental law of life.

"You *will* come back next year?" asked the eager voices, as the boats moved away and the mummers mounted their waggons. I myself had no doubt of it; but when the time of decision came it was the town that was finally responsible for our sad negative.

The decision against a second Market Harborough Festival followed the visit I paid to the town, to discuss the matter. The town indicated that it would like another Festival, but a Festival of its own, with "bowls, amateur dramatics, and something for the old people", and our boats as merely one of the attractions, though no doubt an important one. It seemed likely that active campaigning for the waterways would be as inappropriate as active promotion of art. In any case, it was clear that for the Association the harvest would be unlikely to justify the time, labour, cost, and uncertainty of the ploughing and sowing; especially when the most talented and most energetic of us had a civil war on our hands as well as the proper and supposedly agreed war against official inertia and destructiveness. At Market Harborough, as it seemed, we had followed British colonial tradition: the very success of our efforts had spurred the local population to replace us by themselves and to change our targets. None the less, there has, I think, never been a second Market Harborough Festival of any kind. That too is not unknown as a final non-development in the British colonial tradition.

The 1950 Festival changed the entire prospect for the waterways of Britain; in the main, by simply reminding people, other than specialists, of their existence, and especially by manifesting the enormous potential for pleasure boating. It would hardly be too much to say that an entire new form of public recreation entered history at Market Harborough. Brought in first, amid much controversy, as a somewhat desperate auxiliary in the campaign for a revival of commercial carriage, pleasure boating came to dominate the entire struggle, and ultimately transformed the inner life of the Association. From a body upholding a minority philosophy with almost boundless implications, the Association became a small annexe or tiny cell of the majority way of life and thought. The Prometheans were safely bound to their rocks.

I think we even had a minute influence on the next year's Festival of Britain: an event which it is a particular pleasure to praise, as so many have carped. "Why it's really glamorous!" said an American Indian woman to me as we sat in Misha Black's exquisite waterside restaurant; the feral Thames on the side, the follies on the other: the Gas Fountain, the Tipping Fountain, and all the other chimerae. Her comment was apt both to normal Britain and to this exciting much complained of exception. And really glamorous also, in its minuscule, £70 deficit, degree, was the Market Harborough Festival.

With wild generosity, John Fothergill presented me, on the morning of departure, with an enormous, eighteenth century copper jug. Thereafter, while he lived, I received frequent letters and sudden postcards from him; salty in diction, elegant in calligraphy, and usually bearing exquisite marginal decorations after the style of the wrought iron bracket bearing the Three Swans sign. I grieve to think that epistles so beautiful are now engulfed in the Association's great Sargasso Sea of only semi-sorted paper.

Among many, the spell had visibly weakened even by the morning after the Grand Ball. Those who had lately been transfigured were now to be seen making telephone calls, merely snatching at their food, and greeting with self-conscious effusiveness strangers who had arrived to lead them homewards. "Now I must get back to the real world," they would be heard to say, with an aggression that was all too little assumed.

I myself was still lucky. With Barry Morse and his wife, and others, I sailed away on *Beatrice*, and spent a week travelling by water to her base at Slimbridge. Barry proved to be the most delightful of boating companions.

In the first place, he told endless, and endlessly entertaining stories of the stage. One I remember was of a repertory company actor under notice who, cast as a servant in a play by Lonsdale, was required to answer a question as to where another character had gone, with words to the effect that he did not know. At his final performance, the actor under notice delivered instead a lengthy and wildly scandalous impromptu explanation, involving all the major characters in the piece, and totally impossible for the rest of the cast to deal with. Another actor similarly under notice (I think from the same theatre) was in a costume play by some such writer as the late Gordon Daviot. He too had a humble part, in the course of which he was required silently to deliver a scroll to a council of very weighty noblemen. Instead of handing over the paper, the actor entered and said in ringing, heraldic tones: "My Lords! The Duke of Buckingham is dead." Naturally, there was no Duke of Buckingham among the dramatis personae or even in the historical background.

In the second place Barry was an indefatigable wizard with the tiller, with the engine, and with every situation that arose, human or inhuman. A climax was on the Upper Stratford Canal in King's Norton; where *Beatrice* ran hopelessly aground on a shoal of heavy rubbish in a 'bridge hole'; material discharged by the local residents from the bridge above, according to the national usage. In the end, it appeared that there was no hope of shifting her either by the engine (which was giving trouble, of course) or by the efforts of the entire crew at the ends of lines. Barry unobtrusively took himself off. In no time at all, he reappeared leading a horse; which did the trick in a minute or two. Barry had persuaded a milk roundsman to part with the animal for a few moments. Later the same day, no less a person than Douglas Barwell, soon to be the Napoleon of the Lower Avon, descended from his then eyrie high on the Lickey Hills (I have stayed there in the densest, most Celtic, mountain mist) to the Worcester & Birmingham Canal where we were stuck, in order to wrestle with our engine – natually with transcendant results, at least for the time being. It was the symbol of another opening phase in waterway history.

XVII

Tableau

I have always thought that the truth of fiction is more profound, more charged with meaning than everyday reality. Realism, whether it be socialist or not, falls short of reality. It shrinks it, attenuates it, falsifies it, it does not take into account our basic truths and our fundamental obsessions: Love, death, astonishment. It presents man in a reduced and estranged perspective. Truth is in our dreams, in the imagination.

EUGENE IONESCO

Shortly after the Festival, and before the subsequent civil war within the Association (which raged for more than half a year), Jonathan Cape published "We Are For the Dark", a collection of six original ghost stories by Elizabeth Jane Howard and me. Though we touched up each other's contributions (the spoof obituary notice from "The Times" in Jane's terrifying tale, "Perfect Love", was written by me), three of the stories were basically hers, and three mine. The book was thus not a full collaboration, and subsequently we have both disengaged our names from the other's works.

It is a familiar anomaly of the publishing trade that in Britain collections of short stories can hardly be made to sell at all, even when written by authors of many best-selling novels. Yet if the stories can be described as "ghost stories", there is an immediate market, even if the collection receives very few reviews, as unfortunately, frequently happens; the magical and the metaphysical being at the moment out of literary fashion. That short stories (with one-act plays) should in general be so slenderly supported, shows a lamentable lack of preoccupation with literary art; but the demand for ghost stories, even though sometimes based upon dubious motives, reflects a popular concern that standard education has not so far destroyed, with the things that are of most consequence in life.

As I have sought to demonstrate in at least five published disquisitions on the subject, the ghost story is to be distinguished, and fairly sharply, from the mere horror story on its right and from the science-fiction on its left; and

appertains more properly to the field of poetry. The perils are proportionately great. There are only about thirty or forty first-class ghost stories in the
world's literature (as distinct from the uncounted thousands in the less
demanding realm of fact). In subsequent years I have occasionally found it
cramping to be so *compulsorily* paranormal. People will not accept, as
Shakespeare did, that the "supernatural" is no special enclave in life, but an
all-pervasive element in it. When the slight cramp sets in, I can always
reflect that I am but following Shakespeare.

I doubt whether Cape would have published our six original ghost stories
had not a further item been added to the above considerations: Jane's
beauty and persuasiveness. None the less, when the book appeared
(originally with an enigmatic jacket designed by one of Jane's girl friends),
the reviews were more numerous, more lengthy, and far more laudatory
than I had ever thought possible. The cover of the subsequent paperback
edition (from an American owned enterprise) was less good: I was told by a
spokeswoman for Collins, with which firm I had happy dealings in later
years, that paperbacks sell by the "almost hypnotic reaching of men's arms"
towards appropriately devised cover pictures; and several of my works have
suffered pictorially not a little from this revelation, even though presumably
it has advantaged them commercially.

Many of the critics somehow perceived that the book was not the product
of a complete collaboration; but, having penetrated so far, they commonly
attached the credit for particular stories to the wrong author. Though it was
natural that Jane's marvellous "Three Miles Up" should be attributed to
me, as it is concerned with a canal voyage, many of the other errors were
almost eerie. If one examined the notices, the two authors appeared not so
much to have merged as to have disintegrated. It was extremely odd and
confusing.

The especial award for insight into identity was attachable to the critic of
"The Observer"; who alone among those attempting to distinguish the
authorship, attributed a story called "The View" to me. She was quite
right; and what further she had to say, made that Sunday morning
memorable. "'The View' arouses great interest in Mr. Aickman's future as
a writer, for not only does its element of fable or allegory not offend (as,
when one is expecting a ghost story, it so easily might), it increases the
scope, and depth, and spaciousness of this odd story, which leaves a moving
impression of time, sorrow, and destiny."

As "The View" had been the first seriously intended ghost story I had
ever written, those generous words offered remarkably good cheer to a
young man with a civil war on his hands. They contributed to the
justification of my life purpose. Though I continued to direct the waterways
campaign, with successes and failures, for another fourteen years, they
proved that there was a world elsewhere, as Coriolanus put it.

Other Pearson inland waterway titles

LOCK, STOCK & BARREL
by Shirley Ginger

Canals and self-sufficiency are the twin-themes of this delightful account of a couple's escape from the rat race to a waterside smallholding and general store in the heart of the Midlands countryside. Includes a mouthwatering appendix of country recipes.

"Thoroughly enthralling - top marks" *Canal & Riverboat.*
"Fun to read" *The Lady.*

192 pages, paperback - £4.95.

CANAL CRUISING by John Hankinson

A brand new edition of the classic introduction to canal boating. Up to date with current trends and generously illustrated in both colour and black & white.

96 pages, paperback - £5.95.

CANAL COMPANIONS

Definitive guides to popular canal routes for boaters, walkers and general visitors. Detailed 2 inches to 1 mile maps are accompanied by entertaining and informative commentaries and full classified information on facilities. Currently available: Warwickshire Ring, Cheshire Ring, Four Counties Ring (Staffs., Salop, Cheshire and W.Mids.) and Llangollen & Shropshire Union.

Each 48 pages, paperback - £2.50 or £2.75.

CANALS ARE MY WORLD
by Iris Bryce

Iris Bryce delighted inland waterway enthusiasts with her first two books: "Canals Are My Home" and "Canals Are My Life" which told the story of her voyages throughout the canals with her husband Owen aboard their famous narrowboat "Bix". Now, in her brand new book, "Canals Are My World" she brings the story up to date, chronicling two years of nomadic voyaging on the waterways of the Midlands and North Country.

160 pages, hardback - £9.95

TOWPATH TRAILS
Niall Allsop & Michael Pearson.

A definitive guide to the towpaths of the main canal system. Over forty walks, linear and circular, have been devised to introduce readers to the walking potential of individual canals and navigations. Each featured walk has detailed directions, an informative commentary, information on eating and drinking, public transport, places of interest and tourist information. Additional walks are suggested, enabling the user to compile his or her own itineraries. Lovingly written and generously illustrated in both colour and black & white, "Towpath Trails" is, above all else, a thoroughly practical guide and the authors ask nothing more of their readers than that they "go out there and get their boots muddy"!

124 pages, paperback - £6.95